T0224928

Practical Guide to Salesforce Experience Cloud

Building, Enhancing, and Managing a Digital Experience with Salesforce

Second Edition

Philip Weinmeister

Apress®

Practical Guide to Salesforce Experience Cloud: Building, Enhancing, and Managing a Digital Experience with Salesforce

Philip Weinmeister
Powder Springs, GA, USA

ISBN-13 (pbk): 978-1-4842-8131-4   ISBN-13 (electronic): 978-1-4842-8132-1
https://doi.org/10.1007/978-1-4842-8132-1

Managing Director, Apress Media LLC: Welmoed Spahr
Acquisitions Editor: Susan McDermott
Development Editor: Laura Berendson
Coordinating Editors: Rita Fernando and Mark Powers

Cover designed by eStudioCalamar

Cover image by Pixabay (www.pixabay.com)

Distributed to the book trade worldwide by Apress Media, LLC, 1 New York Plaza, New York, NY 10004, U.S.A. Phone 1-800-SPRINGER, fax (201) 348-4505, e-mail orders-ny@springer-sbm.com, or visit www.springeronline.com. Apress Media, LLC is a California LLC and the sole member (owner) is Springer Science + Business Media Finance Inc (SSBM Finance Inc). SSBM Finance Inc is a **Delaware** corporation.

For information on translations, please e-mail booktranslations@springernature.com; for reprint, paperback, or audio rights, please e-mail bookpermissions@springernature.com.

Apress titles may be purchased in bulk for academic, corporate, or promotional use. eBook versions and licenses are also available for most titles. For more information, reference our Print and eBook Bulk Sales web page at http://www.apress.com/bulk-sales.

Any source code or other supplementary material referenced by the author in this book is available to readers on GitHub (https://github.com/Apress). For more detailed information, please visit http://www.apress.com/source-code.

Printed on acid-free paper

*Dedicated to my mother, Barbara, and my father, Kent,
for always rooting me on and making this journey possible
through a lot of time, energy, and hard work many years ago*

Table of Contents

About the Author

Philip Weinmeister is a Salesforce MVP and a Product Leader at IBM, where he is focused on building innovative components, apps, and bolts that enable industry-driven, transformative experiences on the Salesforce platform. He is 23x Salesforce certified and has delivered numerous Sales Cloud, Service Cloud, and (primarily) Experience Cloud solutions to a variety of organizations on Salesforce since 2010. Phil authored the second edition of *Practical Salesforce Development Without Code* (Apress) in 2018 and has received an average rating of almost five stars on Amazon.com. He has been a Salesforce MVP for over five years and was previously designated the only "Community Cloud MVP" ever named by Salesforce at the Lightning Bolt Trailblazer awards at Dreamforce. Phil has authored three Experience Cloud–related courses on Pluralsight as well.

A graduate of Carnegie Mellon University, with a double major in business administration/IT and Spanish, Phil now resides in Powder Springs, Georgia, USA. He spends most of his "free" time with his gorgeous, sweet wife, Amy, and his children, Tariku, Sophie, Max, and Lyla. When he's not trying to make his kids laugh, cheering on the Arizona Cardinals, or rap-battling his wife, Phil enjoys traveling, playing various sports, and growing in his walk with Jesus.

Stay updated on Phil's most recent insights and blog posts by following him on Twitter (@PhilWeinmeister).

About the Technical Reviewer

Jarrod Kingston is a Salesforce MVP and a Solution Engineering Leader at IBM. He has 15 Salesforce certifications and 12+ years of experience in the support, training, and advancement of Salesforce. He has extensive experience in providing presentations, solution demonstrations, and training. Jarrod has a dynamic ability to provide valuable content in an engaging way. Outside of work, Jarrod enjoys woodworking, house remodeling, and spending time with his family. He lives in Kansas City and is an avid Jayhawks (#RCJH), Chiefs (#ChiefsKingdom), and Royals (#RaisedRoyal) fan.

Acknowledgments

"for all have sinned and fall short of the glory of God, and all are justified freely by his grace through the redemption that came by Christ Jesus." (Romans 3:23-24)

These verses from the third chapter of the book of Romans, found in the New Testament of the Christian Bible, help to convey why I so strongly desire to acknowledge Jesus and what he has done for me. You might be wondering how **Jesus** comes into play with a book on Salesforce Experience Cloud, and that's completely understandable. Simply put, I would have no true, lasting hope if He hadn't given His life for me and provided a way to have eternal security and relationship with the creator of all things. The reality of his saving truth underscores and permeates pretty much every aspect of my life. Behind every page written, every diagram created, and every concept illustrated, there is hope and faith abounding in God's truth and goodness. While I'm eager to talk to people about Salesforce communities, I'm even more excited to talk to them about this topic. I'm easy to find if you ever want to chat...

Amy Weinmeister—My wife has been so supportive and helpful throughout not just this edition but all the editions of all my books. She has served as an editor, a fan, a motivator, and much more. I really can't quantify how instrumental she has been in this process. Thank you, my love.

Paul Stillmank—While Paul was understandably busy with an acquisition-related integration and unable to grant us all his wisdom and insight through another foreword, he continued to lead boldly and serve as an inspiration to me and many others at 7Summits.

John Price—From even before I met John, he has been supporting my authoring endeavors. He continued to be very clear that he was 100% behind me. I think anyone who appreciates a good boss can understand how impactful this support has been.

ACKNOWLEDGMENTS

The Entire Experience Cloud Team—There have been numerous supporters and advocates from this group over the years who have contributed to, promoted, and celebrated this book and its content. A huge thank you to this group, including Mike Micucci, David Green, Adam Weigl, Khush Singh, Anna Rosenmann, Regan Roby, Kimberley Zatlyn, Kate Milne, and many more.

Jarrod Kingston—Thanks for having my back, this time as the guy who ensured I wasn't churning out nonsense.

Bill Loumpouridis—Your support for my first "clicks, not code" book many years ago was one of the factors that kept me going. Thank you!

Introduction

It was 2017. Community Cloud hadn't yet been renamed to Experience Cloud, Salesforce was operating with only one CEO, and "COVID" wasn't a household term. That year, I decided that it was the right time to introduce a meaningful, experience-driven book on Salesforce communities to the technology ecosystem. After almost a year of working on it, *Practical Guide to Salesforce Communities* was released in June of 2018. While I was excited to share what I had learned about building communities with other Salesforce enthusiasts, I had no grand expectations about its future impact; my goal was simply to help others.

It's now 2022, my communities book has been available for over three years, and the impact it has had truly blows me away. At the various Salesforce events I've attended or spoken at over the years, many different people have approached me to tell me about their experience with the book. I must admit that every conversation of this nature really moves me...to hear how the book helped change the trajectory of someone's career or enabled them to become a certified Salesforce professional is very special to me, and I am extremely grateful to be in a position to help.

I thought about what might be useful in the introduction for this second edition of my book, and, while I have some new thoughts and insights about Salesforce Experience Cloud, the most helpful material to illuminate the value of this book should come from readers themselves. So, with that said, I'm excited to share with you some testimonies from those who dove into the first edition and put it into practice in their careers.

I sincerely hope this book provides you with similar help and allows you to create meaningful, impactful digital experiences on the Salesforce platform. I am rooting for you!

Reader Anecdotes (First Edition)

"Practical Guide to Salesforce Communities was a suggested resource from a colleague during a Community/Experience Cloud project. Having minimal experience with communities at the time, I found it to be an invaluable asset to the existing project and found myself referring to it for a better understanding on both security and licensing.

In addition, it became one of my top resources for preparing for the Experience Cloud Consultant Certification. Easily digestible chapters broken down in a logical order was exactly what I needed. I was able to become a certified Experience Cloud Consultant on my first try and Phil's material was critical in obtaining that certification."

Danny Raines

Sr. Manager/Salesforce Lead at Built

Franklin, TN

"I have been working on various communities sites, mostly from scratch. When one develops communities using experience cloud there are varieties of options available and these options grow every year with each new Salesforce release. In the market, there is NO single source available to refer to all those options and use it. Considering these days that communities play a considerably huge role to all the companies, irrespective of the type of business, it's very important to have complete and up-to-date knowledge on this topic. In this era of communities your book helped me to achieve various objectives that I was looking to implement in various communities. To highlight the top items which were most helpful to me:

- How to setup and administer the communities using available templates, themes and styles

- Options available to customize pages and flow based on personas

- OOTB and drag-and-drop functionalities of the builder and how to use them

The very special and unique feature in your book is the visuals, which help to clarify most important areas of communities. I am eagerly waiting for your 2nd Edition of *Practical Guide to Salesforce Communities*."

Maharsh Kapadia

Solution & Integration Architect

Slough, England

"I am a Business Analyst (BA) turned Platform Developer and found that I needed to learn more about Experience Cloud in order to properly perform my job duties. *Practical Guide to Salesforce Communities* was recommended to me by a colleague and it helped me become more competent and confident in relation to my Experience Cloud knowledge and implementations. I loved how the book breaks down key concepts into easily digestible sections and chapters. I also love all of the images in the book as a visual learner, that reference is invaluable. The overview of "Why Salesforce Communities" spoke to my business analysis brain and helped tie the more technical concepts of Communities together in a way that made sense to me.

I used the *Practical Guide to Salesforce Communities* when studying for my Experience Cloud (Community Cloud at the time) exam and it was definitely a key factor in why I obtained that Certification. The chapter on user licenses alone has been a lifesaver and wonderful quick reference as questions have arisen during implementations. In fact, I keep a copy in my office for quick reference. I think this book is perfect for all experience levels and will benefit anyone who wants to gain a thorough understanding of Salesforce Communities and all they entail."

Cece Adams

Manager, Platform Development at 7Summits

Chicago, IL

"Working closely with an incredible partner ecosystem, my holy grail is to discover professionals who are able to articulate the power of our platform and are excited to evangelize the business impact through real world examples.

I've also recognized that the canvas of opportunity with Salesforce Experience Cloud is massive. With all of the capability, it is helpful to have quick reference to proven approaches for not only implementing Experience Cloud, but also the ability to articulate the business value for creating beautiful and reusable approaches on the platform.

I always have Phil's book within easy reference to help inspire ideas and provide pragmatic approaches. I highly recommend his guides to both new and experienced users who want to maximize the impact of using Salesforce for digital experiences."

Rick Gaetano

Global and NA Salesforce Alliance Director at Salesforce

Raleigh/Chapel Hill/Durham, NC

"I really liked reading *Practical Guide to Salesforce Communities* because the language, diagrams, and technical references were concise and easy for me to digest and understand. I also found that the book contained some of the most relevant topics on communities. Even after first reading the book, I continue to use it as a handy reference on my journey to seeking my Experience Cloud certification."

Nancy Jo Brown
Senior Salesforce Consultant at Esor Consulting Group
Orlando, FL

"As the Experience Cloud technical expert for a small company that serves over a million users of our App on the Salesforce Appexchange, I must stay on top of my game to manage the high volume of cases that are in my queue daily. Sitting right next to my keyboard is my bible, *Practical Guide to Salesforce Communities*. As one can imagine, data security, access and visibility make up a high volume of my cases. Every company has a unique use case, and no two companies share the same Salesforce security model. This presents unique challenges in assisting my clients when it comes to Experience Cloud. However, I have found that building a foundation of data security, access and visibility fundamentals is essential and for that, I turn to this book, often referring to Chapter 8: Access, Sharing and Visibility to help build that foundation in a building block format. Starting out with the basics in the section on Object and Field Access, I can use the example provided in this section to show my clients the impact of providing a community user with Read, Create and Edit access. The visualization of global actions when a user has been granted Create and Edit access is an excellent visual learning tool for my clients. It helps them to see the power in their decisions. Once my clients have grasped this fairly basic concept, I can confidently move on to record sharing, Org Wide Sharing and Sharing Sets. I have found that Sharing Sets are a difficult concept to grasp but with the help of *Practical Guide to Salesforce Communities*, I can break it down using the examples provided in the book and relate them to my clients' individual use cases.

Another section that has been a lifesaver is Chapter 3: Licenses and Member Groups: Employees, Partners and Customers. I cannot count the number of times that I have explained to a client, or even just in a conversation about Experience Cloud (formerly Community Cloud), that a community license is not applied the same way as a traditional Salesforce license. I admit that it took me quite a bit of Google searching to figure this out. If I had this book back in the day, I could have saved myself a lot of time. Phil does an excellent job of explaining this in the Customer Community Users section of chapter three.

I refer to this book often and I always keep it close by. It is professionally written, concise and full of examples, figures and valuable information that assist me in handling a high volume of Experience Cloud cases and looking like an expert while I do it. Thanks Phil!"

Jennifer Krutsch

Certified Salesforce Administrator at Chargent

Los Angeles, CA

"I found Salesforce in 2013 when I started working at Appirio, joining my colleagues from WebMethods (Software AG) who had influenced my decision to join them. In no time I became a fan of Salesforce platform and many of the advantages it brought to customers. I am astonished with the speed of innovation on the platform. Working as a consultant on many projects, I got a chance to work on the initial Salesforce communities product. It opened up the Salesforce platform for customers to bring their partners and customers to join business processes. The product evolved quickly with so many useful functionalities. Very soon, I found myself working with Salesforce communities projects exclusively. I joined 7Summits and got a chance to meet Phil personally. I had read his book, *Practical Salesforce Development without Code*. I was totally impressed with his approach to technology and his style to explain it in simple words. When his next book, *Practical Guide to Salesforce Communities*, was released, I knew that I wanted to have my hands on it as soon as possible. The book did not disappoint me. My Salesforce Communities projects topics—understanding licenses, sharing model, automation, templates, audience targeting or anything else—are there in the book. It gave me ideas around the features that I needed to explore more. At times it warned me of gotchas to avoid as well. More so ever he has penned down the business use-case of the communities. These are often my discussions on the project with customers.

I am still working on communities (now called Experience Cloud) projects, this time with Accenture as Technical Architect. The book has greatly influenced my approach on architecting the communities project. And, thus my career. Salesforce has continued to roll out new features at a great pace. And, I find myself asking Phil 'When is the next edition of your book coming?'"

Mitul Patel

Salesforce Technical Architect at Accenture

Houston, TX

CHAPTER 1

Salesforce Experience Cloud

The end product of Salesforce Experience Cloud (previously Community Cloud) can be referred to by a variety of terms: digital experiences, social websites, partner portals, business sites, online communities, etc. While the nomenclature may vary, the end goal is the same: to engage, enable, and empower the customers, partners, and/or employees of one's organization. My goal is to make that engagement, enablement, and empowerment a bit easier.

Some of those reading this guide will be looking to build upon an existing understanding of Experience Cloud, while others will be starting on their journey. I have developed this material to meet each reader along their individual path. For this entire spectrum wanting to grow their knowledge, skill set, career, and more, a foundational baseline is the ideal starting place.

An Introduction

As I see it, a site built on the Salesforce platform is comprised of the following three elements:

- Collaboration

- Process and data

- User experience

These elements are visualized in Figure 1-1. I'll walk through each of these key components and the value they bring to these sites.

1

© Philip Weinmeister 2022
P. Weinmeister, *Practical Guide to Salesforce Experience Cloud*, https://doi.org/10.1007/978-1-4842-8132-1_1

  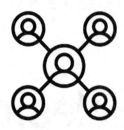

USER EXPERIENCE   **PROCESS & DATA**   **COLLABORATION**

Figure 1-1. *The three key components of an Experience Builder site*

Collaboration

There's a reason many people still refer to Experience Cloud sites as communities; people are at the center of it all. Have you ever heard of a community without people? Merriam-Webster defines types of community as follows:

- *1d*: "A group of people with a common characteristic or interest living together within a larger society"

- *1e*: "A group linked by a common policy

- *1f*: "A body of persons or nations having a common history or common social, economic, and political interests"

- *1g*: "A body of persons of common and especially professional interests scattered through a larger society"

- *3c*: "Social activity"

Sure, every website (in theory) involves people. However, it's not necessarily the case that a website considers the *personas* within the audience. A community needs to consider who is involved and in what capacity or role. It's one thing to have generic viewers and a very different thing to understand who is involved and in what capacity. Faceless "hits" become individuals with personalities, interests, and opinions. People generally desire to be known and heard…and community allows that to happen.

I can take this a bit further and discuss a second, related item, which is the enablement of interactions that these individuals may have within the context of a community. These no-longer-faceless people want to share, learn, influence, collaborate, buy, sell, discuss, and so on; an online community serves as the framework to support all of this. To be clear, however, the focus is not solely limited to system-focused transactions; a healthy, well-designed community always incorporates the individual into the activity.

Process and Data

The concept of member activity within an Experience Cloud site perfectly segues into the next area, which addresses the data with which these individuals are interacting and how those interactions are happening. This business data and the processes related to that data further differentiate standard websites from sites on the Salesforce platform. Intertwining members with meaningful, applicable data through digital interaction and business processes is where the value of a site truly lies.

A traditional business portal minimizes the role and value of the individual members and their activity, while a typical website doesn't have CRM-rich data and business processes behind the scenes that would serve as the foundation for a Salesforce site. Let's take a look at a visual representation in Figure 1-2. This diagram captures the community members, their activity, and the business data and processes.

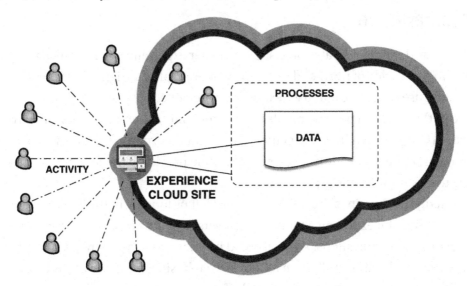

Figure 1-2. *Data and the individuals interacting with that data are essential to digital experiences*

It's important to understand the concept of how both people *and* data play such a key role, so I've provided another view in Figure 1-3. Notice the interconnectedness between members and data; data provides the context for the interactions, not only enriching the interactions between members but providing much more valuable results for the organization as a whole.

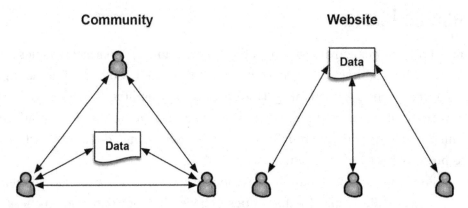

Figure 1-3. *A community changes how individuals interact with data and each other*

User Experience

A third critical element of a Salesforce site is the user experience. For those of us who don't live in the worlds of front-end development or graphic design, it's important to clarify that user interface and user experience are not equivalent. While a user interface (UI) focuses on page elements, layout, and interaction behaviors, effective user experience (UX) puts people at the center of it all. UX incorporates a holistic strategy to support meaningful user actions and activities while providing the desired aesthetic and enabling the relevant business processes.

Admittedly, the "business portals" of the past left us longing in this area. Creating an impressive, impactful experience for business users was just not seen as a requirement by the majority of organizations. While it could be argued that a general website still demands more in the area of UX than a CRM-driven business site, the gap is fairly negligible. In my years of experience as a Salesforce partner focused on community-led, multi-cloud implementations, I have seen the focus on UX firsthand. It is no longer an afterthought or a "nice-to-have"—an eye-catching UX is assumed to be present from the onset of the project. And, fortunately, Experience Cloud is finally delivering this to customers. Instead of seeing a site as a trade-off between business data and user experience, it's fair to expect the ability to have cake and eat it, too—by combining a slick, modern user experience with critical business data and valuable member interactions.

Why Salesforce Experience Cloud?

Now that we've established the basic elements of Salesforce Experience Cloud, let's ask a critical follow-up question: *Why* Experience Cloud? Let me take a moment to explain why this offering warrants close attention.

A Cross-Cloud Approach

It is true that the Experience Cloud has, to a degree, flown under the radar for much of its life. Followers of this "cloud" may have noticed fairly subdued marketing messaging, as opposed to more direct announcements about other areas of the platform. At a glance, this might suggest a minimal role for Experience Cloud on the platform.

However, with a closer look at the situation, those paying attention will see that it's quite the opposite, with online digital experiences playing an increasingly integral part in how organizations manage their business on the Salesforce platform. Instead of focusing on a site as a siloed solution, underlying business-enabling tools for specific areas of sales, service, and marketing are driving the need for these business sites. Businesses need to connect with customers, partners, and employees; Figure 1-4 illustrates the "cross-cloud" nature of Salesforce Experience Cloud.

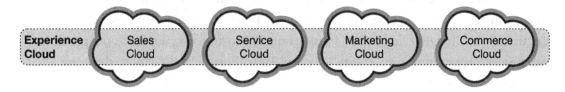

Figure 1-4. *Experience Cloud cuts across the other "clouds"*

Companies are looking to engage and connect with members *in the context of their business*. For example, an organization heavily focused on sales will likely incorporate some aspect of their sales processes into the site. Figure 1-5 shows how a digital experience can bring out this key business context through the means of a site on the Salesforce platform.

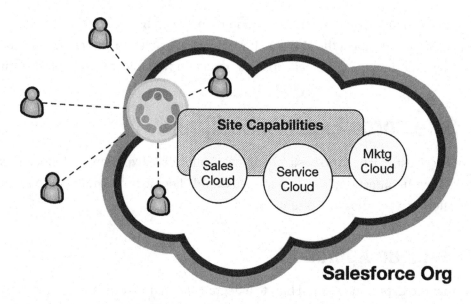

Figure 1-5. *An Experience Cloud site provides the ability to deliver functionality (e.g., sales, service, marketing) to a specific audience*

Transformation, Innovation, and Progress

I am fortunate to have been close to Salesforce's digital experience platform, Experience Cloud, since its inception. My first solo implementation was in 2013. While working for a Chicago-based Salesforce services organization as a senior business analyst, I was tasked with delivering a support-centered community for a global leader in authenticated payments and secure transactions located in Mentor, Ohio. The reality at the time was that the product ("Community Cloud" at the time) was so new and, frankly, so functionally limited that "expertise" loosely equated to knowing what was *not* possible with a Salesforce community. Figure 1-6 provides a glimpse back to those days and what we were working with.

Figure 1-6. *A look at the only "point-and-click" option for building communities, circa 2013*

It's a nice anecdote, but why highlight the shortcomings of the platform about which you are about to read hundreds of pages on the topic? I bring it up because the Salesforce communities of the past are nothing like those of today. Technically, tab-based communities are still around, but they are absolutely not Salesforce's focus. The paradigm shifted to a focus on Lightning years ago, and we've reaped the benefits.

In 2015, Salesforce introduced the Lightning Community Builder and the Napili template to the world. This was a mammoth leap from both tabs-based and Visualforce-based sites. Alongside the benefits of reduced implementation time and increased UX flexibility, an immediately visible effect of this new direction was the extension of control from purely technical resources to include "technofunctional" resources looking to employ declarative methods first. Administrators and business analysts had always been a key part of site implementations, but their postdesign role had historically dwindled when requirements were complex. The reality was that when a significant amount of Apex and/or Visualforce came into the picture, a dependency on technical resources was also introduced.

Don't get me wrong; the picture I'm painting is typical of any customized or personalized software. Big changes mean bringing in the "big guns" in the form of traditional developers. And that is exactly what has fundamentally changed within Salesforce Experience Cloud. Earlier, I carefully used the language "extension of control" as opposed to "shift of control" because as it becomes easier to make changes declaratively, the ability to extend these digital experiences continues to increase. This is not an "admin vs. developer" discussion; it's a discussion on how to best utilize multiple roles and skill sets when building a site on the Salesforce platform.

Ultimately, this shift has benefited customers. It means that a site that has been properly designed, developed, and implemented will result in a streamlined solution that requires minimal maintenance and can be further enhanced or extended without overhauling the existing solution. I'll dive more into the details in Chapter 3.

The huge strides in establishing an accessible platform that uses modern development and design standards are not to be ignored. Fortunately, Salesforce didn't stop there, as they continued to work on the underlying platform for Experience Cloud. Now, with Lightning Web Runtime being the clear focus for the foreseeable future, we can continue to stay ahead of the curve with beautiful, performant digital experiences on the platform.

Nomenclature

Before we take our deep dive into the world of Salesforce Experience Cloud and learn how to leverage this powerful product, I'd like to provide some clarity for readers on an important topic: Experience Cloud nomenclature. These terms have changed over time, and I'd like to set a foundation for their proper use before getting too far.

Keep in mind that, in the recent past, Salesforce renamed "Community Cloud" to "Experience Cloud." This was both a big deal and much ado about nothing. On the one hand, Salesforce "clouds" aren't renamed every day; the term "community" was used ubiquitously by trailblazers for years. On the other hand, the actual product itself technically didn't change one bit when the name changed. Sure, change was in the air, as it always is with all areas of Salesforce, but the name change was a marketing decision, not a technical one. With all of that said, it's important to be clear on our terms going forward.

Previous Term	Current Term	Notes
Community	Site	The reality is, many (actually, most) people still use "community" for this. While "site" is the correct term for the ultimate output from Experience Cloud, "community" still works.
Lightning Community	Experience Builder Site	
Lightning Community <x>	Experience Builder <x>	For example, template, theme, page.

Recap

This chapter provided the foundation for the rest of the book. I addressed the questions of what and why regarding Salesforce Experience Cloud to prepare readers for the more tactical, hands-on sections that follow. Call me crazy, but I think it's important that anyone in this space understands the benefits of building sites with Salesforce Experience Cloud and why this platform is one that will continue to grow to meet the demands of the future.

CHAPTER 2

Planning and Preparing for Success

As tempting as it may be to just dive in and start building an Experience Cloud site—especially considering the declarative capabilities of the Salesforce platform—proper planning and design of your site will firmly establish a much more likely path to success. It is true that, with the power of "clicks," you can build a very basic demonstrable site in a surprisingly short period of time. However, when we're talking about enabling a series of potentially intricate use cases for an enterprise that incorporates various pages, components, and objects, we'll need to go beyond simple examples that highlight the configurability of the platform. To accomplish that, appropriate planning is critical.

In this chapter, we'll explore a few key areas that need to be considered and explored before the actual build takes place. The more thoughtful the planning is, the smoother the implementation is bound to be.

Note Depending on the scope and complexity of a site, the planning phase could range from a few days to months; ultimately, successful planning will establish a clear picture of both *what* an organization will be building…and *why*.

Establishing a Vision

As obvious as it might seem to read in print, true digital transformation is not born out of a list of requirements. We've all seen it before: the meticulously crafted and organized spreadsheet with hundreds of rows describing in detail each of the functions, capabilities, and attributes of a new system. The organization may have even been able to deliver on it, meeting each and every requirement that came along. However, it's important to keep in mind that what a site technically does or allows should not be

© Philip Weinmeister 2022
P. Weinmeister, *Practical Guide to Salesforce Experience Cloud*, https://doi.org/10.1007/978-1-4842-8132-1_2

considered to be the vision or purpose for that site. For example, consider a service-related scenario from both sides. Implementing a specific feature such as Einstein Bots might serve as a key piece of a service-driven experience that will very likely bring quantitative value. At the same time, it's critical to understand that the long-term goals for the service piece of the digital experience will go far beyond a specific feature like Einstein Bots.

Let me try to help you visualize the difference between a vision-led site and a feature-driven site. Figure 2-1 conveys this idea. This visual shows the process of building a site as a supplemental exercise; start somewhere, add some new functionality, and arrive at the intersection of the current state and the added features. This is how many websites are developed.

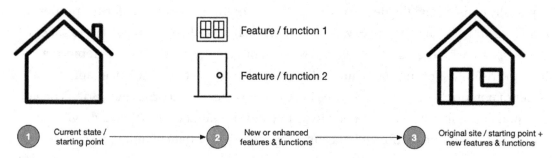

Figure 2-1. *A feature-led approach to building communities*

Now, consider a different path. What if you truly embraced the concept of digital transformation and envisioned the end state first? Instead of focusing on the figurative nuts and bolts that are required to build the machine, you would focus on the machine itself. By first thinking of the goals for the machine, the nuts and bolts needed to build it will naturally come into clear focus. Take a look at Figure 2-2. The "what" (the vision) is then *followed by* the "how" (the supporting elements to achieve that vision). In Figure 2-1, the "what" was simply features and functions without a strategy or vision.

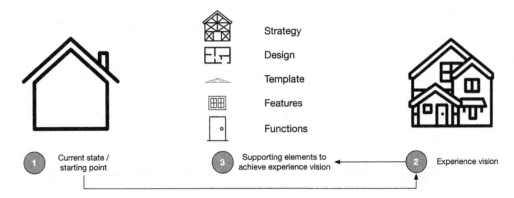

Figure 2-2. *The "how" can—and should—follow the vision for a site*

The depth and breadth of planning needs will vary among organizations. Let's say an individual works for a small firm with an even smaller budget looking to have some form of an online presence via Salesforce Experience Cloud. It's unlikely that this person will have the resources to craft a grand vision for their site—and that's fine. One can still think ahead and come up with a long-term plan that will help to prevent a short-term, feature-focused site that ends up on the shelf after the novelty has worn off.

Validating the Vision

How can site builders tell whether they are on the right track in site planning and preparation? An easy way to identify the common misstep of focusing solely on features or requirements is to do a quick role-play activity. Consider a hypothetical conversation with an executive sponsor about the envisioned digital experience to explain what it's all about in a one-minute summary (i.e., an elevator speech). If the content coming out revolves around page layouts, specific components, or sharing rules, some concern is warranted.

So, what would be compelling to a site's executive sponsor? Take a look at Figure 2-3. In this visual, I convey two very different sets of experience drivers and identify which set shows long-term vision.

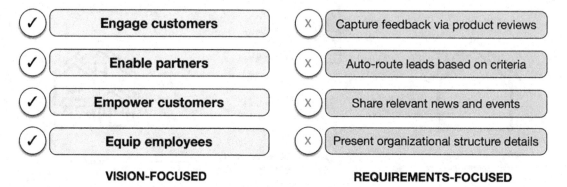

| | VISION-FOCUSED | | REQUIREMENTS-FOCUSED |

Figure 2-3. *Examples of vision vs. requirements*

Even if a builder has already ventured down the requirement-centric path, they can always take a step back to better understand and communicate the purpose of the site. This calls for a moment to focus on site vision crafting. To establish the strategic direction for a site, one will need to identify the corresponding why, what, and who. Figure 2-4 provides a sample of questions that could help formulate this vision.

Know the:	By clarifying:
Why	• Why is an Experience Cloud site being considered? • Why would the expected audience use the site? • Why is the existing solution, if any, unsatisfactory?
What	• What are the known business drivers? • What are the key business challenges? • What is the expected outcome of the experience?
Who	• Who will have interactions via the site? • Who will be impacted by site activities and interactions? • Who could be considered a site stakeholder?

Figure 2-4. *Asking the right questions early in the site planning phase*

The items in Figure 2-4 are just a sample of the types of questions that one will want to ask during your planning phase. With an understanding of information from questions like those shown here, site administrators, managers, and developers will find that the presentation of a compelling, succinct story of an envisioned experience will flow with relative ease.

Note   I'll assume that if someone is involved in building a site in any way, they will understand the basics (and criticality) of gathering detailed requirements and establishing use cases. This chapter is not intended to provide an overview on business analysis; rather, it is to provide the right mindset when establishing an Experience Cloud site to ensure that builders think of key elements and ask the right questions.

Key Planning Areas

As you gather, analyze, assess requirements and use cases, and prepare to build an Experience Cloud site, there are a number of functional and technical topics to potentially address:

- Licensing

- Org strategy (multi-org, new vs. existing org)

- Site type (templates)

- Reporting and analytics

- Security (access, visibility, sharing, permissions)

- Topics and knowledge articles

- Branding

- Process automation

- Deployment

- Management and moderation

- Activation, onboarding, and training

- Login/SSO

- Page variations and dynamic branding

I will dive into many of these topics in the coming chapters. However, in this chapter on planning and preparation, I want to call out a few specific areas that warrant particular attention early in the process:

- Site audiences

- Data sources and systems

Experience Audiences

Identifying all relevant audiences is a key step in preparing for a site build. Site administrators might not yet have all related users categorized, but they should have a sense for the individuals who play a direct or indirect role in the experience. It may be fairly straightforward to determine the active "doers" within the site (although there are definitely exceptions to that statement); however, it's critical not to forget the "receivers" of site activity. For example, site activity may result in data that is routed to users who are not obvious, direct participants. These impacted users *are* still part of a relevant audience and need to be considered. Figure 2-5 gives a visual representation of audiences associated with both primary and secondary user groups within an Experience Cloud site.

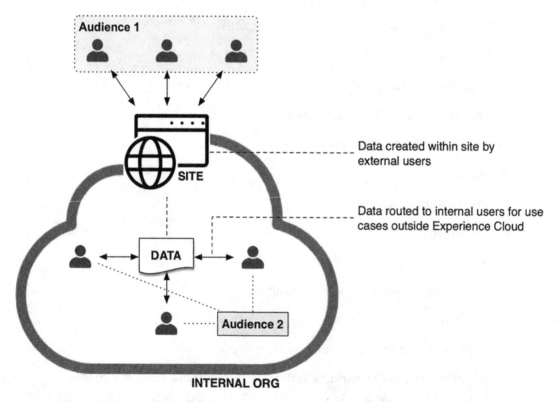

Figure 2-5. *Make sure to consider all potential audiences within the site*

Data Sources and Types

Site builders must know their data. Along with members, data will serve as the lifeblood of a site. Requirements and use cases should help to extract this information, but a systematic approach is needed to ensure that all bases are covered. Admins should step through the following and identify which of these components will come into play in your site:

- Standard objects

  - Standard fields

  - Custom fields

  - Field types

- Custom objects

  - Standard fields

  - Custom fields

  - Field types

- External systems

  - Data types

  - Data fields

  - System of record

While your organization's setup may not require having to peer outside Salesforce, it's unlikely that 100% of your data will reside in your Salesforce org. Sites frequently leverage data from outside sources. Figure 2-6 gives a picture of what this might look like.

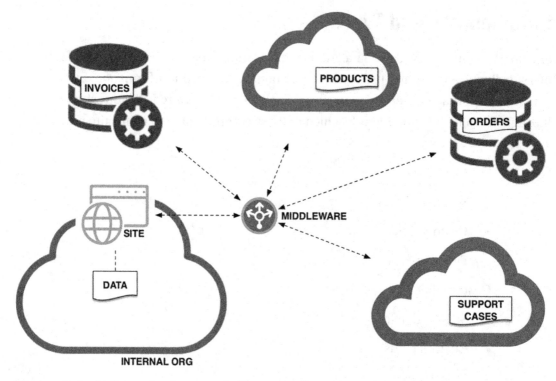

Figure 2-6. *Take an inventory of all potential sources of data when planning your site*

I stress having this familiarity with the site data because unaddressed issues at the data level—be it missing data, improperly mapped data, or data integrity issues—will plague your experience from day one. Inevitably, an initial negative perception will adversely impact the adoption of the site. Like a famous dandruff shampoo brand once stated, "You never get a second chance to make a first impression."

Measuring Success with KPIs

Even with a moving vision for an experience and an extremely comprehensive set of detailed requirements and user stories, success is not guaranteed. While an organization may have positioned its experience well to make a positive impact, there is one way to ensure that it has achieved your goals: by establishing key performance indicators (KPIs) and monitoring corresponding site activity over time. With quantitative, measurable goals, those building Experience Cloud sites can eliminate subjective conjectures and provide facts on how the site is operating, at least to a degree.

Your KPIs will do more than you might realize to help you achieve success in your Experience Cloud implementation. KPIs will benefit your site, its members, and you by

- Measuring success through objective means

- Aiding communication by revolving around data and facts vs. feelings

- Guiding decisions on future investments through revealed insights

- Establishing benchmarks to assist with monitoring and interpreting trends

- Meeting standard by aligning with stakeholder expectations

While the measuring comes post-implementation, one can start thinking about defining the KPIs as early as desired. Figure 2-7 shows examples of some metrics that warrant consideration, depending on the site's audience(s) and use cases.

Sample site metrics / KPIs	
Member registration	Call volume
Member login / engagement	Case volume, response times
Page views	Opportunity volume, amount, closure %
Likes, post, comments	Lead volume, quality, conversation rate
File views, downloads	Custom satisfaction score (CSAT)
Reputation activities	Net promoter score (NPS)
Data interaction / activity	Order volume, amount

Figure 2-7. *Examples of metrics to consider before the site build starts*

Note   The high-level metrics in Figure 2-7 are a sample of potentially relevant metrics. It's likely that some of these won't be applicable to your site, while other, unlisted metrics should be added to this list.

Make sure to think carefully about what an effective KPI is before you hastily throw together a list of metrics. Here are some best practices and considerations that should be factors in your development of solid KPIs:

- They are objective and consistently measured.

- They are clear and meaningful to stakeholders.

- They are almost always time-bound.

- They represent key data, trends, activity, or behavior.

Establishing a Road Map

A common pitfall in the implementation of software is the equating of the initial launch, or "go-live," with the software's end state. This applies to the development of Experience Cloud sites as well, and failure to consciously avoid this mistake can have significantly detrimental effects. In other words, the path doesn't end when your site launches; you'd better have a plan before you get to that point.

The good news is that a simple road map for your site can do wonders in this area. First, ask yourself some key questions:

- How do we see interactions and behavior evolving over time?

- What's our long-term goal or vision?

- How can we continue to engage and compel the audiences of our site?

- What's next (postlaunch)?

- What are additional use cases that would complement those available now?

Considering your available human and financial resources, you should at least be able to construct a high-level road map for the future of your Experience Cloud site. From here, you'll want to focus on ensuring the successful delivery of your road map. To do so, I would suggest three action items to help you stay on track:

1. Stick to the mission. Always have the guiding principles and vision in mind.

2. Be flexible. Don't lock yourself into an unchangeable road map. Pivot, as needed.

3. Communicate. Share the latest road map and associated progress with stakeholders regularly.

Establish a Development Lifecycle

One of the Salesforce platform's greatest attributes—its support of low-code development, allowing powerful business solutions to be built rapidly through configuration—can also be one of your biggest obstacles to success. How so? Since progress can be delivered so quickly with clicks, the temptation to focus on a project's build phase is undeniable. I would caution you, however, to fight that temptation and, instead, establish a proper development lifecycle for your Experience Cloud site. That doesn't mean adopting a bureaucratic, rigid process that adds unnecessary red tape; it means that you should apply the appropriate amount of attention to the various phases of your project to achieve the following:

- Timely identification of appropriate project resources

- Reduction or elimination of repeated or redundant activities

- Clear and complete communication of progress and status to stakeholders

- Long-term success via preparation and plan thoroughness

There is no exact lifecycle formula that can be applied to all Experience Cloud implementations, of course. You will need to assess what will work best for your individual site build. However, you may consider an approach that looks something like this:

1. *Discovery*: Identify the business challenges and drivers that warrant change.

2. *Design*: Identify what needs to be built and how.

3. *Development*: Build (configure, code, etc.).

4. *Launch*: All activities associated with publishing/activating the experience.

5. *Management*: Everything that would follow launch, including ongoing tasks.

Of course, other phases (e.g., Strategy) may be needed as well. Again, think through what your organization needs and craft a lifecycle accordingly. As you determine the development lifecycle for your site, I would suggest two key points of advice. First, you need to be flexible. The fluid nature of these projects (and the Salesforce platform as a whole) requires that you are prepared to adjust your plans as you move forward. Do not chain yourself to a plan that isn't working. Second, do not neglect postlaunch activities. It is surprisingly easy to find yourself at the point of launch without a thorough plan in place to manage the site for some time into the future. That can be a catastrophic mistake for your site, as it will inevitably encounter a growing number of challenges without the proper attention and care.

Assembling the Ideal Team

Unless you've been through a full Experience Cloud implementation a few times, the picture of the ideal team to bring your site to life might be a bit fuzzy. Just like with the development lifecycle, there is no plug-and-play formula that I can suggest for every build. However, there are definitely some key roles to consider:

- *Strategist/Consultant*: Crafting a vision and outlining the path to success

- *Business Analyst/Functional Architect*: Capturing and analyzing requirements, establishing clear user stories

- *Designer (UI/UX)*: Providing perspective on the user experience (look and feeling, styling), creating wireframes for the site

- *Configurator/Declarative Developer*: Handling the "clicks" side of the build

- *Developer (Front End, Back End, Full Stack)*: Supporting all customization required for the site, including developing Apex, Lightning components, etc.

- *Technical Lead*: Managing and overseeing the customization

- *Technical Architect*: Guiding the team on big-picture architectural items

- *Quality Engineer*: Ensuring the quality of the delivered site

- *Content Specialist*: Handling key data and/or content for the site

- *Community (Site) Manager/Administrator*: Managing the members and related activity, owning the site road map

As you assess your needs and which roles will be critical for your project, I would suggest that you carefully consider each individual's responsibilities and how to best leverage their strengths. I understand that some people can tackle multiple project roles and that can, at times, work out for the best. However, the proverbial "Swiss army knife" can quickly become overloaded without clear delineation of what is expected of time or boundaries on their responsibilities. Also, stick with the experts, when possible. Try to avoid scenarios like having your developers conduct functional testing. Even if they have some solid QA experience, that can often lead to less-than-ideal results. Let each individual shine in their area of expertise.

Recap

This chapter explored a critical, but oft-underestimated, phase of the site development lifecycle: planning. A general foundation was provided for achieving success upon deployment of an Experience Cloud site, although you will need to go much deeper with your own organization's specific needs, requirements, and use cases. The other main takeaways from this chapter should be grasping the criticality of a vision for a digital experience and knowing where you are headed...and *why*.

CHAPTER 3

Experience Cloud Licenses and Member Groups

A critical element of any site-building journey is the identification of corresponding groups of members who will be direct participants in the digital experience. In particular, site builders will need to identify which individuals will comprise a particular group (e.g., employees, partners, or customers), which capabilities and functions will be needed for each group in order for the corresponding individuals to achieve success or fulfill a desired role within the site, and how members will mesh with new or existing business processes in the context of system behavior. To a degree, this relates to the access and permissions that will be granted to each member group. However, the focus in this chapter will primarily reside at a more foundational level: user licensing. While the constitution of an organization's mix of Experience Cloud licenses can evolve over time, an unplanned shift in a set of licenses will come at a cost. Fortunately, such impacts can be avoided by establishing a proper understanding of license types and how they apply to a site early on in the project lifecycle.

Note Two questions that must be addressed early by an organization using Salesforce Experience Cloud are "Which licenses do we need?" and "How many of each license do we need?". Delaying or avoiding these questions can have significant financial ramifications for your organization.

25

P. Weinmeister, *Practical Guide to Salesforce Experience Cloud*, https://doi.org/10.1007/978-1-4842-8132-1_3

Experience Cloud User Licensing

An essential aspect of building a successful Experience Cloud site is the understanding and application of appropriate licensing. To assist with those activities, I will explore a few areas:

- *License types*: The types of licenses that grant Salesforce users access to Experience Cloud sites

- *License functionality*: The access and permissions that each license type provides for corresponding users

- *License application*: How licenses are applied to Salesforce users

- *License duration*: Named (long-term) vs. login-based (short-term) licensing

- *License management*: Optimization of the license mix over the life of a site

License Types

Before we proceed into specifics of Experience Cloud licenses, I feel obliged to say something that will become clear to you over time, if it's not already apparent: Salesforce licensing can be frustratingly unclear at times. I think the largest contributor to that sentiment is the frequency at which licenses types are retired, renamed, or newly introduced. Look, I get it; Salesforce evolves rapidly and their set of licenses will change accordingly as well. I will cut them a bit of slack for that. However, I believe it's important for me to communicate this to you. You're not the exception; licensing can be a challenge. The one piece of good news for Experience Cloud is that the "core" or "standard" licenses have been fairly stable for some time.

To clearly explain the various licenses that are available to Experience Cloud users, it's helpful to first group them:

- Standard Experience Cloud licenses (external users)

- Legacy Experience Cloud/portal licenses (external users)

- Standard Salesforce licenses (internal users)

Standard Experience Cloud Licenses

I have been building Experience Cloud sites for a number of years; I have seen a wide variety of different use cases that need to be solved and different constituencies that make up a site audience. The vast majority of site-related licensing, as one would expect, comes from this bucket. However, it is critical to understand that these licenses are for *external users* only; none of these license types will enable access to an "internal" Salesforce org. Equally important to understand is the fact that you would not (and should not) purchase these external license types for employees.

There are three license types that fall into this group:

- Customer Community

- Customer Community Plus

- Partner Community

Note   Each of the primary three license types for external Experience Cloud users houses two underlying child license subtypes: User (named member) and Login. I will address these later in this chapter.

Technically, there are a few other license types that enable external Experience Cloud users. I am categorizing these as "secondary," as they are much less commonly used than the three previously mentioned:

- External Apps

- Channel Account

Legacy Experience Cloud Licenses

There do exist site user licenses that are no longer available to new organizations looking to build an Experience Cloud site, but are grandfathered for active use in some previously created orgs. I won't dissect the access or functionality associated with these licenses since you cannot newly acquire these license types for your Salesforce org, but having a list may be useful for reference. As of the publication of this book, legacy license types related to external Salesforce users of which I am aware include the following:

- Customer Portal Manager Standard

- Customer Portal Manager Custom

- Customer Portal—Enterprise Administration

- Gold Partner

- High Volume Customer Portal

- Overage High Volume Customer Portal

- Service Cloud Portal

- Authenticated Sites Portal

Standard Salesforce Licenses (Internal)

While there are no license types for internal users that are specifically and only for the purpose of granting access to Experience Cloud, many do allow for external access in addition to internal org access. I'm grouping a number of licenses into this bucket. Most notably, the most typical/common license for internal users is found here. Users with these licenses can be granted access to an external site; an additional license is not needed. I won't go into all the types in the "other" bucket, but know that there are other license types that provide internal users with the ability to log in to sites:

- Salesforce ("full" internal users)

- Salesforce Platform* (limited internal access; e.g., no leads, opportunities, or products)

- Other/Legacy license types

Please note a few items, especially if you have had confusion over these license types before. First, the names of some of these licenses have changed multiple times (e.g., Force.com ➤ Salesforce Platform; Employee Apps ➤ Lightning Platform ➤ Platform (Starter/Plus)). Additionally, the label shown on marketing pages doesn't always match what you see within an org (e.g., Platform Starter/Plus vs. Salesforce Platform). Finally, some of these consist of a license *and* an add-on license via a permission set license. You might have seen "Company Communities" before; that is now a permission set license that is associated with the Platform license. The bottom line here is that any user with a Salesforce or Salesforce Platform license may be a member of any site within the same org.

License Functionality

A key aspect of the licensing around Experience Cloud sites is the set of capabilities and functionality that each license type provides.

External Experience Cloud Licenses

The most common question I get about licensing is about the difference between the various license types and what each type grants a user, in terms of access, permissions, and system capability. This question is typically asked for the purpose of making a wise decision on a forthcoming purchase of licenses. In general, organizations want to purchase the least expensive license(s) that will support their given use cases. When the focus is on ensuring maximum capability instead of the financial expenditure, organizations may be inclined to simply purchase premium licenses (i.e., Partner Community). Even then, though, the organization will need to consider user volume, which could impact the decision.

Let's take a step back and look at the picture from a high level. It's important to understand which Experience Cloud capabilities are enabled through these license types. Figure 3-1 shows the access each type provides to "standard" Salesforce (internal) and to sites (external).

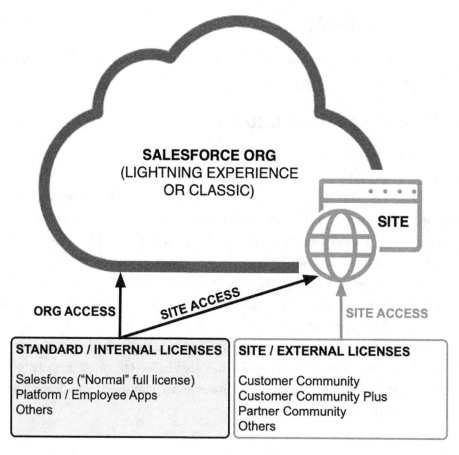

Figure 3-1. *Site licenses do not provide "internal org" access*

The main takeaway of Figure 3-1 is that a number of licenses provide internal org access (via classic and/or Lightning Experience) and access to the sites that live within that org, while external user licenses are intended only for access to Experience Cloud sites.

Now, I'll zoom in and take a closer look at Experience Cloud licenses to understand what makes sense for different use cases. Figure 3-2 shows a layered view of functionality available to users with each of the three Experience Cloud licenses.

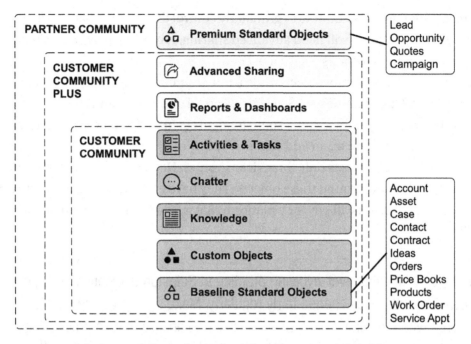

Figure 3-2. *Enabled capabilities by external Experience Cloud license type*

Based on my personal experience working with organizations to build a site on Salesforce, a substantial portion of licensing decisions—outside of financial constraints, of course—come down to two requirements:

- Advanced sharing

- Access to opportunities (i.e., the Opportunity object)

I'll go into detail on access, sharing, and visibility in Chapter 8, but it's important to understand what "advanced sharing" means in the context of licensing here. With Customer Community licenses, the sharing model and sharing settings that we've all come to know and love within the classic or Lightning Experience interface is, for the most part, not available. That's correct: users with Customer Community licenses are not able to benefit from any of the "advanced" elements of standard sharing. That means that while admins *can* grant general read-only or read/write access for a specific object to external users, they *cannot* manually share records with them, set up sharing rules for them, or even set one of these users as the owner of a record through the UI. User sharing is extended with Sharing Sets, which can aid with automated sharing but provide significantly less flexibility than standard sharing. The bottom line is that, if an organization needs to be able to granularly control the records that external users can see, that organization will need advanced sharing, requiring *at least* the Customer Community Plus license for its external users.

Access to the Opportunity object, while a much simpler concept, is no less critical on the platform. Opportunities are Salesforce's bread and butter, and Salesforce isn't sharing this loaf for pennies anytime soon. It might seem odd that access to a few objects (Lead, Quote, Campaign, etc., in addition to Opportunity) would command a separate license in a model that boasts only three license types. However, think of it this way: the real money is made around these objects. They have everything to do with driving revenue, and companies will pay for a platform that will help them to do that effectively and efficiently.

Note   Licensing is an ever-evolving practice at Salesforce. License types, names, functionality, and prices change fairly regularly. Make sure to directly contact Salesforce when making a purchasing decision to ensure that your licensing information is accurate and up to date. One likely example of change is the probable replacement of "Community" with "Experience" in external user license names at some point.

Employee License Functionality

While employee licenses don't technically fall in an "Experience Cloud licensing" bucket, they are an ideal option for providing employees with low-cost access to both the internal org and one or more communities that are a part of the org. Figure 3-3 shows a high-level view of functionality in the two types of employee licenses.

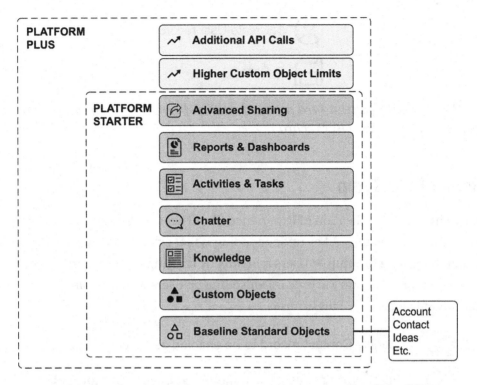

Figure 3-3. *Additional custom objects are a major reason for "Plus" licenses*

License Application

The actual application of Experience Cloud licenses is not intuitive, as it fundamentally varies from the process of applying a standard license to a user. Let's walk through the process for each scenario.

Note   There are different tactical ways to carry out the application of licenses (e.g., via the UI, via Data Loader, etc.). The focus here is to provide more of a conceptual understanding of how site user records are created.

Standard/Internal User Setup

To create a standard/employee user, an administrator can follow a simple, traditional approach, as shown in Figure 3-4.

1. Create User record

 2. Save

Figure 3-4. *Creating a standard internal user is simple and straightforward: create and save the new User record*

Customer User Setup

When we shift to the application of Experience Cloud licenses for external users, other steps come into the picture. A key understanding is that external site licenses are never applied by navigating to Setup ➤ Users and directly creating a User record, as we saw in Figure 3-4. Figure 3-5 shows the process for setting up users with Customer Community and Customer Community Plus licenses.

 1. Identify Contact record to be enabled as a Customer User

 2. Enable Contact as a Customer User (**Enable Customer User**)

 3. Create User record

 4. Save

Figure 3-5. *Creating a Customer User record involves starting with a Contact record*

Figure 3-6 shows the specific action to be selected to create a User record for a customer from the Contact record.

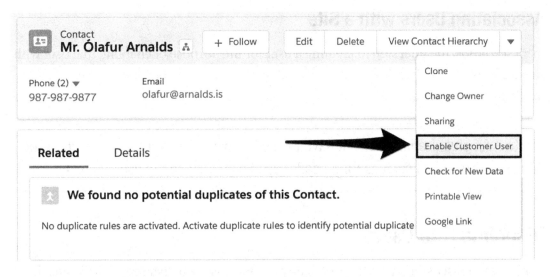

Figure 3-6. *Before a User record can be created for an external site user, an administrator must click Enable Customer User on the Contact record*

Partner User Setup

To create a partner user, there is an additional step. For partners, you will need to first establish the related Account as a Partner Account. Figure 3-7 shows the steps to set up a partner user for sites.

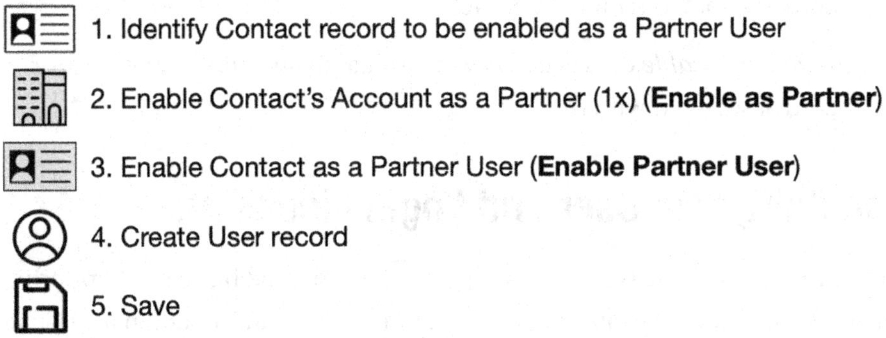

1. Identify Contact record to be enabled as a Partner User

2. Enable Contact's Account as a Partner (1x) (**Enable as Partner**)

3. Enable Contact as a Partner User (**Enable Partner User**)

4. Create User record

5. Save

Figure 3-7. *Creating Partner Community User records involves both Contact and Account records*

Associating Users with a Site

In all scenarios, the final step to creating a user for the purpose of enabling that user with site access is to associate the profile or permission set of that user with the site. I'll cover this in more detail later in the book.

Note   An organization does not have to use Classic or Lightning Experience to set up site users; a tool such as Data Loader can be used to create users in bulk.

Disabling Site Users

While it's not discussed or performed nearly as much as the activation of site users, the act of disabling site users is also an important activity to be familiar with. Four primary functions exist, two at the account level and two at the contact level:

- *Account ➤ Disable Partner Account*: This deactivates all partner user records associated with contacts on the account.

- *Account ➤ Disable Customer Account*: This deactivates all customer user records associated with contacts on the account.

- *Contact ➤ Disable Partner User*: This deactivates the partner user record associated with the contact.

- *Contact ➤ Disable Customer User*: This deactivates the customer user record associated with the contact.

License Subtypes: User and Login Licensing

Each of the three site license types that we previously covered has a corresponding "login" license subtype. For example, both Customer Community Login and Customer Community licenses are available for providing users with customer-level access to a site.

The idea is simple. For users who do not log in frequently, providing them with a "named user" license is unnecessarily costly. On the other hand, providing a regularly active user with a login license is not sensible either, as they will also incur avoidable costs. Salesforce suggests that the crossover point is 3:1, based on the list price of these two license subtypes. This means that if a user logs in three or more times per month, they should be a named user. Figure 3-8 shows this decision point.

Note   The cost ratio of named-to-login site licenses is subject to change. Confirm with Salesforce where the recommended line exists before making a decision.

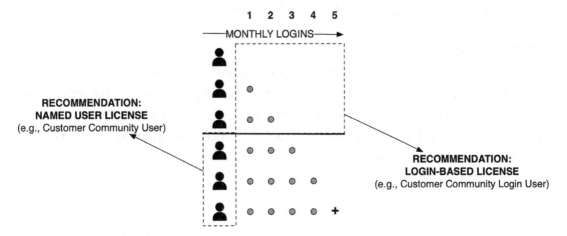

Figure 3-8. *Users who log in three or more times a month should be set up as named users*

Choosing wisely between named users and login-based users is critical and can significantly impact the bottom line. Let's walk through this with an example org from our example company, WeinCo. Assume that WeinCo has six external site users with varying login activity. Figure 3-9 shows the login activity by users over a given month.

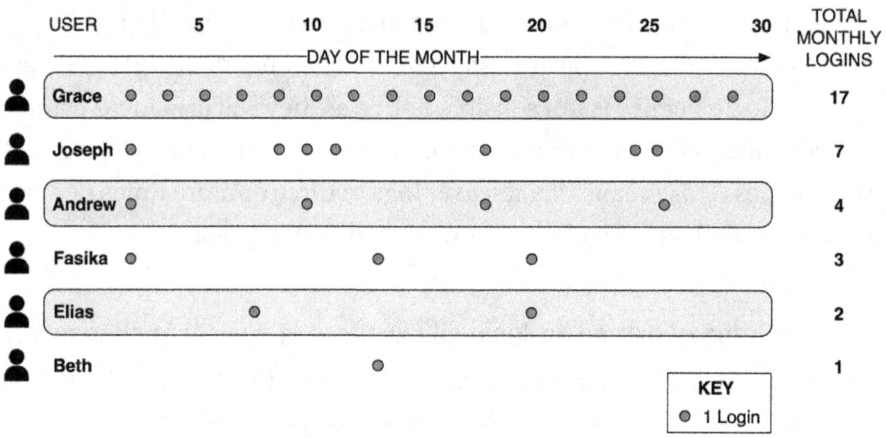

Figure 3-9. *Login activity for WeinCo external site users*

While the licensing decision may seem simple, success is dependent on an organization's ability to predict future activity and apply licenses accordingly. This is obviously a bit more variable than having a set of users with completely repetitive, predictable behavior. In Figure 3-10, I show four possible approaches for WeinCo to apply license types and the ramifications of each. The high-cost option would cost the organization more than twice the optimal option!

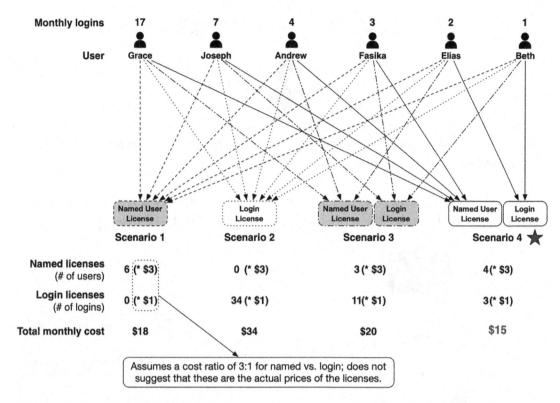

Figure 3-10. *The optimal licensing scenario (4) comes in at less than 50% the cost of the least optimal scenario (2)*

License Management

A final key point specific to licenses is that there are specific capabilities regarding a change in licensing for a specific user. I will place these types of changes into two buckets: *named vs. login* and *license type/level*. A user can be switched, with relative ease, between named and login user licenses, as shown in Figure 3-11. Of course, this assumes available licenses of each type, which would be necessary for the switch.

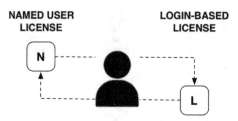

Figure 3-11. *Assuming license availability, an admin can move a user between named and login-based licenses*

Named vs. login is a fairly straightforward concept. Changes of license *type* are a bit trickier. Figure 3-12 shows what is possible between standard site license types.

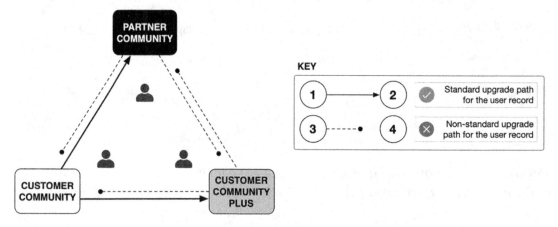

Figure 3-12. *The upgrade and downgrade paths between community licenses are not intuitive. Know these before making a license purchase*

Note   The nonstandard upgrade path does not completely prevent a site member in that scenario from being migrated from one license type to another (e.g., Partner to Customer). It does, however, mean that the process is much more involved, requires more time and analysis, and may result in data loss.

The Concept of Member Groups

Familiarizing oneself with the various site licenses and what functionality those licenses encompass is necessary for Experience Cloud success. However, I can't simply leave the conversation there; the concept of "member groups" goes beyond a license label. It is critical to clearly understand what it means when you see labels such as "Employee Experience," "Partner Experience," or "Customer Experience."

Technically, organizations do not exactly "buy a [member group] experience" although Salesforce's marketing engine can imply that, at times. I'll explain what I mean in the rest of the chapter. Consider our fictitious company, WeinCo, for a moment. True, WeinCo can subscribe to an Experience Cloud license bundle that has 100% employee licenses—with zero partner and customer licenses—for a site named WeinCo Employee Community. In that sense, WeinCo just purchased an "employee experience"; however, it's important to understand that the site name is arbitrary and doesn't necessarily have anything to do with functionality or capabilities, and the mix of licenses can be changed at any time. If a Partner license is added and leveraged for this site, is it still technically an "employee experience?" This question is rhetorical; the point is that it's up to the organization to determine whether this community is still labeled as an "employee experience" or not.

Some may be thinking, "Wait, I thought Salesforce had a Partner offering for Experience Cloud…so you *can* buy a type of site that is based on a user group!" That is a partner *template*, which technically can be leveraged with a variety of license types; it is not necessarily limited to partner licenses. Additionally, nonpartner functionality can easily be added to a site using this template. I'll discuss templates, or Lightning Bolts, more in Chapter 12.

The key takeaway in this section is that the labels of *employee*, *partner*, and *customer for a site* do not directly relate to off-the-shelf Experience Cloud SKUs from Salesforce; the supporting licenses do. In the context of the site itself, these labels are descriptors and serve two purposes by clarifying the following:

- The spirit/essence of the experience

  - Functionality, capabilities

  - User experience/presentation

- General licensing structure

  - Distribution of available site licenses in the org

  - License distribution of users actively logging in to the site (e.g., a site leveraging only Customer licenses would be considered a "customer experience")

As an organization's need to connect with employees, partners, and customers expands, it becomes easier to see that Experience Cloud is a true digital experience platform that allows for a spectrum of site manifestations that aren't limited to one specific audience type. I created Figure 3-13 to assist in that line of thinking. This figure shows potential overlap between function, vertical, and site member group; notice that each vertical and function includes more than one member group.

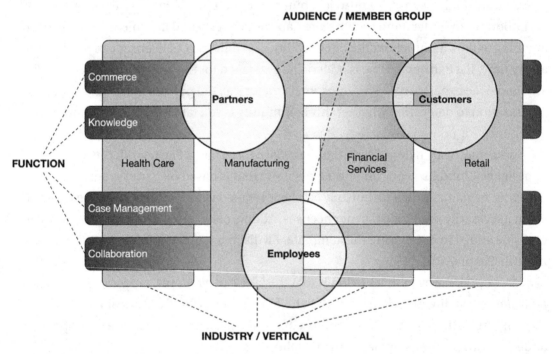

Figure 3-13. *Experience Cloud sites can support various combinations of audience, function, and industry*

With all this said, I need to be clear on one point. I said quite a bit about understanding the concept of member groups, specifically clarifying what exactly it means to label an experience as a certain type (e.g., "employee experience"). It is extremely common to label sites or communities in this way, and I am not discouraging the application of these labels whatsoever. Ultimately, it is by far the simplest way to describe the purpose of a site, even if the mix of licenses is not homogenous. My main goal here is to provide you with a deep comprehension of what a site comprises that goes beyond a simple label.

Blending Member Groups Within Sites

We benefit from a couple major paradigm shifts that occurred when Salesforce introduced sites—at the time, communities—and started moving away from portals. First, multiple member groups can be enabled within a single site. Second, an individual user, regardless of member group, can be enabled in multiple sites and can do so *at no additional cost* to the enabling organization. Let's dive into both and better understand how they impact the development of an Experience Cloud site.

Multiple Member Groups Within a Single Experience

Within an Experience Cloud site, multiple member groups can coexist. This is no small revelation, as legacy "portals" did not allow for this. At that time, an organization would build a "partner portal," and it would be limited to a few license types associated with the partner portal. The concept of mixing multiple license types did not exist. Well, the game has changed, and we are all beneficiaries of that change.

If one does want to slap a label of "employee," "customer," or "partner" on an experience, let's at least open it up to the full gamut of possibilities. While both admins and users will definitely hear those three labels most commonly, there are four additional member combinations that need to be considered:

- Customer and Partner Experience

- Customer and Employee Experience

- Partner and Employee Experience

- Customer, Partner, and Employee Experience

Figure 3-14 shows how these member groups can come together to form blended experiences.

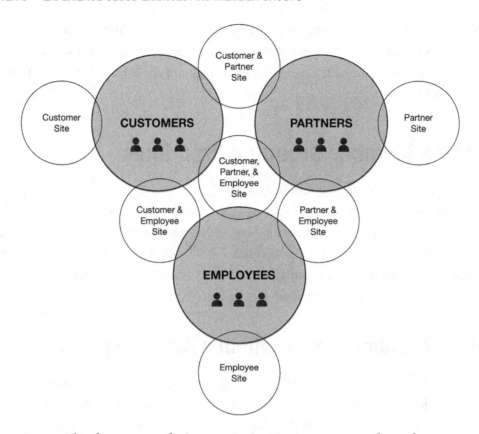

Figure 3-14. *The three most obvious experience types are not the only ones available to you; 4, 5, 6, and 7 are hybrid experiences*

One User in Multiple Experiences

Another major revelation in Experience Cloud is that a single user, regardless of member group, can be enabled in multiple sites. Additionally, this can be done *at no additional cost* to the enabling organization. Not only is this ideal from a financial perspective, it means you can manage a single identity for an external user who may need to be part of multiple sites. No one wants multiple user accounts anymore, especially on the same platform for similar use cases. Figure 3-15 depicts what this potentially means for an individual user.

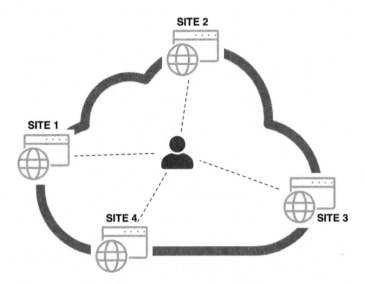

Figure 3-15. *One user can be granted access to an internal org and all the sites within that org*

Recap

In this chapter, I dove headfirst into the world of licensing and how licenses come together with the concept of member groups such as customers, partners, and employees within Experience Cloud sites. I reviewed various aspects of licenses, including types, functionality, application, and management. Additionally, I explained the idea of named users vs. login-based users and how to approach your licensing purchases in light of these options. Finally, I opened up the concept of multisite users, as well as sites with multiple member groups.

CHAPTER 4

Experience Cloud Template Types

Technically, the first choice one is required to make when creating a new site is selecting an appropriate template, or "Experience Builder template." One could argue that this decision is even more critical than the selection of license types, as those can be changed without impacting the site itself (see Chapter 3 for some caveats to this statement). As I see it, a template has three primary purposes:

1. Establishing an overall theme for the digital experience (e.g., focusing on customer service, commerce, manufacturing, etc.)

2. Providing technological foundation and scope to guide expectations and drive site road map

3. Accelerating site development through inclusion of preconfigured Lightning pages and components

In this chapter, I will walk through the specific templates that are available, the decision-making process that should precede template selection, and other considerations and factors that are important when selecting a template in Experience Cloud.

Template Terminology and Lightning Bolts

Before I dive in, I want to eliminate potential confusion around Salesforce terminology, specifically "Experience Builder template," or "template," and "Lightning Bolt Solution," or "bolt." While Salesforce has not provided an official stamp on this, I would propose that the terms be considered and interpreted as follows:

© Philip Weinmeister 2022
P. Weinmeister, *Practical Guide to Salesforce Experience Cloud*, https://doi.org/10.1007/978-1-4842-8132-1_4

- *Template*: A standard, out-of-the-box template that is provided by Salesforce and is available in a new org

- *Bolt*: A custom template that is created by a Salesforce partner or customer and is not available in a new org

In this chapter, we'll be focused on templates. However, I will walk through how to develop a Lightning Bolt Solution later in this book.

Another area of potential confusion lies in the option to select a Visualforce-based site from the template selection screen. While "Salesforce Tabs + Visualforce" remains a valid selection (and will be discussed in this chapter), I would not group it with other templates. First, considering that the official, full term for templates is "Experience Builder template," it would be nonsensical to apply this label to a template that can't leverage Experience Builder. Second, while it is a starting point for a site, it is really not a "template," per se. If we consider a template a starting point that contains specific elements and tools out of the box, you'll find almost none of those with the Visualforce selection.

Introduction and High-Level Categorization

The specific template choices available when creating a site can be split into two primary categories (Tabs and Visualforce are not separated, but are presented as one consolidated option). At the time of this book's publication, the available templates from Salesforce are

- Experience Builder templates (Lightning)

  - Aloha

  - B2B Commerce*

  - B2C Commerce*

  - Build Your Own

  - Build Your Own (LWR)

  - Customer Account Portal

- Customer Service

- Help Center

- Manufacturing*

- Partner Central

- Insurance Agent Portal

- Financial Services Client Portal

- Salesforce Tabs + Visualforce

Your first choice will be selecting an Experience Builder template or the "Salesforce Tabs + Visualforce" option. For that decision, I will review the Lightning templates as a single, general template choice. Although differences do exist between Customer Service, Partner Central, and the other Lightning templates, they are fundamentally similar and leverage the same core tools for site building. I will review the template-specific differences later in this chapter. See Figure 4-1 for some potential options that may be available to you when first creating an Experience Cloud site.

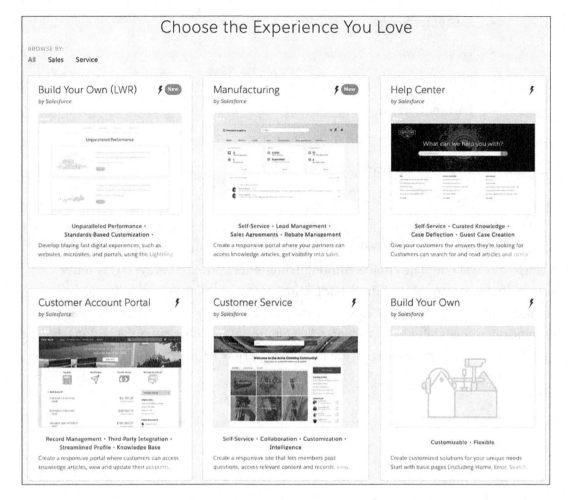

Figure 4-1. *Some Experience Builder templates that may be available at the point of initial site creation*

While "Tabs" and "Visualforce" are actually part of one template, I will look at these as two distinct choices in this chapter.

When I mention a "tabs-based site," I am specifically referencing a site created with the *Salesforce Tabs + Visualforce* template that uses the standard, out-of-the-box navigation menu and sidebar. It's possible that the site leverages Visualforce pages *and* tabs, but the shell of the site is declarative, not custom. Figure 4-2 provides an example of a tabs-based site.

Figure 4-2. *A tabs-based site*

When I discuss a "Visualforce site," I am referring to a fully custom site that does not employ a standard, out-of-the-box navigation menu or sidebar. Everything in a site like this would be custom, with the exception of a few default Visualforce pages that can be leveraged (e.g., "Page not found" page). See Figure 4-3 for an example of a Salesforce site built on Visualforce.

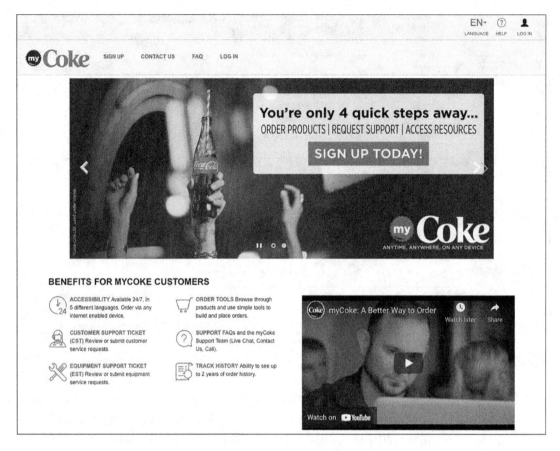

Figure 4-3. *A Visualforce-based site*

This leaves us with three template "groups" to walk through:

- Tabs
- Visualforce
- Lightning

Overview and Assessment

I am going to spoil the ending and tell you now: you should exhaust all reasonable scenarios in which you select a Lightning template when building out a site for yourself or a client before you consider a Salesforce Tabs + Visualforce site. However, these are still available options, so I will walk through each one and outline pros/cons of each.

Salesforce Tabs + Visualforce

Tabs

Tabs provide a declarative, no-code option with which one can build a site. However, I cannot with a good conscience suggest to anyone—for any reason—to build a tabs-based site. Even in the situation where you want to create an extremely basic site and don't plan on using technical resources, a Lightning-based template is going to be your best choice. The user experience within a Lightning site is significantly better than that of a tabs-based site; additionally, the ease with which you can drag and drop your way to a finished masterpiece with Lightning puts tabs in the rear-view mirror, once and for all. See Figure 4-4 for a view of a key administration page within a tabs-based site (I will cover administration in detail in Chapter 7).

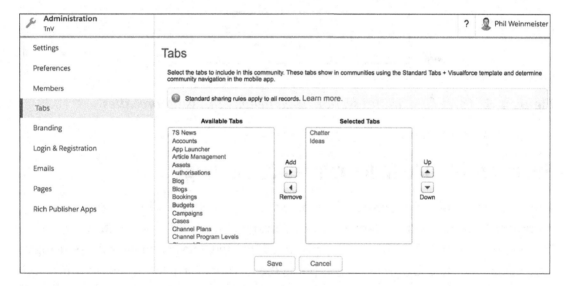

Figure 4-4. *Adding tabs to a tabs-based site (no drag-and-drop options available)*

Visualforce

By nature, Visualforce allows for an essentially limitless palette. Since a Visualforce site is built almost solely on code, you can granularly control the user experience and functionality. However, it's important to understand that this does come at a cost. With Visualforce sites, one will find a solid correlation between the output and the investment required to get there. If you want extremely complex business logic with a bespoke UI, you'd better be ready to pay for it. In other words, "clicks" won't get you to where you need to go, shrinking the pool of resources that can build this type of site. Figure 4-5 shows the administrative area that one would frequently use when building a Visualforce site.

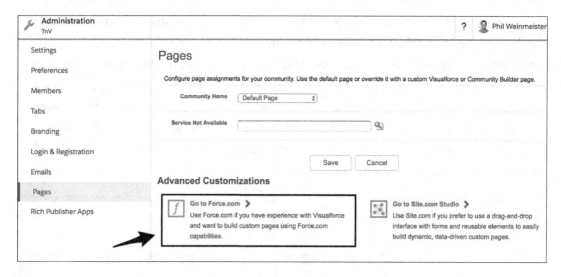

Figure 4-5.   *Force.com admin section, used heavily in Visualforce sites*

Experience Builder Templates (Lightning)

The introduction of Lightning-based templates to the Experience Cloud portfolio a few years back truly changed the game. Furthermore, it has matured significantly over the last few years, closing the few gaps that previously existed. I have built many sites using tabs, Visualforce, and Lightning. At this point, there is not even a thought as to which path I will take for a new site (for any set of potential use cases); it will undoubtedly be a Lightning-based Experience Builder template. Why? I'll provide a few reasons.

Extreme Productivity for Noncoders

To say that Lightning does not require code or technical resources in general is a bit misleading. Yes, technically, like with tabs, an individual can create a site with fairly useful functionality from scratch in short order without a line of code. However, to truly deliver digital transformation, it is highly likely that custom Lightning components will come into the picture. As we all know, those custom components will require code. To be clear, though, this will be the case with any highly transformative solution, whether delivered with Visualforce, Lightning, or another front-end platform.

I think it's more appropriate to say that Lightning sites enable and empower those of us who are not programmatic developers (i.e., noncoders) in ways never before possible within the world of Salesforce sites. Not only can a "functional" resource efficiently configure a Lightning site, but they can assemble something much greater than the individual parts. I will share a few personal examples of this to illuminate the concept.

Since starting to work with Lightning sites, I have found myself in multiple situations where availability of technical resources was extremely limited or nonexistent, but an inventory of existing assets (in the form of custom components) was at my disposal. I have been able to take these assets and, through reassembling and reconfiguring them, create a different application. Of course, the ability to do this depends on the flexibility of the original components, but this scenario is not a pipe dream.

I'll provide a few specific examples of taking disparate solutions and declaratively combining them. I have taken commerce and CPQ elements from different providers and, by leveraging the related components and some additional platform tools, created an end-to-end configure/price/quote → checkout/purchase application in a Lightning site. Another example is with Lightning Flow; I have taken custom components built for one specific purpose and, without any communication with the original developer, leveraged these components within a flow as part of a Lightning site. I simply learned what attributes were available and set them according to the need within the site.

In general, the concept here is that you can take individual Lightning components and create something that is greater than the individual parts; that "something" is a digital experience in the form of a Lightning page. Figure 4-6 provides a visual of what I'm describing.

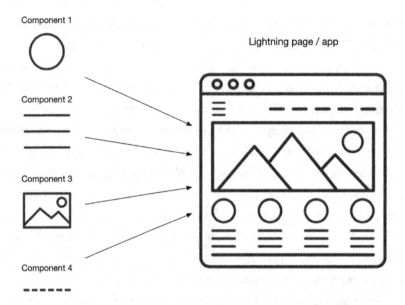

Figure 4-6. *Lightning allows the efficient creation of new or enhanced applications by consolidating and configuring components from disparate applications*

WYSIWYG Editor with Drag 'n' Drop Control

Neither tabs nor Visualforce offers a WYSIWYG ("what you see is what you get") site editor. That is a fairly significant limitation when you consider that you are building an online visual experience for your audience(s). Sure, you can preview the site, but to have little or no visual context while you are building is not a desirable situation.

Lightning offers this with Experience Builder, which I will dive into in the next chapter. It's important to understand that this is a major advantage over tabs and Visualforce. Seeing what is being built along the way saves a significant amount of time in the long run.

Additionally, with Experience Builder, administrators can drag and drop components onto and off of Lightning pages. Administration UX has made a major shift in this direction over the past decade, and it's fairly intuitive to most of us in an admin or developer role. This is also helpful for efficiency; what's faster than clicking, dragging, and unclicking to make a new element appear on a page?

Salesforce Lightning Design System

The Salesforce Lightning Design System (SLDS) (`www.lightningdesignsystem.com`) means that even a rudimentary Lightning site will provide a largely acceptable level of aesthetic pleasure for users. SLDS is used out of the box within all Experience Builder templates, as one would expect. This means a much slicker, more modern look and feel than you'll find with tabs or most Visualforce sites. So, what's included in SLDS?

- *Component blueprints*: Building blocks for Lightning component development

- *Utilities*: Utility classes that apply a single rule or simple pattern to components

- *Design tokens*: Elements that store visual design attributes and are used in place of hard-coded values

- *Icons*: Library of icons that support the Salesforce interface

True, SLDS is at least partially supported within Visualforce. It is not recommended by Salesforce for retrofitting into existing pages, but is an option for new Visualforce pages.

Focal Point for New Functionality and Innovation

Since it's not an immediately impactful area, the future road map and potential innovation related to a template choice can be easily overlooked. However, it should be a key factor in any organization's decision when selecting a site template. Salesforce is only investing in Lightning, at this point; it should not come as a surprise that Salesforce is not spending anything on Visualforce innovations or enhancements these days.

So, what does that mean for an organization looking to build a Salesforce site? It means that the decision to build with an Experience Builder template will reap benefits well beyond the launch date. No organization launches a site without hope of long-term success; it's fair to look a few years out when thinking about how a technology decision could impact the future. Sure, Visualforce might suffice today and allow your experienced developer who knows Visualforce to whet their appetite for some old-school development challenges. However, this approach is shortsighted. It's not a wise bet to overlook the continued maturity and expansion of Lightning and, likewise, not insightful to bet on an aging technology that is relatively stagnant. Figure 4-7 provides a conceptual view of how innovation has played out among these three template types over time.

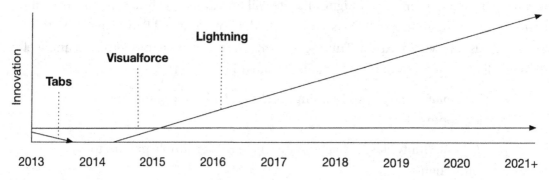

Figure 4-7. *Lightning is where the innovation is at on the Salesforce platform*

Impact of Template Selection

Why is template selection so critical when creating a new site? I will walk through a few areas that warrant serious consideration and explain why.

Relevant Functions and Features

Even with setting aside the almost limitless world of customization to extend a site, there exists a plethora of site-specific and site-enabled functionality that is provided out of the box on the Salesforce platform. While many organizations leverage some custom functionality and others may even want a completely tailored, pixel-perfect site, the vast majority want to maximize the platform and what is possible without reinventing the wheel or spending unnecessary funds.

To that end, templates come with and/or support specific functionality. As one may be able to deduce, that means that some templates *don't come with or support* specific functionality, making your template choice that much more critical. For the most part, this is a fairly clear delineation.

Let's take a look at a few examples:

- *Ideas*: Unavailable without customization in an Experience Builder template.

- *Featured topics*: This component doesn't exist in Tabs or Visualforce and wouldn't be available without building something similar from scratch.

- *Flow*: While Flow can be used in Visualforce pages, Lightning Flow, which has significant advantages, cannot.

Accelerated Site Development

The last section addressed how to ensure that what you will need in your site is supported and/or enabled. Let's now shift to focusing on how your template selection can get you to the finish line as quickly as possible. While different templates may support various functions, notable work might be required to get them up and running.

I need to make sure that a key point is not missed here; only Lightning sites can come with site elements prepositioned and preconfigured. With Tabs + Visualforce sites, you always start from scratch. Figure 4-8 gives an idea of the overall concept.

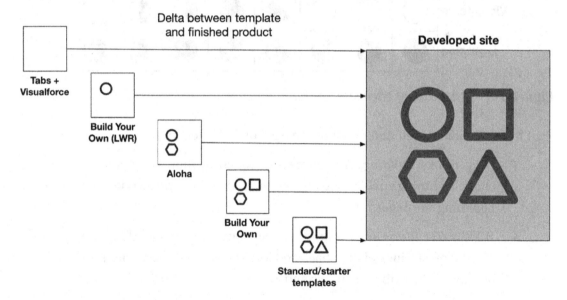

Figure 4-8. *Each site template brings with it a certain amount of out-of-the-box functionality*

Technological Foundation

Choosing the appropriate template is much more than a consideration of available or supported functions and features. With Lightning now on the scene, your choice has an immense impact on how your organization will develop and maintain your site. Figure 4-9 provides some of the corresponding factors that you'll want to consider.

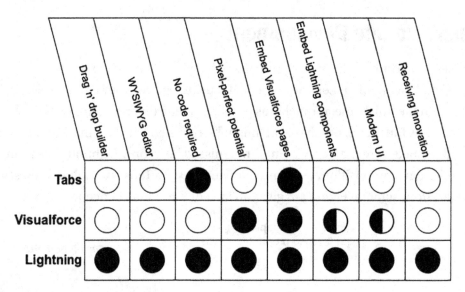

Figure 4-9. *Attributes of each site template type*

I'll provide some additional thoughts on each of these items:

- *Drag 'n' drop building*: Visualforce requires code; Tabs requires clicks. Lightning enables one to drag and drop components onto Lightning site pages.

- *WYSIWYG editor*: Only Lightning (via site builder) provides this. Plan for a lot of clicking/tabbing back and forth between screens when building a site with Visualforce and/or Tabs.

- *No code required*: Tabs and Lightning hit the mark here, requiring zero code. Visualforce is completely the opposite, as it requires code.

- *Pixel-perfect potential*: I believe we have finally reached the point where we can legitimately say that Lightning allows for pixel-perfect site building. A site admin will have to build their own custom theme and custom Lightning components, but it is possible. On the other hand, Visualforce has always been known as the option that allows one to "do whatever they want."

- *Embed Visualforce pages*: Of course, there's no issue with leveraging these in a Visualforce site. It's possible to leverage the "Visualforce Page" Lightning component to wrap Lightning-enabled Visualforce pages for use within Lightning sites. Also, an admin can create a Visualforce tab for a Visualforce page and use that tab in a Tabs-based site.

- *Embed Lightning components*: There are no options for using components in a strictly Tabs-based site, although one can leverage Lightning Out to potentially place components within a Visualforce page. You lose all ability to configure that component via the property editor GUI, however. Components, of course, can live in a Lightning site template.

- *Modern UI*: Tabs clearly do not have a modern UI. Visualforce technically can, but that requires significant customization. The standard Visualforce look to show data is outdated. On the other hand, Lightning clearly shines through here with a slick, modern look that aligns with Lightning Experience.

- *Receiving innovation*: Tabs and Visualforce are, for the most part, in maintenance mode and do not receive significant updates or enhancements. Anything new is being built for Lightning.

Flexibility and Extensibility

A factor in choosing a template that can be easily overlooked is the aspect of flexibility and extensibility. Think of flexibility along the lines of configurability; how easily can a resource make changes without customization (a.k.a. code)? Extensibility stresses the ease with which one can add to, or extend, the solution.

Again, Lightning stands out here. Virtually every aspect of a Lightning site can be modified without code. Of course, to change the essence or nature of a specific Lightning component, a resource will have to modify the code in that component; however, one can easily configure the site and the components contained within via clicks. As far as extensibility goes, new Lightning components can be added with extreme ease.

As for the other options, not so much. Yes, a site administrator can configure a tabs site and make changes without code. However, the ceiling of what they can change is much lower. Extending a tabs solution also doesn't leave a ton of options without requiring a dip into the world of code.

Visualforce sites are inherently inflexible, unless significant time was spent up front to inject configurability into the solution. They can definitely be extended (back to the "do whatever you want" mentality), but customization will be required for almost any extension that is considered.

Experience Builder Template Types

I've spent a good portion of this chapter explaining why you should build your digital experience on the Salesforce platform with a Lightning-based template over a Tabs- and/or Visualforce-based template. However, there's a bit more to the selection process; you still need to decide which specific Lightning-based template to start with. Now, I'll walk through the groups of currently available templates and help to inform you which specific template might fit your requirements and vision most appropriately. First, let's create buckets for each group of templates:

- Horizontally focused

  - Customer Account Portal

  - Customer Service

  - Help Center

  - Partner Central

- Product or vertically focused

  - B2B Commerce

  - B2C Commerce

  - Manufacturing

  - Insurance Agent Portal

  - Financial Services Client Portal

  - Others

- Build Your Own

  - Build Your Own

  - Build Your Own (LWR)

- Other/Niche

  - Aloha

- Retired

  - Koa

  - Kokua

I think it's important to share that one of these templates stands out—way out—beyond the others in terms of usage. For a "typical" site, the *Customer Service* template (previously Napili) is by far the most commonly selected and utilized template for building an Experience Cloud site. As for the reason, it's pretty straightforward. The Customer Service template is loaded with available components. In my opinion, its popularity is less about the default layout and configuration than it is about the fact that organizations want to have all available tools for potential use at some point in the lifecycle of their site. To me, that makes sense. Consider it an "instant road map"; while an organization might not utilize all of the available components on day one, they can plan future use and also leverage components as opportunities arise.

As for the other horizontal templates, Customer Account Portal and Partner Central are fairly similar. They are missing some of the components found in Customer Service, but they do boast a different styling and layout perspective, as well as prebuilt pages that map to the use cases for each scenario. To be clear, however, there is absolutely no issue using the Customer Service template for partners or employees; while you may feel more comfortable with "Partner" in the title of the template, it may cause you to miss out on certain functionality. Do note that there are a few items (e.g., Account Brand) that can only be found in the Partner Central template.

The templates focused on verticals or other Salesforce products are fairly straightforward, but with one catch. Each of these does require some specific licensing for use, so some organizations will not see these in their Salesforce org(s). However, if you're using Salesforce B2B Commerce or Salesforce B2C Commerce, you'll know what to do here. Manufacturing is dependent on the Partner Community license and might make sense for organizations looking to build a partner-focused manufacturing site.

The "Build Your Own" templates are stripped-down, bare templates that remove the potential clutter that one might feel exists in the standard horizontal templates. The biggest difference is that there are almost no pages prebuilt or preconfigured; these templates are intended for custom-built solutions. I would not suggest these as "accelerators" or quick start tools; these are to set you up for a specific, tailored community that will likely take much thought and time to build. The "LWR" version works on the Lightning Web Runtime platform. What does that mean for you? It means that the template is only compatible with Lightning Web components; it is not compatible with Aura components. Also, it means that users will experience a notable performance over the equivalent community built with the non-LWR template. As of 2022, however, there's one major drawback to the LWR template; only a handful of out-of-the-box components exist. This means that the vast majority of standard components are not available, creating an immense technical burden on organizations using the template to build a significant amount of custom functionality in the form of Lightning Web components.

Lastly, there is one "niche" template to consider: Aloha. Aloha is intended for identity/login use cases. It can serve as an app launcher, just as you've come to know and expect in Lightning Experience. If you are simply looking for a hub that offers authentication and can direct users to relevant apps that are connected to the Salesforce platform, Aloha is a good choice. You would not use Aloha for standard site interaction and use cases, as you would the other templates that are available.

Recap

In this chapter, I reviewed the three top-level options for building a site: Tabs, Visualforce, and Lightning. Considering criteria such as efficiency, flexibility, and available capabilities, I looked at each template type and provided pros, cons, and recommendations. The clear takeaway? An organization should heavily consider Lightning first; if Lightning doesn't satisfy a showstopping requirement, the organization should have a look at Visualforce. However, the long-term trajectory of the different template types and the likely impact of future Lightning innovation need to be considered; a short wait to jump on Lightning might be worth it in the long run.

CHAPTER 5

Experience Builder

For those who have decided to leverage a Lightning-based template as a starting point for a new Experience Cloud site, a major bonus awaits. That bonus is the opportunity to leverage Experience Builder, the primary tool with which all Lightning-based sites are constructed. Experience Builder, as shown in Figure 5-1, is found as a unique section within the site workspaces and provides the paintbrush, paint, and canvas for those creating a site from Customer Service or any other Lightning-based template. This tool has significantly changed the site creation process and has enabled and empowered many "declarative developers" in the Salesforce ecosystem to develop functional, effective, and vibrant sites.

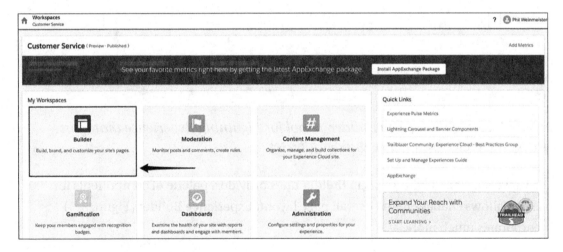

Figure 5-1. *The Builder workspace*

Note   Tabs + Visualforce-based sites do not use Experience Builder.

P. Weinmeister, *Practical Guide to Salesforce Experience Cloud*, https://doi.org/10.1007/978-1-4842-8132-1_5

Overview

Experience Builder is a visual tool that allows those responsible for building a site to see it come to life during the creation process. It is a what-you-see-is-what-you-get (WYSIWYG) editor that provides the ability to drag and drop the main building blocks of a Lightning site—Lightning components—to achieve the desired end state. The closest equivalent on the Salesforce platform is Lightning App Builder (another WYSIWYG tool), which allows administrators to construct apps for Lightning Experience. Lightning Experience is for users of "internal" Salesforce, not of sites. See Figure 5-2 for a view of Lightning App Builder.

Figure 5-2. *Lightning App Builder, a tool for Lightning Experience that most closely resembles Experience Builder for sites*

However, while Lightning App Builder does provide a palette of components for use and allows changes to the overall page layout, Experience Builder (Figure 5-3) incorporates much more.

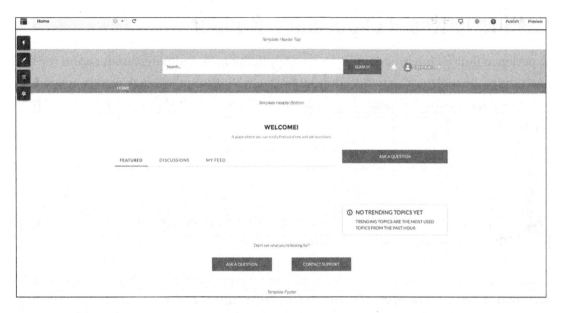

Figure 5-3. *A look at a just-created, "Customer Service"–based site from within Experience Builder*

Within Experience Builder, administrators can perform the following functions, among many others:

- Add, remove, position, and configure standard and custom Lightning components

- Create site pages and configure page attributes (e.g., layout)

- Select an overarching site theme

- Manage sitewide branding colors, fonts, and images

- Create audiences for page variations, branding sets, navigation menus, and components

- Preview and publish a site

In this chapter, I will walk through each of the sections, describe how to use them, and explain how they contribute to the overall creation of an Experience Cloud site using Experience Builder.

Getting to Know Experience Builder

Experience Builder is a broad, multifaceted application. To intimately understand the ins and outs of the tool, a systematic, comprehensive walk-through of each area is needed. I will divide it into two main sections, as shown in Figure 5-4: the left sidebar/tabs and the top menu bar.

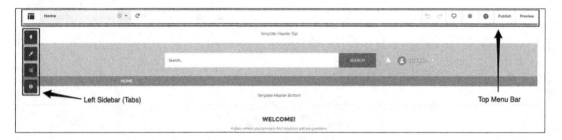

Figure 5-4. *Basic structure of controls in Experience Builder*

Left Sidebar (Tabs)

A significant amount of time building sites is spent using the left sidebar. This sidebar within Experience Builder houses four tabs:

- Components

- Theme

- Page Structure

- Settings

Figure 5-5 shows where each of these tabs is located.

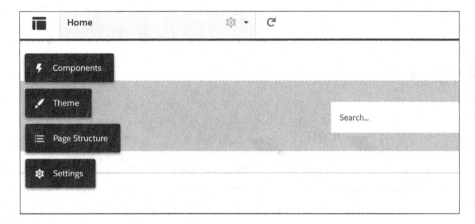

Figure 5-5. *The tabs in the left sidebar within Experience Builder*

Components Tab

An Experience Cloud template provides a basic assortment of prepositioned components already placed on pages to be configured. However, it is inevitable that site creators will eventually want to tap into the available pool of additional components to fill out their site and plug functional gaps. Insert the Components tab.

If I go with the analogy that a component is to a site as an individual Lego piece is to a finished Lego project, then the Components tab serves as a bag of various Lego pieces. The tab is essentially a list of available Lightning components that can be used as core functional pieces in a digital experience. Each component is represented by three items: a text label, an icon, and a description that is shown upon hovering over a component. See Figure 5-6 for an example.

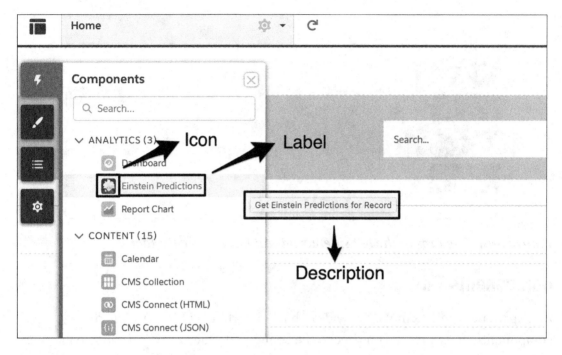

Figure 5-6. *Each component listed in the Components tab has a label, icon, and description*

The Components tab has two primary groupings: standard components, listed first, and custom components, listed last. However, admins will not see both of these exact section headers; Salesforce displays subgroupings within the standard component section. So, while site administrators may see a Custom Components section, they will definitely see sections such as the following that comprise the standard component group, depending on the page context. Figure 5-7 shows the categories on the Home page, also listed as follows:

- Analytics

- Content

- Feeds

- Files

- Gamification

- Messages

- Process Automation

- Records

- Sales

- Support

- Topics

Figure 5-7. *Component categories displayed within the Components tab*

Additionally, one can search by a text string to filter for any component that contains that string. As a bonus, the section headers persist in the search results. See Figure 5-8 for an example of a possible component search.

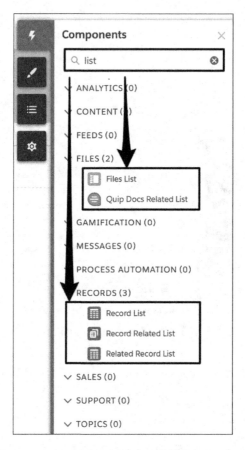

Figure 5-8. *Search results for "list" from within the Components tab*

To add a component from the Components tab to your site, simply perform the following steps (see Figure 5-9 for an example):

1. Click and hold the desired component.

2. Drag the component to the appropriate section and position on the page.

3. Place the component by "dropping" it (releasing from the click).

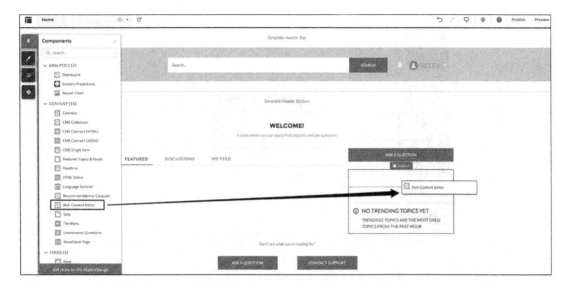

Figure 5-9. *Dropping the Rich Content Editor component on an Experience Builder page*

Don't worry; if a component is placed in the wrong section on the page, it can be easily moved later. I'll discuss the details of handling and configuring components following a drag and drop from the Components tab in detail later; for now, I'll continue walking through the sidebar tabs within Builder.

Theme

While the Components tab focuses specifically on page-level content, the Theme tab generally provides sitewide configurability. Theme includes five distinct sections, as shown in Figure 5-10:

- Overall Theme

- Colors

- Images

- Fonts

- Theme Settings

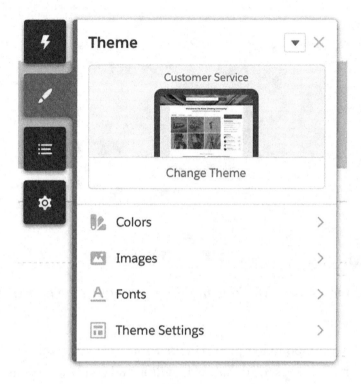

Figure 5-10. *The Theme tab*

Overall Theme (Template)

With the creation of every new site, a set of available theme "templates" come ready to go within Experience Builder. By using these theme templates, it is possible for an administrator to select a prebuilt theme that quickly and broadly expands what is possible with the declarative Experience Cloud UX. See Figure 5-11 for the Change Theme page.

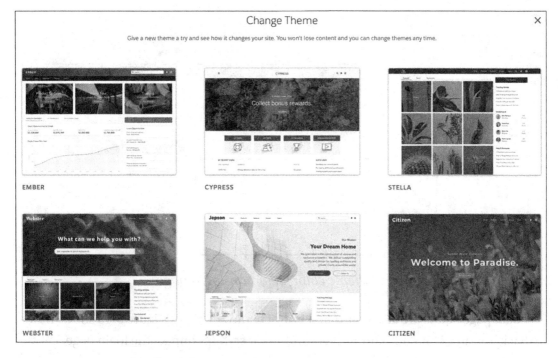

Figure 5-11. *Out-of-the-box site themes*

Colors

The Colors section of the Theme tab defines the colors of specific elements on site pages. The settings in Colors apply to all site pages that leverage the impacted standard components. Figure 5-12 shows the different color settings available and examples of where one can find them on an actual page (in this example, a Home page with minimal variance from the out-of-the-box configuration). This screenshot encompasses "general" and "navigation" colors.

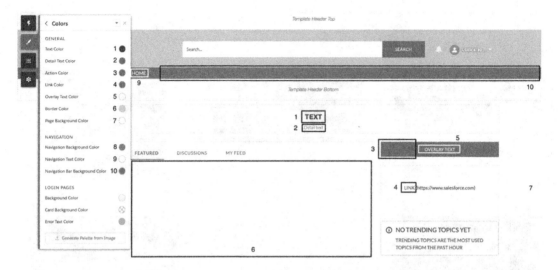

Figure 5-12. *Application of theme colors to a non-login page*

Login page colors are also controlled from Theme ➤ Colors. Figure 5-13 shows how the Background Color and Card Background Color settings impact the login page.

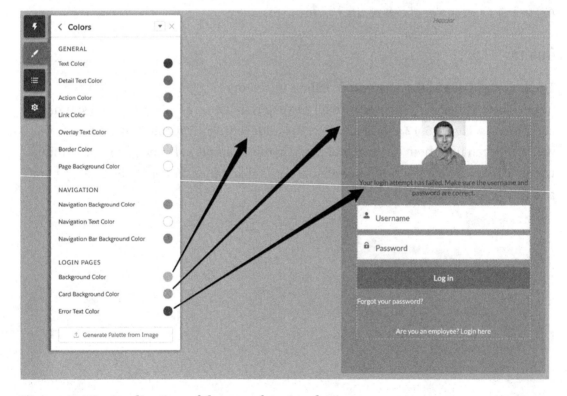

Figure 5-13. *Application of theme colors to a login page*

Images

The Images section impacts the standard header, which is included in all Salesforce-provided templates (other than Build Your Own), as well as the login page. Figure 5-14 shows Theme ➤ Images.

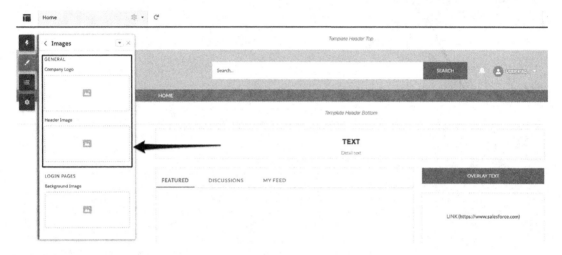

Figure 5-14. *Management of site theme images for non-login pages*

If the standard header is used (as opposed to replacing it with a custom header), two specific elements come into play that are updated in Theme ➤ Images:

- Company Logo

- Header Image

To add either a company logo or header image, click the placeholder image underneath the image type (e.g., Company Logo) and then identify an image. An image can be uploaded from the user's local computer or selected from Salesforce. External data sources that are configured will be displayed as well, allowing users to select images from sources such as Quip, Office365, or Google Drive, among others. See Figure 5-15 for a look at how uploading an image works.

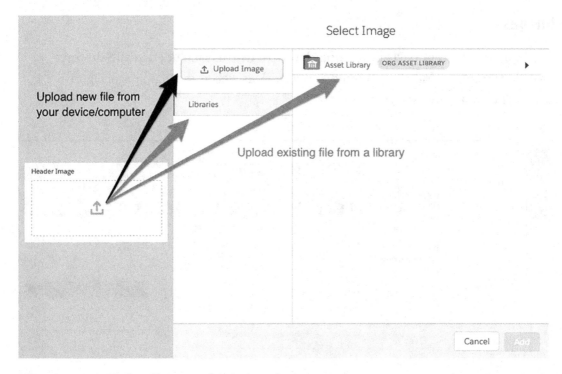

Figure 5-15. *Uploading or selecting an image*

Figure 5-16 shows the final result after uploading both a company logo and a header image.

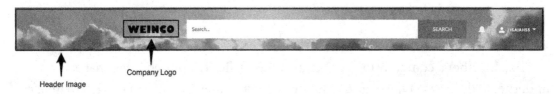

Figure 5-16. *Uploaded images*

Figures 5-17 through 5-19 show three examples of how the header might look in the Customer Service template.

Figure 5-17. *Header example 1*

Figure 5-18. *Header example 2*

Figure 5-19. *Header example 3*

The Images section also allows for the upload of the login background image, if desired. Figure 5-20 shows an example of an uploaded image for the login page.

Figure 5-20. *Uploaded image*

One common area of confusion is the source of the logo on the login page. While it's not clear to me why Salesforce decided to set it up this way, the login logo is managed in a different area from the login page itself. I'll dive into that area later, but I'll mention it now for context. It can be found in Workspace ➤ Administration ➤ Login & Registration ➤ Logo. See Figure 5-21 for a look at where you can modify the logo.

Login & Registration

Brand, configure, and customize your site's login experience, which includes pages used to log in users, verify identities, reset passwords, register members, and for login flows. Tip: To view your login pages as you work, use your browser's private browsing mode to access your site.

Branding Options

Customize your site's login experience to reflect your brand. You can use dynamic branding URLs to change how login and related pages appear at runtime. Learn about Dynamic Branding URLs

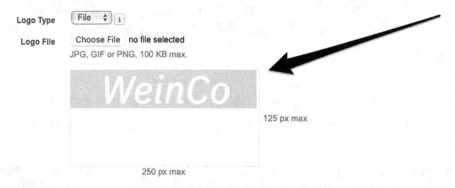

Figure 5-21. *Use the Login & Registration section within Administration to modify the displayed logo on the login page*

Note   The images used for the header image and background image should be Web-optimized versions of high-resolution images. While it's ideal to have clear/vivid images, it's not ideal to "break the performance bank" by forcing a large image to load when the site is accessed.

With the right theme/branding settings, the login page can be transformed into a bright, welcoming page for site members. Figure 5-22 shows a customer-branded login page.

Figure 5-22. *Fun with the login page*

Fonts

The Fonts section impacts the font of all text that does not explicitly have a font already specified. An admin can modify the font for paragraph text (Primary Font) and header text (Header Font). Figure 5-23 shows an example of text impacted by the Primary Font setting.

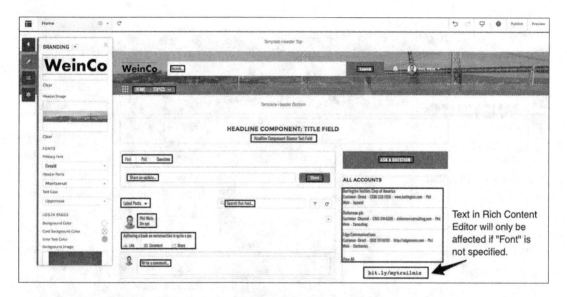

Figure 5-23. *This image shows a number of examples of how the primary font impacts the text on a site page (the Home page, in this case)*

Figure 5-24 shows an example of text impacted by the Header Font setting.

Figure 5-24. *This image shows a number of examples of how the header font impacts the text on a site page*

Additionally, the case of certain text can be configured via the Text Case setting, allowing an admin to set text formatting as Uppercase, Lowercase, or Capitalize or to leave it unformatted. Figure 5-25 shows the text impacted by this setting.

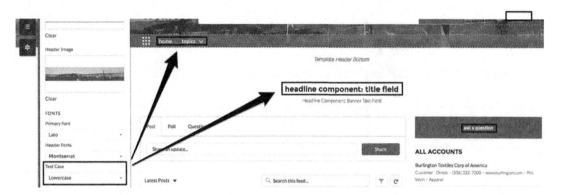

Figure 5-25. *This image shows how the text case impacts the text on a site page (in this case, with lowercase text)*

Theme Settings

The fourth section within the Theme Branding tab is Theme Settings. This allows for modification of some sitewide settings of the theme that apply to all pages. For the standard "Customer Service" theme, the following settings are available, as shown in Figure 5-26.

- Hide the header region and navigation (includes header image, search box, user profile, and navigation menu)

- Hide notifications icon in the site header

- Set max page width

- Search Component (allows replacement of the standard search component with a custom component)

- User Profile Component (allows replacement of the standard user profile component with a custom component)

- Navigation Component (allows replacement of the standard navigation component with a custom component)

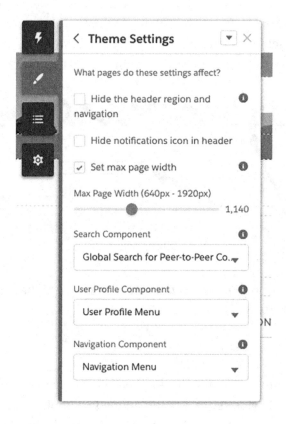

Figure 5-26. *Theme Settings section*

Note Technically, branding sets live within the Theme tab as well. However, this tool is really about audience targeting; I will discuss branding sets in Chapter 11.

Page Structure

Unlike the three other tabs within Experience Builder, the Page Structure tab is largely informational; actions that can be performed from the tab are limited. Page Structure displays two types of data:

- Each layout section that is present on the page currently being displayed

- All Lightning components present within each of those layout sections

Figure 5-27 shows an example of the Page Structure tab contents for a site Home page.

Figure 5-27. *Page Structure tab*

I want to point out a few specific items within the Page Structure tab in the example shown in Figure 5-27:

- *Empty sections*: Some content sections may be empty. This is not a problem; it's common to have a completed page with multiple page sections that do not contain any components.

- *Lock icon*: While the template header shows three components, these components are locked. This means that admins cannot manually remove components within this group through standard means (clicking an X to delete a component). The Napili header, in particular, can be removed by navigating to the Theme Settings (to be described later in this chapter).

- *Hidden components*: Some components will not show up at all if the corresponding feature is not enabled or set up. Some examples of components that won't initially display for this reason include Reputation Leaderboard and Recommendations Carousel. Other components, like Trending Topics, are dependent on data and won't appear until corresponding data exists.

- *Trash can symbol*: As you might expect, this icon allows you to delete a corresponding component from its corresponding section on the page. This is actually very useful. I've had Builder lock up on me a few times, preventing me from deleting a specific component. This icon always allows an alternative way to delete the component successfully.

- *Aura vs. LWC/Code symbol*: A little-known trick, at least as of Summer '21, for identifying whether a custom component on a page is Aura or LWC is to go to page structure and look for the code symbol ("<>"). If that is present, the component is Aura, and clicking the symbol will open the component within the Developer Console. This may change in the future, if LWC becomes editable within the Developer Console.

While I personally access the Page Structure tab the least often of the four tabs on the left of Experience Builder, it is worth being aware of. It allows administrators to confirm page contents; whether a component is hidden or simply hard to distinguish, it can help to verify exactly what is in a specific section. Additionally, it is useful for confirming whether a specific component is present on the page at all. And, finally, it allows for quick editing of certain components.

Settings

The Settings tab within Experience Builder hosts a multitude of configurations that broadly impact your site, as opposed to correlating directly to a specific page or component. The Settings tab includes nine sections:

- General
- Theme
- Languages
- Navigation
- CMS Connect
- Advanced
- Security & Privacy
- Developer
- Updates

I will review each section and explain its purpose and how to manage it.

General

The General section serves as a hub to consolidate key sitewide information. It includes two primary subsections, Site Details and Topics.

The Site Details section houses five pieces of information:

- Site Template
- Public Access
- Site Title
- Published Status
- Guest User Profile

The Site Template setting is purely informational; it is a quick reference to confirm, with certainty, which template is currently being used for the site. Public Access is an important setting that, surprisingly, was not available for quite some time after sites were initially released. This setting allows you to open up access to your site to guest users (i.e., public, unauthenticated users who have not logged in). By default, a site does not allow public access; unless settings are changed from the default, anyone trying to directly access a page in the site would be redirected to a login page.

Note   Here are two key points about public access. First, visibility can be controlled at the page level as well. Even if the site as a whole is restricted, a page can be opened up to guest users. Second, making the site public means that guest users are granted access to all asset files on a public page; you can restrict this in Administration ➤ Preferences (see Chapter 7).

Site Title displays the title of the current site.

Published Status is purely informational and lets you see one of two statuses: "Not published" or "Published." A "Published" status is followed by the URL of the site's Home page.

Guest User Profile is also informational and allows you to access the guest user profile (the profile used by unauthenticated users) much more easily than following the traditional page via administration settings. See Figure 5-28 for the five aforementioned settings.

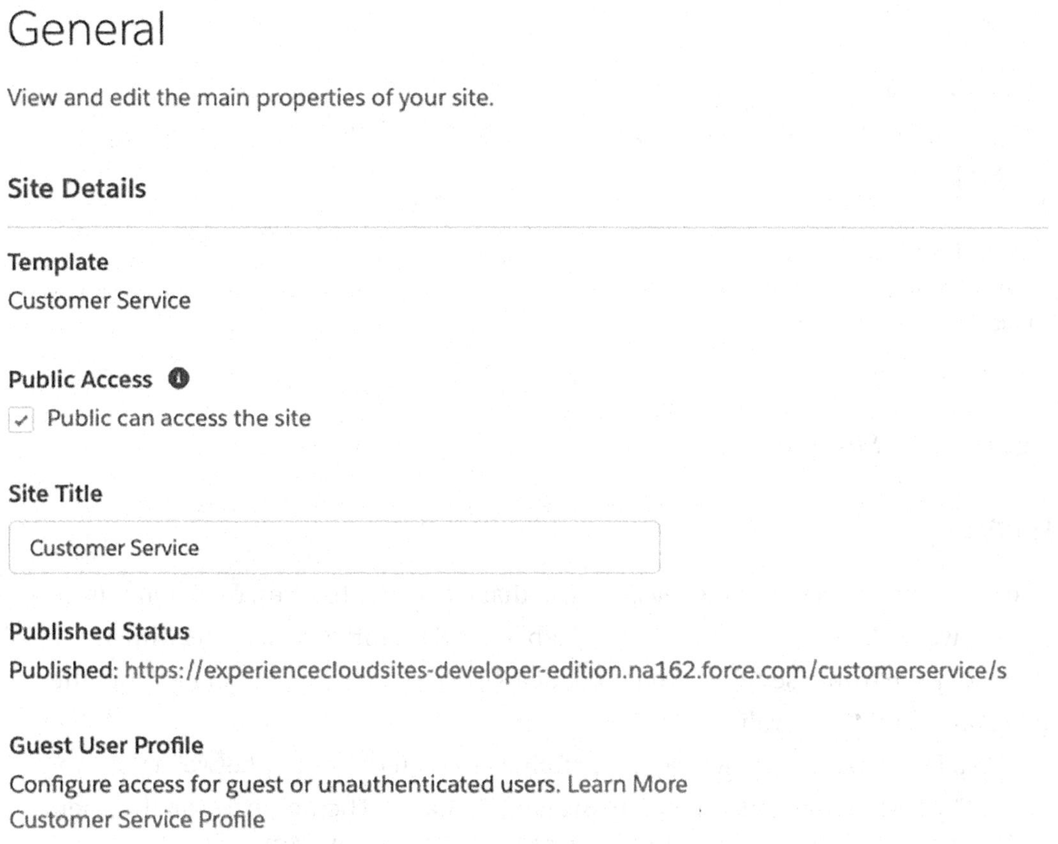

General

View and edit the main properties of your site.

Site Details

Template
Customer Service

Public Access ❶
✓ Public can access the site

Site Title

Customer Service

Published Status
Published: https://experiencecloudsites-developer-edition.na162.force.com/customerservice/s

Guest User Profile
Configure access for guest or unauthenticated users. Learn More
Customer Service Profile

Figure 5-28. *Site Template, Public Access, Site Title, Published Status, and Guest User Profile settings/fields*

In the second section of General settings, the Navigational Topics and Featured Topics links are displayed. See Figure 5-29 for a view of this.

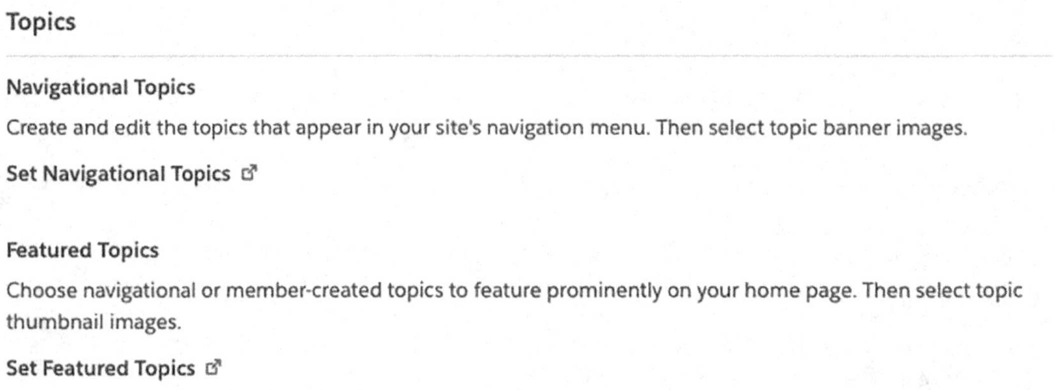

Topics

Navigational Topics

Create and edit the topics that appear in your site's navigation menu. Then select topic banner images.

Set Navigational Topics ⬀

Featured Topics

Choose navigational or member-created topics to feature prominently on your home page. Then select topic thumbnail images.

Set Featured Topics ⬀

Figure 5-29. *Site topics*

Theme

If you're having deja vu, let me reassure you that it's warranted. Yes, earlier in this chapter we walked through the "Theme" tab; now, Salesforce presents us with a "Theme" page within settings. What's the deal? There is an explanation here, but the question is completely valid.

First, I must point out that there is definitely some redundancy between the two pages. The first button/link on the Theme tab is "Change Theme"; here, on the Theme page within the Settings tab, the "MANAGE" tab duplicates the "Change Theme" functionality.

Duplication aside, the Theme tab primarily impacts the look, feel, and usability of a site by controlling settings such as fonts, colors, and images. Within Theme Settings, specifically on the "CONFIGURE" tab, a site administrator can assign and configure the Theme Layout components associated with a particular theme layout. Site themes can be an area of some confusion because of how they are managed and configured. To help clarify how theme layouts and Theme Layout components work with pages, see Figure 5-30.

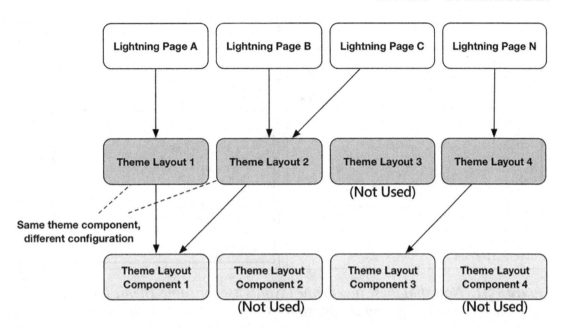

Figure 5-30. *An overview of how Lightning pages, theme layouts, and Theme Layout components work together in a Lightning site*

I'll walk through Figure 5-30 starting with the Theme Layout component. Three sources exist: Salesforce (to use an included Theme Layout component such as Customer Service), one's own development team (to build a homegrown theme), and a third-party provider. All sites use what is provided by Salesforce by default, so that will always be an option. If that is not sufficient, an organization may consider building its own custom Theme Layout component. The Theme Layout component is literally just that: a Lightning component. It has to be developed intentionally for this purpose; it may include an interface, a design resource, and a CSS resource. I won't dive down into code-level details in this book, but that information can be found at http://developer. salesforce.com. Alternatively, a custom Theme Layout component could be obtained from a third-party provider and installed for use.

Once the appropriate Theme Layout components have been installed or identified within the site's org, a site admin would determine how the Theme Layout component (or components) should be applied to specific pages; this is where theme layouts come into the picture. Two different theme layouts most commonly leverage different Theme Layout components. However, this is not a given; the same Theme Layout component could be used in different theme layouts but just configured differently. Figure 5-31 shows two configurations of the same Theme Layout component, manifested as two different theme layouts.

Figure 5-31. *Note that these two theme layouts use the same Theme Layout component but with different configurations*

As part of setting up theme layouts, individual Lightning pages within the site will need to be mapped to a specific theme layout. Figure 5-32 shows an example of how a specific site page (in this case, Quip Docs Related List) could be configured. To modify the associated theme layout, the setting "Override the default theme layout…" must be checked; that will reveal theme layout options below.

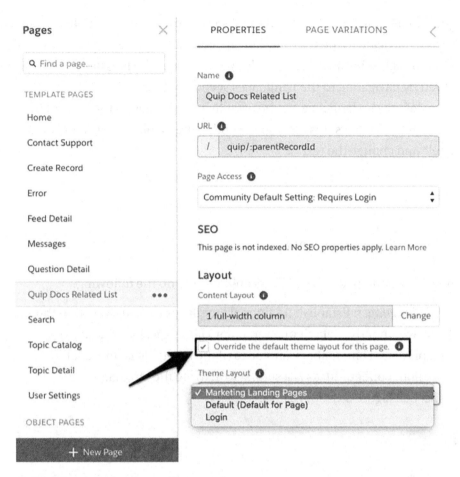

Figure 5-32. *Setting the theme layout for a page*

Be aware that you can create new theme layouts from standard or custom themes. In other words, for a site using the out-of-the-box Customer Service template, the Customer Service theme will be the default. Theme layouts can be created from that theme. However, if a custom Theme Layout component exists in the org, an admin can create a new theme layout from the custom theme vs. just using the Customer Service Theme Layout component.

Languages

Language setup within Salesforce is not exclusive to sites; it is a platform activity that touches various parts of an org. I won't dive terribly deep into all things language within Salesforce, but I do want to at least cover the aspects specific to sites here.

For quite some time after the inception of sites, the only way to configure languages for a site was to navigate to the well-hidden Site.com settings and make changes there. Fortunately, for Lightning sites, that is no longer the case. The languages for your site can be configured by navigating to the Languages section of the Settings tab.

First, the default site language can be established, along with the label of that language. Figure 5-33 shows this setting. To modify the display label, simply click "Edit display label" and change the text.

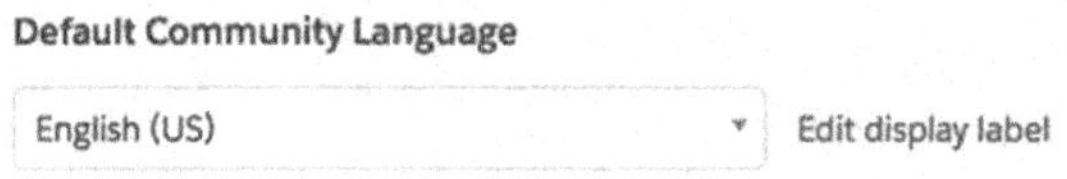

Default Community Language

English (US)   ▼   Edit display label

Figure 5-33. *Default Site Language setting*

The bottom section of the page allows an admin to do the following:

- *Add languages*: Establish additional languages to be used within the site, whether the default or a secondary language. Once added, the display label and fallback language (if the language is unavailable) are both configured, as is a setting to activate the language for the site. See Figure 5-34 for details.

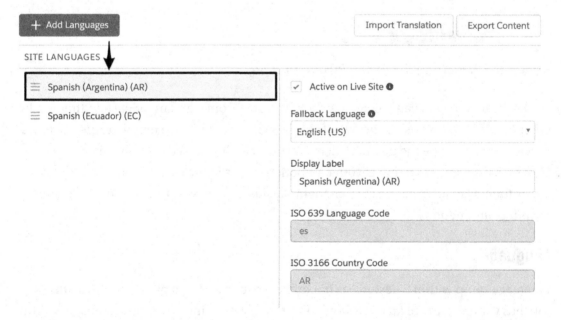

Figure 5-34. *Adding a language*

- *Import translations*: Bring in properly formatted translations as XML to use for a specific language being used within the site. See Figure 5-35 for the modal that is displayed to allow a user to import content.

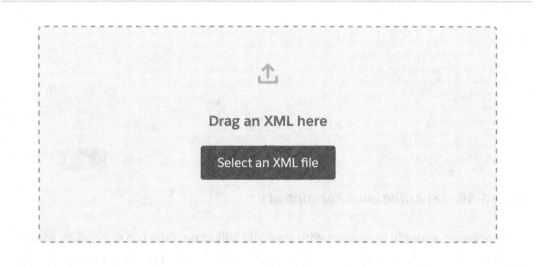

Import Translated Content

Import overwrites the current translation values in your site. Ensure that the XML file matches the expected format and is well formed. Learn more

Drag an XML here

Select an XML file

Figure 5-35. *Importing language content*

- *Export content*: Export existing translation content for a specified language to be used externally (see Figure 5-36).

Export Content for Translation

Select All   Deselect All

English (US)
Spanish (Argentina) - español (AR)
Spanish (Ecuador) - español (EC)

Save as:

Languages   .xml

Cancel   Export

Figure 5-36. *Exporting language content*

Associating multiple languages with your site will impact the top navigation within Experience Builder, introducing one additional button/control (shown in Figure 5-37) to manage your languages.

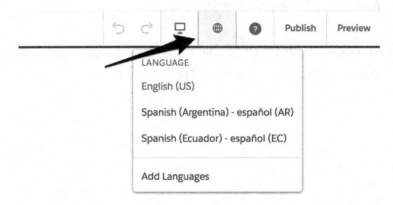

Figure 5-37. *Language management within Builder*

Navigation

Salesforce did us all a major favor by adding a "Navigation" section to the Settings tab. While it hasn't always been available, it's now a tough one to live without. The Navigation section allows admins to create multiple navigation menus for use within the site. Not only can you create multiple navigation menus for the purpose of personalization (i.e., audience targeting), but you can associate a navigation menu with a custom navigation component and, in turn, associate that custom component with a specific theme layout. That means that you can have specific navigation menus available for all pages that leverage a particular theme layout. Take a look at Figure 5-38.

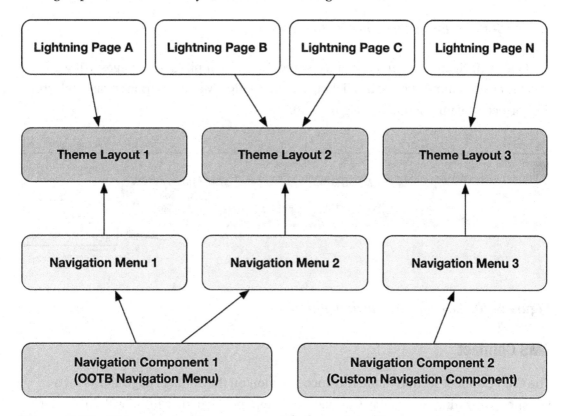

Figure 5-38. *Using navigation menus with theme layouts*

The process to create and associate a navigation menu using the out-of-the-box Navigation Menu component is fairly straightforward. First, you create a new navigation menu. See Figure 5-39.

Navigation

Create and manage navigational menus for your site. Menus can be used in Navigation, Tile, Profile, and custom menu components.

[+ Add Navigation Menu] ⬅

NAME

Philly

Default Navigation

Figure 5-39. *Adding a new navigation menu*

Once a navigation menu has been created, it can be applied to all pages using a specific custom theme layout by clicking the Navigation Menu component and selecting the correct "Default Menu." See Figure 5-40.

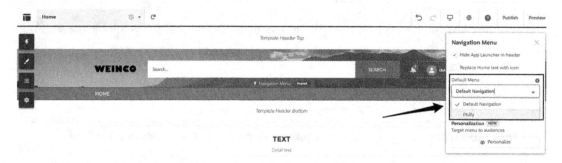

Figure 5-40. *Selecting a new navigation menu*

CMS Connect

The CMS Connect section of the Advanced section on the Settings page allows for a few sitewide settings from CMS Connect to be applied. I will dive into CMS Connect in general later in the book; for now, I'll address this area of Builder only. Specifically, an administrator can control the header and footer via CMS Connect using the Settings tab. Once a CMS Connection is set up, that connection, along with the corresponding URL, can be used to serve up a header or footer for the site. Figure 5-41 shows how the header might be set via CMS Connect.

Settings

General

Theme

Languages

Advanced

CMS Connect

Updates ①

Developer

CMS Connect

CMS Connect Header and Footer
Use a header and footer from a connected CMS source in your community.

| Header Source | Header Path | Use Personalization ❶ |
| Weinforce ▾ | wp-blog-header.php | ☐ |

| Footer Source | Footer Path | Use Personalization ❶ |
| --None-- ▾ | Example: content/example/site/footer.html | ☐ |

Figure 5-41.   CMS Connect within site settings

Advanced

The Advanced section on the Settings tab allows the ability to enable and gather additional analytics, to control the head markup of all pages within the site, adjust visibility of components on the Components tab, and tweak performance-affecting factors.

Google Analytics

For an organization that isn't yet set on a web analytics tool for its Salesforce site, I highly recommend using Google Analytics. The reason is not a secret; Salesforce supports Google Analytics out of the box with ease. After updating your site's Content Security Policy security level from "Strict CSP" to "Relaxed CSP" (more on that later in this chapter), you can simply create a new Analytics property in Google Analytics and then enter the corresponding Tracking/Measurement ID in Builder. See Figures 5-42 and 5-43.

Administration
Phil Weinmeister / Complete Guide to Communities

| PROPERTY | **Tracking ID** | **Status** |
| Complete Guide to Commun... ▾ | UA-87468862-3 | No data received in past 48 hours. Learn more |

Figure 5-42.   Obtaining your Google Analytics Tracking ID

Google Analytics™

Enter your Google Analytics Tracking ID to track page views.

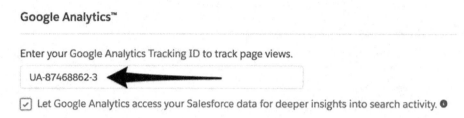

UA-87468862-3

☑ Let Google Analytics access your Salesforce data for deeper insights into search activity. ❶

Figure 5-43. *Entering your Google Analytics Tracking ID*

Note that your tracking ID may not be in the format suggested by Salesforce. You'll notice that the ghost text shown by Salesforce is formatted as "UA-YYYYY-XX." However, if you have a newer type of property (e.g., Google Analytics 4, or "Web + App"), it may be formatted differently (e.g., "G-VTB7EK0XN8"). Don't worry, it will still work.

After setting up Google Analytics for Salesforce sites, an admin will need to wait for site activity to occur. Once that happens, the analytics will start to come to life. Figure 5-44 shows an example of real-time tracking analytics from a Salesforce Experience Cloud site.

Figure 5-44. *Google Analytics in action*

Head Markup

While Google Analytics tracking won't change your site's perceivable user experience, the Head Markup section may. This section is primarily to help inform search engines and browsers how to label, report on, and present a site, but some markup can actually change its behavior and the user experience. The markup set here is applied to each page within your Lightning *site*. Entire books are dedicated to this topic, so I won't be covering it in much more detail here. However, it is important to understand what is allowed within the head markup; see Figure 5-45.

ALLOWED TAGS	ALLOWED ATTRIBUTES
<base>	href, target
<link>	as, charset, crossorigin, disabled, href, hreflang, id, import, integrity, media, relList, rev, sheet, sizes, target, title, type, rel (allowed values for rel are alternate, apple-touch-icon, apple-touch-icon-precomposed, apple-touch-startup-image, author, bookmark, canonical, external, help, icon, license, manifest, mask-icon, next, nofollow, noopener, noreferrer, pingback, prefetch, preload, prev, search, shortcut icon, stylesheet, and tag)
<meta>	charset, content, name, property, scheme, http-equiv (allowed values for http-equiv are cleartype, content-type, content-language, and default-style)
<noscript>	Within <noscript> only the following elements are supported: <img>, <a><img>, <iframe>
<script>	Use for custom content
<style>	type, media, nonce, title
<title>	None allowed

Figure 5-45. *Allowed head markup in a Salesforce site*

Here is an example of what the head markup could look like:

```
<base href="https://philwein.my.force.com/s/" target="_blank">
<link rel="stylesheet" type="text/css" href="theme.css">
<link rel="icon" type="image/png" href="https://weinforce.files.wordpress.com/site-favicon.png">
```

This markup provides the following results:

- Establishes **https://philwein.my.force.com/s/** as the base URL for all relative links

- Uses **https://philwein.my.force.com/s/theme.css** as a stylesheet for the overall site

- Sets **https://weinforce.files.wordpress.com/site-favicon.png** as the icon for the site

Components Panel

If you need to address your FOMO issues related to components, Salesforce has a solution for you. By default, some components do not appear in the Components tab; this is because the components are not relevant or eligible for the given page. However, you can enable the "Show All Components" setting to ensure that you can always see all components, regardless of whether they can be used on a certain page or not. Personally, I wouldn't recommend it, as components incompatible with specific pages will appear, causing potential confusion for a site administrator. However, if you want to see the full list, do know that you have the option.

Performance

The last section is Performance. There is actually only one true configuration setting: progressive rendering. Enabling this allows you to control the sequence of how components load on a page. It's very useful if content higher on your page takes a while to load, resulting in a jarring experience when that content finally loads and pushes everything on the page down. In addition to that setting, you have access to a couple links:

- Experience Cloud Content Delivery Network (CDN)
- Page Optimizer

The CDN will allow you to decrease page load time by leveraging a content delivery network to optimize the delivery of performance-impacting content to your site. Page Optimizer will help you to identify potential issues with your Lightning page that could impact performance.

Security & Privacy

Security & Privacy settings include three subsections:

- Clickjack Protection
- Content Security Policy (CSP)
- Site Cookie Usage

Each of these sections is critically important to be aware of for your site.

Clickjack Protection

If you're using a public page in your site, it's possible that a third party could load your page within an iframe outside your site. While it may appear harmless for users to click on elements on your page within the iframe, the page that contains the iframe can record and/or modify your input and interactions for nefarious purposes. Salesforce provides a few setting levels to prevent this from potentially occurring. The settings are

- Allow framing by any page (no protection)
- Allow framing of site or community pages on external domains (good protection)
- Allow framing by the same origin only (recommended)
- Don't allow framing by any page (most protection)

Unless you have a specific need to change the settings, the recommended setting ("Allow framing by the same origin only") should suffice.

Note   The "good protection" setting ("Allow framing of site or community pages on external domains") only applies to Tabs + Visualforce sites.

Content Security Policy (CSP)

While clickjacking doesn't often need specific attention or configuration outside the default setting, CSP often requires a review and updates by the site admin. First, you'll need to determine the appropriate security level. You have two options:

- Strict CSP: Block Access to Inline Scripts and All Hosts
- Relaxed CSP: Permit Access to Inline Scripts and Allowed Hosts

By default, your site will be configured for Strict CSP. However, it is a common scenario to require access to inline scripts and allowed hosts. The idea here is fairly straightforward; if you need to run a script that is host on a domain other than that of your site, you'll need to approve that domain for script use. You can approve the base domain (`https://www.example.com`) to allow all scripts on that domain, or you can be more restrictive and narrow down the allowance to a specific subfolder (`https://www.example.com/folder/subfolder`). Figure 5-46 provides an example of domains that may be needed for CSP whitelisting. These specific domains are included automatically when Google Analytics is enabled for a site.

Trusted Sites for Scripts

Third-party hosts listed here can be accessed by scripts in your site. Third-party hosts required for non-script resources such as images, videos, and stylesheets must be added to your CSP Trusted Sites in Salesforce Setup. More Details

TRUSTED SITE NAME	TRUSTED SITE URL	STATUS	
www.google-analytics.com	https://www.google-analytics.com	Active	▼
stats.g.doubleclick.net	https://stats.g.doubleclick.net	Active	▼
www.googletagmanager.com	https://www.googletagmanager.com/gtag/js	Active	▼

+ Add Trusted Site

Figure 5-46. *Trusted Sites for Scripts ensure that domains listed are whitelisted for use in scripts referenced in your site*

Do note that the preceding instructions are just for scripts for your site; images, videos, and other media hosted outside your site must be approved in the CSP section in the main Salesforce setup menu. Figure 5-47 shows what occurs if you reference an image hosted externally within your site before including a corresponding CSP entry.

Can't Access Resources

Access to resources from an unapproved, external host violates the Content Security Policy (CSP). To allow access to these resources, add the host to the list of trusted hosts in CSP Trusted Sites in Salesforce Setup. More Details

Blocked URI: https://www.evernote.com/l/AMkvuB5Y_MJCj5G6cRAAy-pXOtoEBDQBtXoB/image.png
CSP directive: img-src

☐ Don't show me CSP violations

OK

Figure 5-47. *You will receive an error message when a resource is stored externally and its domain is not listed as a trusted domain in the CSP settings*

Fortunately, Salesforce provides an easy path to whitelisting images and similar file types hosted externally. In addition to presenting the "Can't Access Resources" message, CSP errors from the last 30 days are provided, as displayed in Figure 5-48.

CSP Errors

View and resolve resources that are blocked due to conflicts with your site's CSP settings.
Note: This page lists new CSP issues from the last 30 days.

BLOCKED RESOURCE	RESOURCE TYPE	STATUS
https://www.evernote.com/l/AMkvuB5Y_MJCj5G6cRAAy-pXOtoEB...	img-src	Allow URL

Figure 5-48. *Salesforce gives recent errors to allow for easy and quick whitelisting by clicking on "Allow URL"*

After clicking "Allow URL," the associated domain will be whitelisted on the CSP page within the main Salesforce setup menu. See Figure 5-49.

Content Security Policy Trusted Sites   Help for this Page

Below is the list of Web addresses (URLs) that your organization can use to access resources for Lightning components, either within your organization's Lightning Experience or CSP-Secured Lightning Communities. To use third-party APIs that make requests to an external (non-Salesforce) server, add the server as a trusted site.

To use the Salesforce Console Integration Toolkit JavaScript from within a third-party domain, add that third-party domain as a trusted site here and in the Security settings of the Builder in your Lightning Communities.

View: Main View ✓   Edit | Create New View

A | B | C | D | E | F | G | H | I | J | K | L | M | N | O | P | Q | R | S | T | U | V | W | X | Y | Z | Other | All

Action	Trusted Site Name ↑	Trusted Site URL	Active	Context	Created Date
Edit	Del	stats_g_doubleclick_net	https://stats.g.doubleclick.net	✓	Experience Builder Sites	5/21/2021, 4:31 AM
Edit	Del	www_evernote_com	https://www.evernote.com	✓	Experience Builder Sites	5/26/2021, 3:51 AM
Edit	Del	www_googletagmanager_com	https://www.googletagmanager.com	✓	Experience Builder Sites	5/21/2021, 4:31 AM
Edit	Del	www_google_analytics_com	https://www.google-analytics.com	✓	Experience Builder Sites	5/21/2021, 4:31 AM

Figure 5-49. *Clicking "Allow URL" in the CSP errors list adds the domain as a CSP trusted site*

Getting CSP set up correctly can actually be a bit painful at times. If you reference third-party content a lot, you will, at some point, find that you can't seem to get that content to display correctly. My suggestion is to add the broadest access possible for your content (i.e., the base domain) to the CSP whitelist on the Security page in Builder *and* to the CSP page in Salesforce setup. Once you have the image or content showing, work back your configuration to make it more restrictive (if necessary).

Note   An additional setting for CSP script whitelisting ("Allow Inline Scripts and Script Access to Any Third-party Host") exists for older sites, but will be deprecated in 2022. In light of that change, it is recommended to leverage one of the two standard options.

The next setting on the Security page is Lightning Locker. I am not going to dive too deep here, but I will provide some basic guidance. Unless absolutely necessary, leave Lightning Locker enabled. Locker basically ensures that components on your page don't interact with other components in unexpected or undesired ways (the ramifications of which could be significant). And, if you are not fairly technical, do not assume you have the expertise or authority to change the setting without consulting technical resources. Salesforce has some great information on this that should be reviewed before making a decision on what to do with this; search for "Develop Secure Sites: Lightning Locker and CSP."

The final Security & Privacy configuration setting is Site Cookie Usage. Salesforce currently provides two options:

- Allow cookies deemed either "required" or "functional."

- Only allow cookies considered "required"; do not allow cookies considered "functional."

The first option, where both cookies are supported, is the default setting. See Figure 5-50 for a look at the default configuration.

Figure 5-50. *Cookie usage can be restricted to required cookies only*

You should review all Salesforce cookies considered functional before disabling them, as your overall site experience may suffer, as a result. Make sure you have a compelling reason/justification before disabling "functional" cookies.

Developer

In my opinion, the naming of the Developer section of the Settings tab is a bit of a misnomer. This page could be leveraged by individuals in a variety of roles, not just developers. Also, the focus is not really development; the focus here is the ability to "templatize" and reuse specific aspects of your site. Currently, the page allows for exporting three types of Experience Cloud elements:

- Templates (i.e., Experience Cloud templates or Lightning Bolt Solutions)
- Themes
- Pages

All of these options are specifically centered around Lightning; no aspects of a Tabs + Visualforce site are eligible. Figure 5-51 shows the initial view of the Developer section; the template/bolt export page is in focus by default.

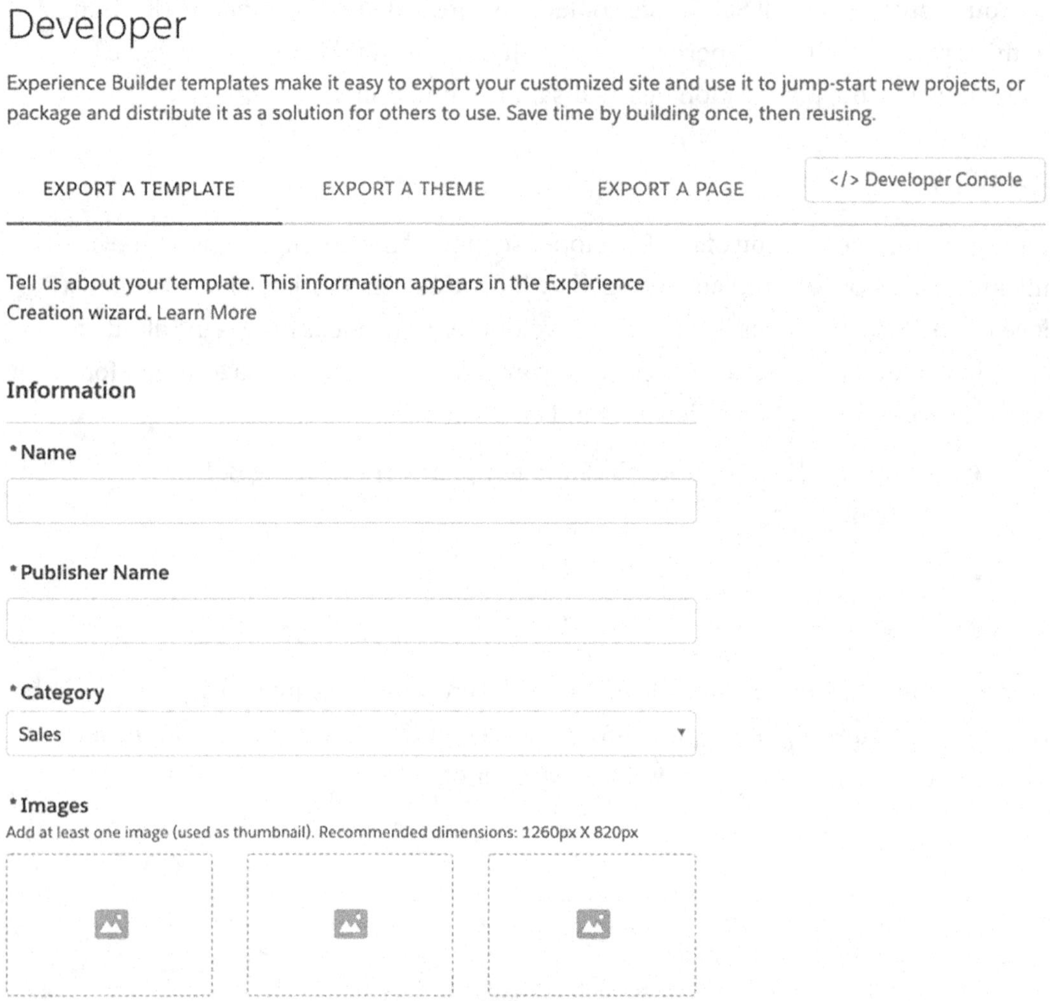

Developer

Experience Builder templates make it easy to export your customized site and use it to jump-start new projects, or package and distribute it as a solution for others to use. Save time by building once, then reusing.

EXPORT A TEMPLATE   EXPORT A THEME   EXPORT A PAGE   </> Developer Console

Tell us about your template. This information appears in the Experience Creation wizard. Learn More

Information

* Name

* Publisher Name

* Category

Sales   ▾

* Images
Add at least one image (used as thumbnail). Recommended dimensions: 1260px X 820px

Figure 5-51. *The Developer section of the Settings tab in Experience Builder*

The Developer tab essentially allows you to create templates from an overall site, the theme, or a single page. These templates can significantly speed up site configuration, as they offer preconfigured site elements that can be used in place of multiple manual steps. I will dive into Experience Cloud templates, or Lightning Bolts, in granular detail in Chapter 12. For now, I'll just mention that exporting a template allows you to "clone" your site for the purpose of creating a new site from that cloned experience. It's very useful if you plan on building multiple sites that are similar.

Exporting a theme allows an administrator to quickly and easily capture the overall theme, related theme layouts, and associated settings for reuse. Again, this is very useful if you are planning on spinning up multiple sites and you'd like to reuse at least part of your original site's theme.

Exporting a page allows an administrator to copy a page in the existing site, including the layout, component placement, component configuration, and metadata associated with that page. The administrator can immediately reuse that page quickly within the existing site or another site in the same org. Furthermore, that page can be exported, via Change Set, package, or IDE, to another org; this allows the use of that page template within any site in that destination org. See Figure 5-52 for a look at this tab.

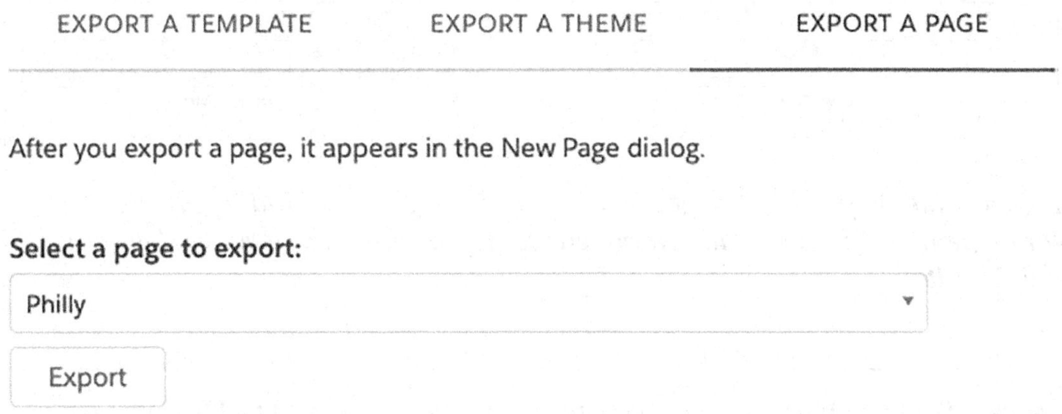

EXPORT A TEMPLATE   EXPORT A THEME   **EXPORT A PAGE**

After you export a page, it appears in the New Page dialog.

Select a page to export:

| Philly | ▼ |

| Export |

Figure 5-52. *Exporting a Lightning page from a site*

Do keep in mind that this page, when exported, is not actually connected to a site. It is a page template, essentially, that can be used to create a new page in a specific site. Figure 5-53 provides another view of the contents included in a page export.

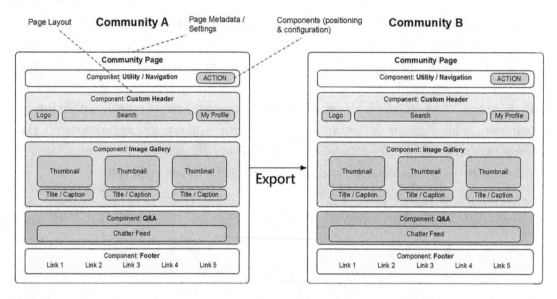

Figure 5-53. *Exporting a page allows the page contents, including layout, component positioning, and component configuration, to be leveraged within another site*

Note   Configurable metadata, such as name, description, and featured images, are required for template and theme export; page export includes only the selection of the page to clone.

Updates

The Updates section of the Settings tab provides information on template updates and allows upgrades to be performed from the same location. See Figure 5-54 for an example of a pending update. If no update is available, a message will appear formatted like this: "You're already using the latest version of your template: [Template/Bolt] [Release Name]."

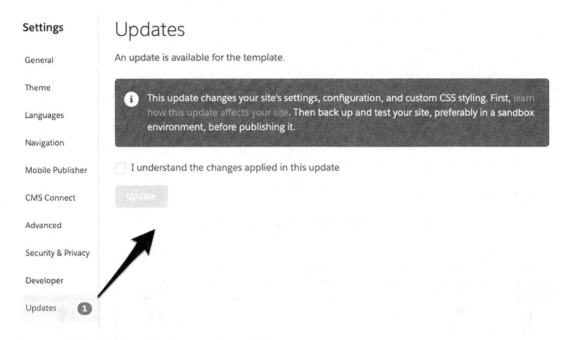

Figure 5-54. *Presentation of a pending template update*

After selecting "I understand…" and clicking Update, a warning message appears. See Figure 5-55 for the message.

Update site?

You can't reverse the update. Some parts of the site can be reverted if you've exported a backup. Make sure you understand all the implications before continuing. Learn More

Figure 5-55. *Template update warning*

Top Navigation Bar

While the left sidebar is a major focus for activity within *Experience Builder*, the top navigation bar also boasts a number of commonly used controls, menus, and actions. It contains the following elements:

- Site menu (site navigation/control center)

- Pages menu (page management)

- Builder controls

- View mode

- Help

- Publish

- Builder mode

Figure 5-56 shows where each of these elements is located.

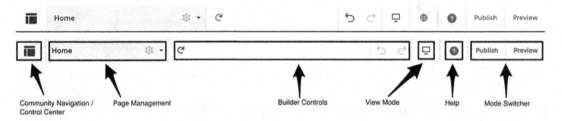

Figure 5-56. *The top navigation bar within Experience Builder*

Note   The Languages button is present only if multiple languages are configured for the site.

Site Menu

The Site menu allows for navigation not only to all administrative areas of the current site in focus but to all other sites within the org. There are three main sections:

- Top-level navigation

- My Workspaces

- My Experiences

Figure 5-57 shows the panel with these three sections.

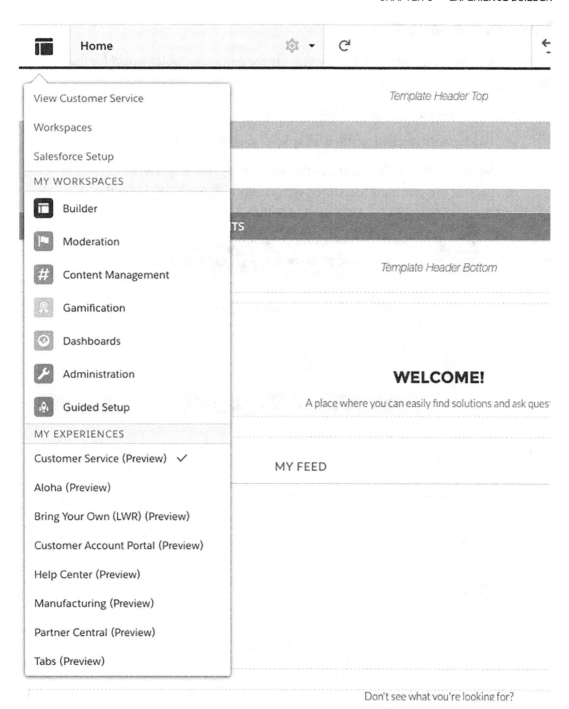

Figure 5-57. *The Site menu within Experience Builder*

Top-Level Site Navigation

The top-level site navigation section provides three common "quick links" for the
following purposes:

- *View [site name]*: View the site "live" (i.e., as a user in production).

- *Workspaces*: Accessing the workspaces page for the site in focus.

- *Salesforce Setup*: Navigating to the All Sites/Digital Experiences
  page in the standard Salesforce setup menu. Figure 5-58 shows the
  destination pages for a site named Self-Service Site.

Figure 5-58. *A look at the destinations of each of the links in the top section of the*
Site menu

My Workspaces

This area of site administration involves a modular approach to managing a site, segmenting different key areas that drive site functionality. There are currently seven modules, although that may change as new administrative elements are added. As of the Winter '22 release, the following modules are available:

- Builder (the focus of this chapter)

- Moderation

- Content Management

- Gamification

- Dashboards

- Administration

- Guided Setup

See Figure 5-59 for a view of the site workspace screen.

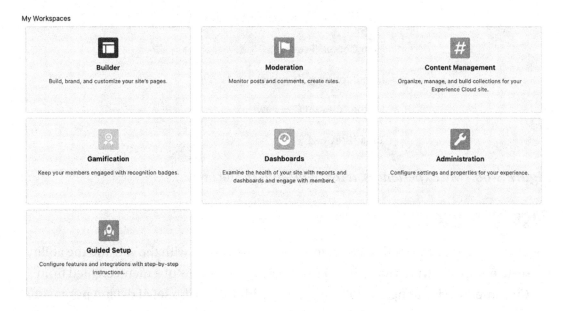

Figure 5-59. *Site workspaces*

I will cover each of the other workspaces in more detail later in this book.

> **Note**   The specific workspaces that appear may differ, depending on the template being used and the version of that template.

My Experiences

In the third and last section of the site navigation/control center, users will find a list of all sites, whether Tabs + Visualforce, Lightning, preview, active, or inactive. You'll see something like the list shown in Figure 5-60.

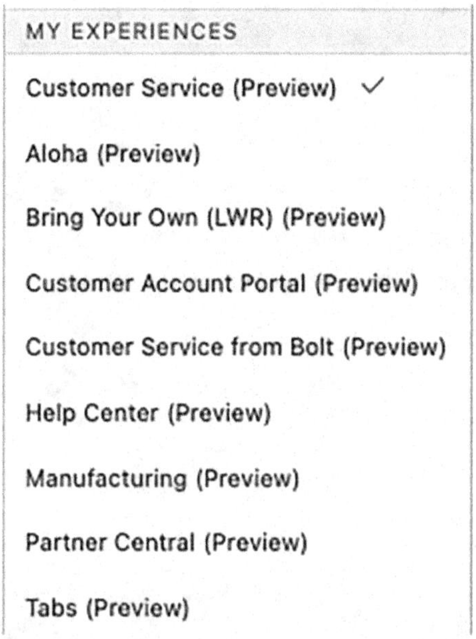

MY EXPERIENCES

Customer Service (Preview) ✓

Aloha (Preview)

Bring Your Own (LWR) (Preview)

Customer Account Portal (Preview)

Customer Service from Bolt (Preview)

Help Center (Preview)

Manufacturing (Preview)

Partner Central (Preview)

Tabs (Preview)

Figure 5-60. *My Experiences, a list of all sites in the org*

Page Manager

Page Manager allows for quick access to all pages associated with the site and the ability to create new pages with a few clicks. Figure 5-61 shows a view of a menu created from the Customer Service template, following a few additions to the set of default pages site.

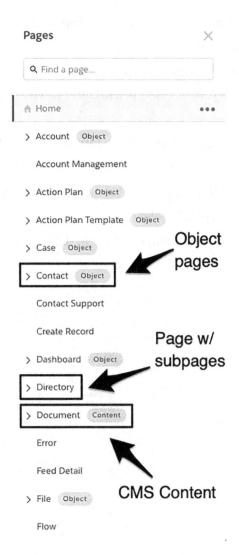

Figure 5-61. *The Pages menu*

This menu does not prioritize pages based on a page's prominence on the site or criticality within the standard site navigation; it simply lists every page that exists in that site, whether or not the page is technically being used. Salesforce used to categorize pages into multiple sections, but now lists the pages alphabetically. Personally, I think this was the right move; as an admin, you think of your page name, you don't first think of the appropriate category that it falls into.

It's important to be aware that some pages are grouped together. You'll see the following bundles in your page list:

- *Object pages*: When you create object pages, you'll get pages for a list, a related list, and a record detail page. These will be bundled under the object name.

- *Pages with subpages*: Subpages will be bundled under the top-level page; the page name shown will be that of the top-level page.

- *Content pages*: Content pages are bundled under the content type (e.g., "Document," "Image," etc.).

I will dive into the page setup screen/interface in detail in the next chapter (shown in Figure 5-62).

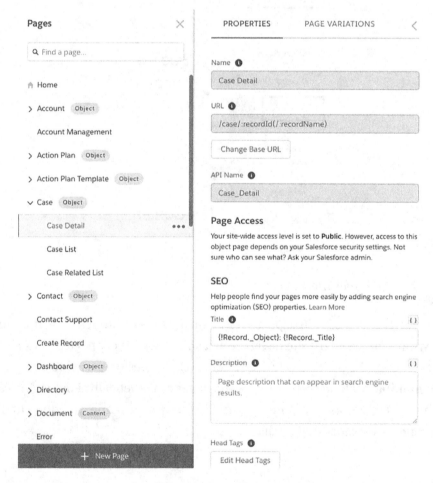

Figure 5-62. *Page setup, to be discussed in Chapter 6*

Builder Controls

Builder controls, as I refer to them, allow a site administrator to perform some basic actions to assist with site development. See Figure 5-63 for a glance at the three controls in this group.

Figure 5-63. *Builder controls in Experience Builder*

The Refresh button allows for back-end updates to be reflected in Builder. Let's say that a few Salesforce records that are being displayed on the site page shown in Builder are updated by a user while you're working on the page; those updates won't automatically be reflected within Builder. However, clicking Refresh will display the latest, most up-to-date version of the applicable site page. See Figure 5-64 for the button location.

Figure 5-64. *The Refresh button, useful for updating a page based on data changes*

The additional controls are Undo and Redo. These can be huge time savers for site builders. For example, let's say a component with a large number of property editor configurations is deleted. The site administrator then realizes that they made a mistake and actually does need the component. With one click, the component can be reinserted on the page in the same position and with the same configurations. See Figure 5-65 for a view of the Undo and Redo controls.

Figure 5-65. *Undo and Redo buttons*

View Mode

The View mode that is built into Experience Builder is extremely useful for site managers or builders to determine what the site will look like on a variety of device types. Specifically, three options are provided:

- Mobile

- Tablet

- Desktop

With one click, the view can be adjusted to validate the responsiveness and positioning of components within the site. Figures 5-66 to 5-68 show the same site page in all three modes to convey how the View mode changes the display.

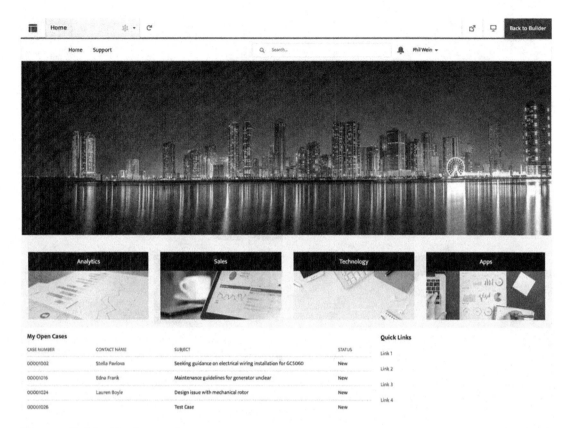

Figure 5-66. *Desktop view*

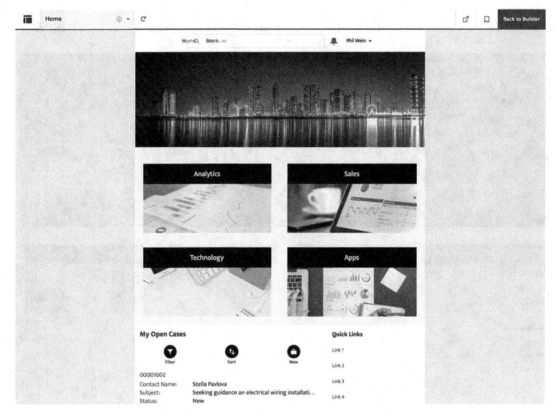

Figure 5-67. *Tablet view*

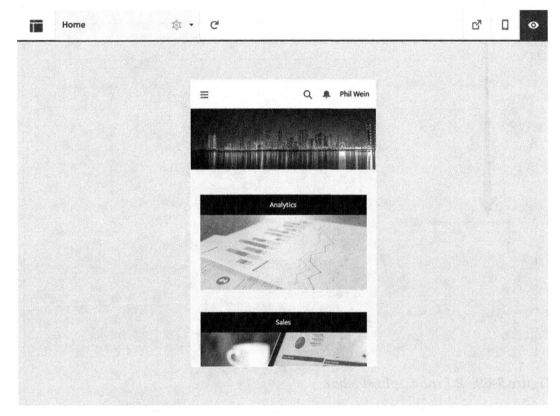

Figure 5-68. *Mobile view*

It's great to see the different responsive views, but don't miss what's actually happening with the page display. The "algorithm" to determine the view is structured and logical, making it easy to build a site with different views in mind. For example, let's take a look at a specific page layout (Figure 5-69).

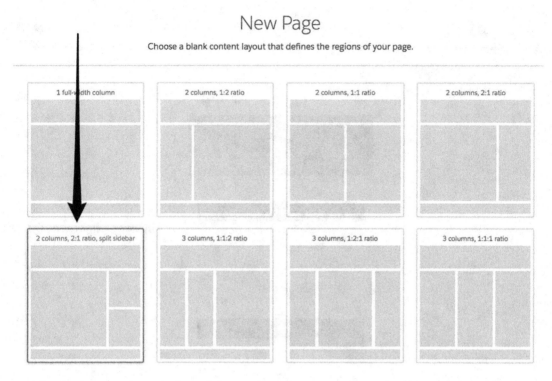

Figure 5-69. *2:1 ratio, split sidebar*

To clarify what's happening, I set up one component in each section below the header—the Rich Content Editor component. In each instance of the component, I display the name of the page section. See Figure 5-70 for the desktop view.

	Content Header	
Content		Sidebar Featured
		Sidebar
	Content Footer	
	Template Footer	

Figure 5-70. *Sections clearly labeled for the purpose of viewing sequence in a mobile view*

I take the desktop view and modify it to the mobile view to show how these sections are sequenced; see Figure 5-71.

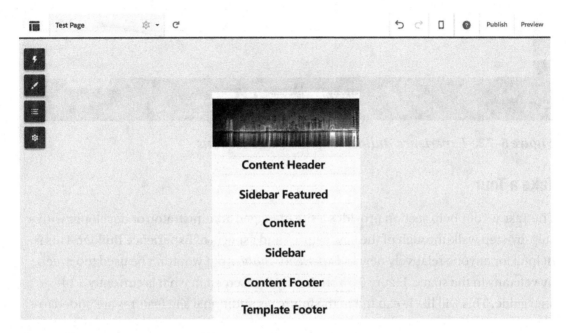

Figure 5-71. *Mobile view of the page shown in Figure 5-70*

The main takeaway here is the positioning of sidebar content relative to the main "content" section: Sidebar Feature comes first, followed by Content and, finally, Sidebar.

Help

Salesforce has you covered on help documentation relevant to **Experience Builder**; even better, the available help documentation doesn't require that you exit Builder to read it. There are currently three help sections provided:

- Take a Tour

- What's New

- Help & Training

Figure 5-72 shows where these different areas of help can be selected.

Figure 5-72. *Experience Builder help has three sections*

Take a Tour

The Take a Tour help section provides a site manager, administrator, or developer with a step-by-step walk-through of the key features and aspects of Experience Builder. This is helpful for anyone relatively new to *Experience Builder* but wouldn't be used too much by veterans in the space. Figure 5-73 shows the first screen in what is currently a 14-step guide. This will likely expand in the future, as additional site features are added to Salesforce.

Figure 5-73. *Take a Tour of Salesforce Experience Builder*

What's New

The What's New section within help provides a "bullet list" overview of some significant enhancements and changes delivered in the most recent of the triannual releases. Figure 5-74 shows what was made available via What's New in Spring '18.

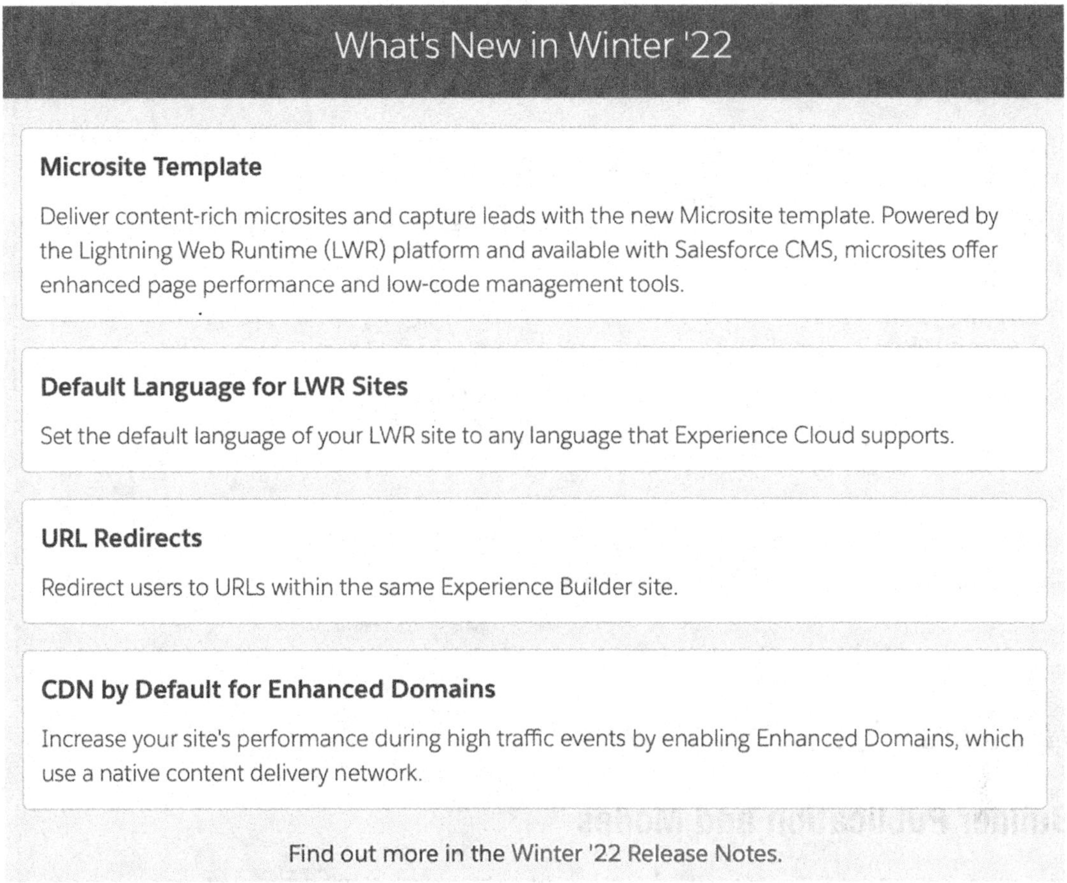

What's New in Winter '22

Microsite Template

Deliver content-rich microsites and capture leads with the new Microsite template. Powered by the Lightning Web Runtime (LWR) platform and available with Salesforce CMS, microsites offer enhanced page performance and low-code management tools.

Default Language for LWR Sites

Set the default language of your LWR site to any language that Experience Cloud supports.

URL Redirects

Redirect users to URLs within the same Experience Builder site.

CDN by Default for Enhanced Domains

Increase your site's performance during high traffic events by enabling Enhanced Domains, which use a native content delivery network.

Find out more in the Winter '22 Release Notes.

Figure 5-74. *What's New shows what came out in the last Salesforce release related to sites*

Help & Training

The Help & Training links take users to the standard Salesforce help documentation and, specifically, to the *Experience Builder* Overview article. Figure 5-75 shows the article that appears.

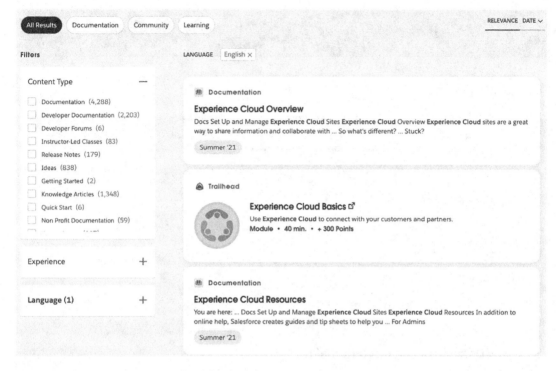

Figure 5-75. *Experience Builder help*

Builder Publication and Modes

The final area of the top navigation menu within *Experience Builder* allows administrators the ability to perform two key actions:

- *Publish*: Publish the site

- *Preview/Back to Builder*: Toggle between preview and Builder modes

Publish

With the exception of changes made to the navigation menu, no Builder changes are immediately/directly exposed to external users. To make site changes visible to end users, the site must first be published. Clicking Publish (Figure 5-76) does the following:

- Pushes "live" any changes since the last publication of the site; the user-facing version of the site will then reflect what is in Builder as of that moment.

- Sends an email to the publisher notifying them that the live site has been updated.

- Clears any undo/redo cache.

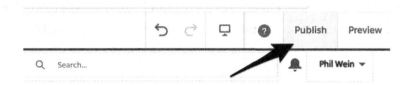

Figure 5-76. *Publish a site to push draft changes to the site's audience*

Figure 5-77 displays the three-step process that occurs once an administrator clicks the Publish button:

1. The administrator is presented with an information modal before proceeding by clicking another Publish button.

2. The progress indicator is shown (or "No changes to publish" is shown).

3. Notification of publication completion is displayed.

Figure 5-77. *Steps involved in publishing a site*

Note   As of the time of this book's publication, it's all-or-none when it comes to publishing an Experience Cloud site (i.e., when you publish, you publish all pages in your site). Page-specific publication would be a welcome enhancement to Experience Cloud, but we'll have to wait for that.

Preview

While it is true an admin can fairly easily view the live site from Builder (referenced earlier in the chapter), those live changes might not reflect the latest changes made in Builder. To quickly view those changes as a user would actually see them in a production-like environment, the admin can click Preview at the top right (see Figure 5-78).

Figure 5-78. *Preview a site*

Preview will remove all section indicators, minimize controls, and provide an easy toggle back into Builder. Figure 5-79 shows that the Preview button is replaced with once entering Preview mode.

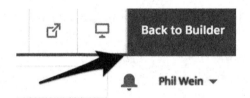

Figure 5-79. *When previewing, an admin is provided with an option to return to Experience Builder*

Figure 5-80 shows a "normal" (nonpreview) image of a site page in Builder. Note that section boundaries and names (when blank) are shown.

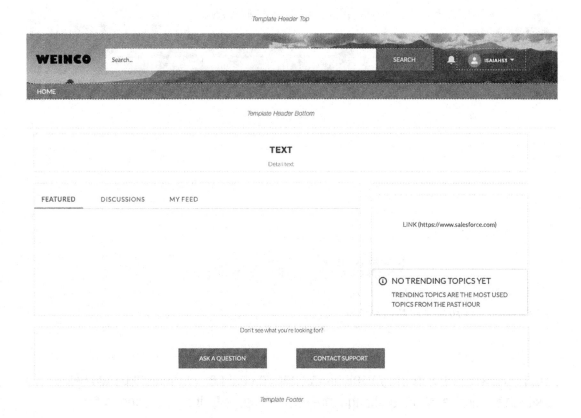

Figure 5-80. *A standard, Builder page view*

Figure 5-81 shows a preview image of the same site page.

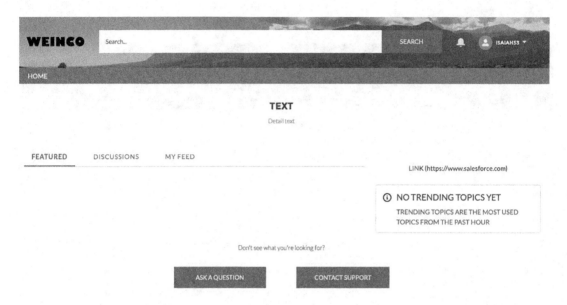

Figure 5-81. *A preview page view*

Note   Preview is extremely useful for separate changes to multiple pages within a site in sequence. Make a change, preview, navigate to the next page, return to Builder, and repeat as often as needed. This process is much easier than navigating through the site within Builder.

Recap

This chapter on Experience Builder was extremely lengthy, warranted by the high volume of content and detail associated with this powerful tool. I reviewed every aspect of the Experience Builder user interface. The first major section covered was the left sidebar/tabs, which revealed multiple layers of functionality, starting with the Page menu, theme controls, page structure, and settings. Additionally, I walked through the top navigation bar, which houses the main site menu, page manager, and various Builder controls. You should feel fairly comfortable with how to navigate Builder and be able to start to construct a basic Lightning site.

CHAPTER 6

Pages and Components

For anyone planning to build an Experience Cloud site on the Salesforce platform, understanding the associated creation and management of the corresponding pages and components is essential for success. In this chapter, I'll build upon the Experience Builder framework that was covered in detail in Chapter 5 and provide insights on how to make the most of what comes out of the box in an Experience Cloud site, as well as how to extend that with additional pages and components.

Before I jump in and walk through the ins and outs of page publication and component configuration, I want to make sure the concept of the journey—as it relates to pages and components within Experience Builder—is abundantly clear. Let's first take a look at a starting point: a standard, Salesforce-provided site template. Figure 6-1 shows this starting point, which includes standard objects, standard Lightning pages, and standard Lightning components. "Standard" is simply Salesforce's term for out of the box (i.e., available to all organizations using Experience Cloud).

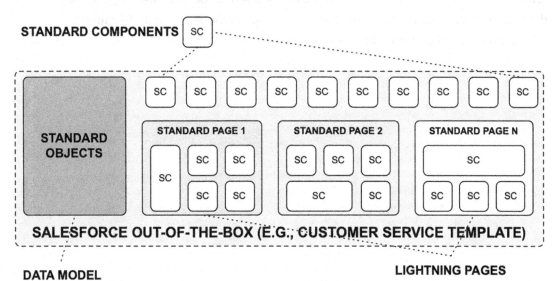

Figure 6-1. *The starting point for an Experience Cloud site, based on a template, includes the data model, pages, and Lightning components*

© Philip Weinmeister 2022

P. Weinmeister, *Practical Guide to Salesforce Experience Cloud*, https://doi.org/10.1007/978-1-4842-8132-1_6

Right out of the gate, Salesforce provides a slew of existing pages and components to work with. It's extremely likely, however, that a site administrator or developer will want to build upon this initial inventory of assets that are available to address requirements and use cases specific to their organization. Figure 6-2 provides the next high-level step, which is supplementing existing objects, pages, and components, as needed.

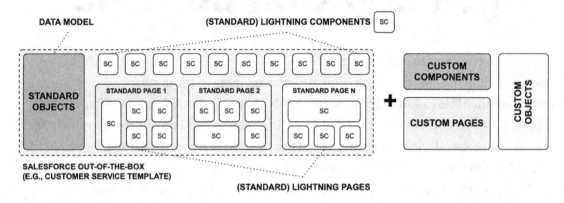

Figure 6-2. *The objects, pages, and components that are initially available in an Experience Cloud site can—and usually should—be supplemented*

Assembly and configuration now follow as the final step in the implementation process. Once the conceptual "Lego pieces" are made available, they need to be put together and placed appropriately on the corresponding Lego boards. Figure 6-3 shows the final picture of a site, following the addition, placement, and configuration of relevant pages and components.

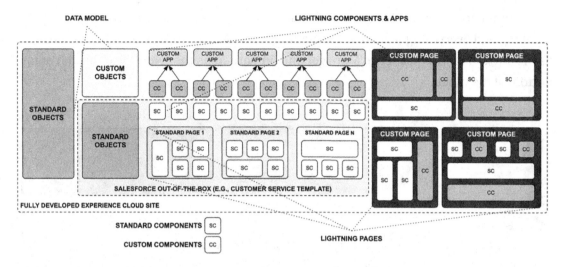

Figure 6-3. *Representation of a customized, configured Experience Cloud site that has gone beyond the assets initially available at site creation*

Note   The Build Your Own templates come out of the box with minimal pages and components, providing only what is absolutely required for a basic Experience Cloud site solution.

I will not be covering actual development of Lightning components in this chapter and, generally, will not be providing guidance on programmatic aspects of the platform. There are abundant resources on how to build custom components in the Salesforce ecosystem; I will be focusing on how to use these components within your Experience Cloud site.

Lightning Pages

Before delving into Lightning components for Experience Cloud, one must understand a corresponding element: Lightning pages. Why? A component's utility is minimal (even nonexistent in a purely declarative framework) without a page to actually house the component within a site. To break down the details of a page, we will start at the beginning with page creation.

Within Experience Builder, an admin can access the Page Manager menu for anything and everything related to the management of a Lightning page within a site. See Figure 6-4 for a look at Page Manager and, in particular, the "New Page" button at the bottom of the menu.

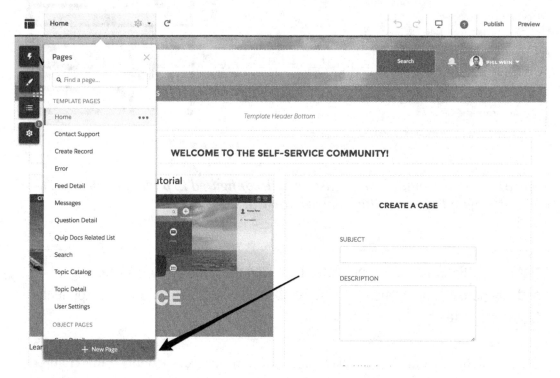

Figure 6-4. *Selecting "New Page" at the bottom of the Pages menu starts the page creation process*

To create a new page, a site administrator clicks the "New Page" button. The first step is a critical one: selecting the page type. Figure 6-5 shows the three choices (Standard, Object, and CMS Content) that are available when creating a new page.

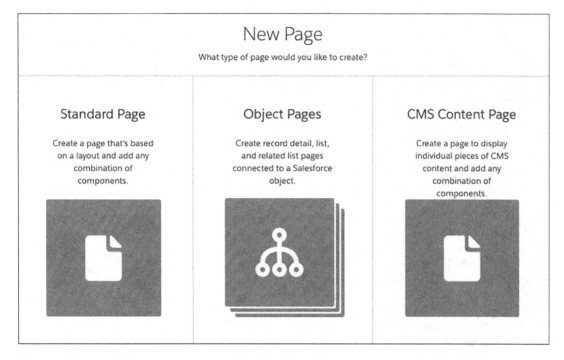

Figure 6-5. *The New Page dialog provides three choices: Standard, Object, and CMS Content*

During page creation, the admin will need to determine whether the page will need to be bound to data (a specific object) or content (a specific CMS Content type). If not, a standard page will suffice. See Figure 6-6 for the thought process critical to making this decision.

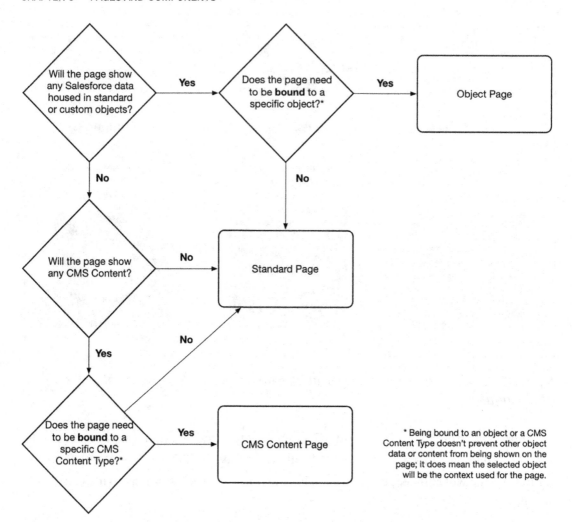

Figure 6-6. *Decision tree for creating a page in Experience Cloud*

When creating a standard page, the next choice is to determine whether to start from a preconfigured page or from scratch. The preconfigured pages that are available (Figure 6-7) are sourced from the "Export a Page" option on the Developer page within the Settings tab. Once a page is exported (and, if from a different org, imported), it will appear as a candidate starting point for any new page.

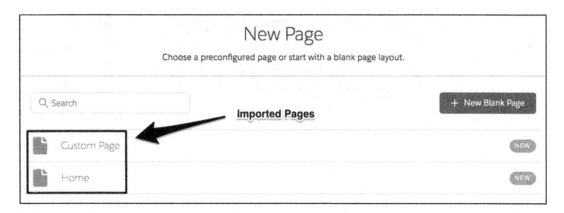

Figure 6-7. *When creating a new page, an admin can select a blank page or select from available imported pages as a starting point*

It is critical to understand what it means to create a page from an existing, preconfigured page, instead of creating a new, blank page. With a new, blank page, an administrator can select the page layout, but no content will exist on the page (with the exception of anything that is part of the overall theme). When a preconfigured page is selected, however, any components that are present on the selected page will be on the page at inception. Not only will the components be present, they will be positioned and configured exactly as they are on the selected page. Think of this as a page-level template. Figure 6-8 shows the page creation process and the various selection points and activities.

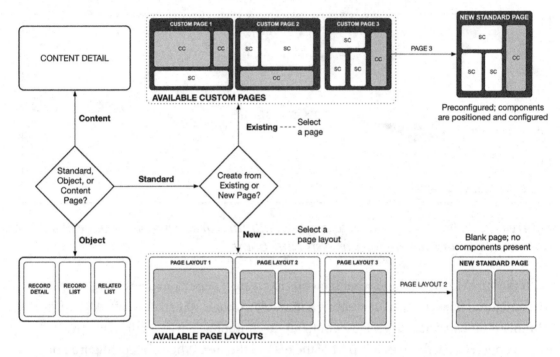

Figure 6-8. *Decision-making flow for Experience Cloud page creation*

For those selecting a new standard page, an option to select the page layout will appear. The layouts that are available will include a number of out-of-the-box layouts, but may also include some that are custom. In Figure 6-9, a combination of both standard and custom layouts is shown.

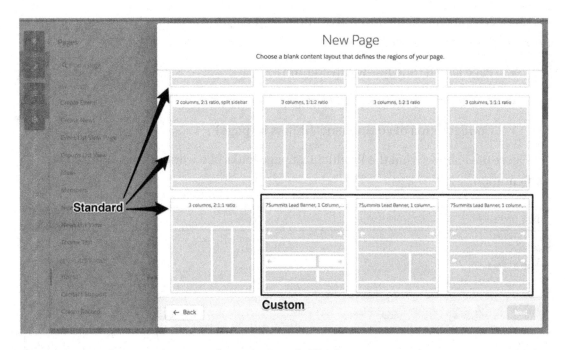

Figure 6-9. *The page layouts that are available during page creation can include a selection of custom page layouts*

Creating a new object page is fundamentally different from creating a new standard page. An object page actually results in three new pages, not just one:

- Record Detail

- Record List

- Record Related List

As an example, I'll create an object detail page for the product object (Figure 6-10).

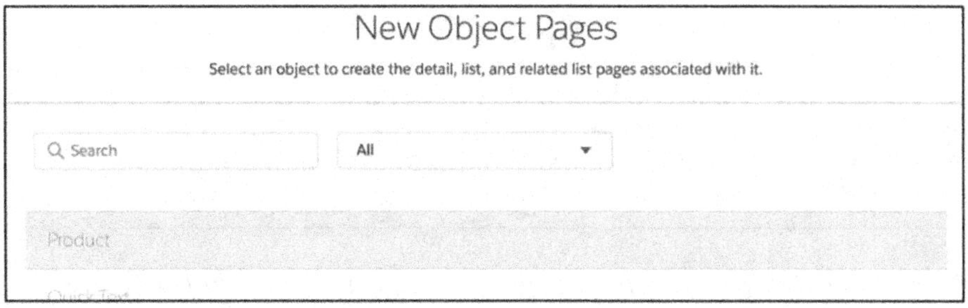

Figure 6-10. *Creating new object pages for the product object*

141

Once completed, this action will result in the following activities being completed via automation for the product object:

- Page layout (one full-width column)

- Applied components (differs by page)

- Configuration of components (differs by page)

Figure 6-11 shows what the Product List page looks like without any additional configuration.

Figure 6-11. *New, unmodified Product List page following creation*

Creating a new CMS Content page is similar to, but not the same as, creating a new standard page. CMS Content page creation results in one page:

- CMS Content Type Detail

As an example, I'll create a CMS Content page for the Image content type (Figure 6-12).

New Page

Select a content type for the page

Image

Figure 6-12. *Creating new content pages for the Image content type*

Once completed, this action will result in a flexible page being created for the purpose of dropping and configuring content-related components on the page.

Navigation Menu Bar

The navigation menu bar that is available in Experience Cloud sites goes hand in hand with Lightning pages. The navigation menu bar is a highly configurable component that drives the overall site navigation. While Lightning pages (standard or object) are the most common targets of menu items, the navigation menu bar supports a variety of destination types. Figure 6-13 shows the navigation menu bar.

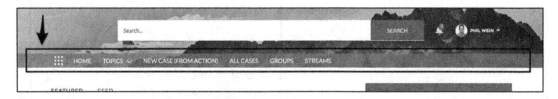

Figure 6-13. *Standard navigation menu bar*

The standard navigation menu bar has a couple top-level settings, relating to App Launcher and the home page, as shown in Figure 6-14. The App Launcher icon can be hidden, and the home page icon can be shown as text or a small house icon.

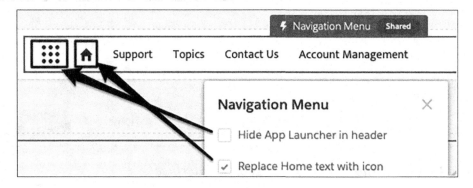

Figure 6-14. *Navigation menu bar top-level settings*

The Navigation Menu configuration settings provide significant flexibility for modifying the navigation menu items. Figure 6-15 shows the six types of menu items that can be added.

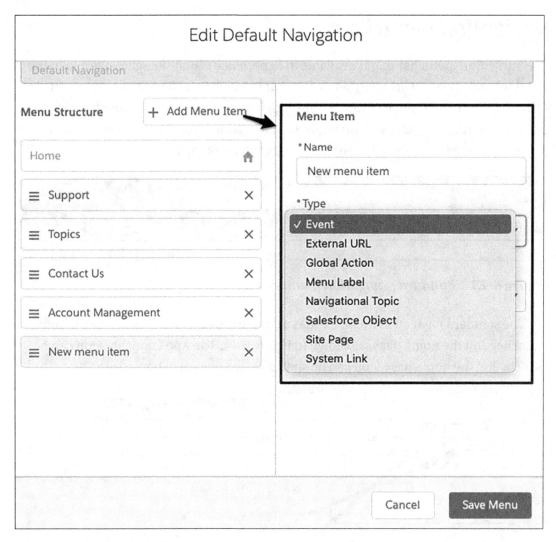

Figure 6-15. *Navigation Menu management interface*

To help with understanding all available options, refer to Figure 6-16 for details on the navigation menu item types.

Type	Name	Event	URL	Open link in the same tab	Action	Add the "More Topics..." link	Object Type	Default List View	Page	System Link	Publicly Available	Image	Notes
Event	✓	✓									✓	✓	Specific system events, such as login, logout, account switch
External URL	✓		✓	✓							✓	✓	Any URL outside the site
Global Action	✓				✓						✓	✓	Directly load a global action (e.g., a form)
Menu Label	✓										✓	✓	Grouping of other menu items
Navigational Topic	✓					✓					✓	✓	Allow users to navigate to existing navigational topics pages
Salesforce Object	✓						✓	✓			✓	✓	Provide links to a specific object list view
Site Page	✓								✓		✓	✓	Any page within the site
System Link	✓									✓	✓	✓	Certain system links/page (e.g., Experience Builder, setup, etc.)

Figure 6-16. *Navigation menu bar item types, settings, and notes*

One significant change to come to the Navigation Menu is that Experience Cloud now supports multiple navigation menus. This is a major leap, as it gives administrators the ability to associate each navigation menu from a set of multiple menus to its own custom theme layout. In other words, the displayed list of pages can differ based on which theme layout is being leveraged. See Figure 6-17 for the property editor setting that allows selection of a navigation menu.

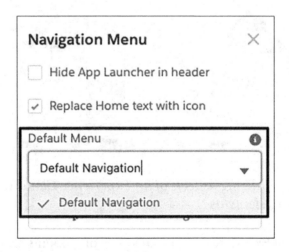

Figure 6-17. *Select a default navigation menu from a list of menus*

The power of the navigation menu can be taken even further with personalization, allowing an admin to show different menus to different site audiences. I'll cover that in more detail when we dive into audience targeting.

Lightning Components

I find it helpful to use metaphors in the context of Experience Cloud sites (hence my previous example of referencing Legos). I'd like to use a slightly different one here. This time, let's use a neighborhood as the example for an Experience Cloud site. Pages serve as the "slabs" under homes, while components represent structural and functional elements of the homes that are supported by those slabs. While both slabs *and* the supported elements are absolutely essential, owners of houses really don't care about the slabs too much; the slabs exist to support and provide a layout for the house, but they don't provide much functional value to the owners.

It's the same with Lightning components and pages; most users don't think too much about the page itself, but, instead, they care about the content (components) on the page. Don't misinterpret what I'm saying here; pages are an absolutely critical piece of an Experience Cloud site (and they have their own configuration and metadata), but, from an end user's perspective, it's the components that get all the credit. See Figure 6-18 for a visualization of the site-to-home concept.

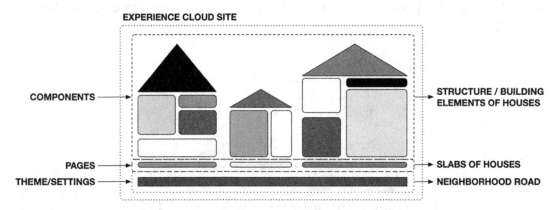

Figure 6-18. *Conceptualizing aspects of an Experience Cloud site as neighborhood housing elements*

When we talk about Experience Cloud sites, the components are at the core of the functional experience. In Chapter 5, I covered the Components tab within the left tab/ sidebar and discussed the presentation of the components (with standard components being grouped functionally/logically and custom components being consolidated in their own group). Here, I will go a little deeper to help site administrators go from concept to application in their journey to create the perfect site, specifically at the point of determining what to do with the plethora of components that are available.

Understanding Components Within Sites

Assuming a component is built properly for its intended purpose, the value of a component within an Experience Cloud site is predicated on these three factors:

- Placement (the page on which the component is placed)

- Positioning (the page section in which the component is dropped)

- Configuration (the configured settings of the component)

If any of these is not appropriately considered, the value of the component will decrease for site users. I'll briefly walk through each to ensure the concept is clear.

Component Placement

Before an admin can start configuring a component for its particular use, they must decide which page (or pages) it should be associated with. The absence of a high-value component on a particular page can be extremely impactful; similarly, the extraneous presence of a component on a page can be distracting and create a convoluted experience for a user. While many components can be placed anywhere within a site, it is critical to understand context and the fact that some components have a limited number of suitable page habitats. See Figure 6-19 for some examples of where and how components might apply to pages.

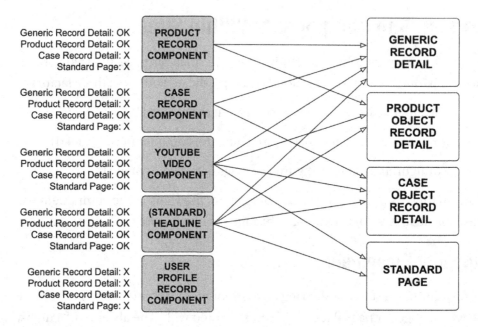

Figure 6-19. Components have context and will not function properly on all Lightning pages

Component Positioning

I discussed page sections in Chapter 5 and will let you revisit that section for corresponding details. Here, I want to help answer the question, where on a page should a component be placed? There is typically no shortage of options; see Figure 6-20 for an example of what a site admin might be faced with when choosing a component's positioning within a Lightning page.

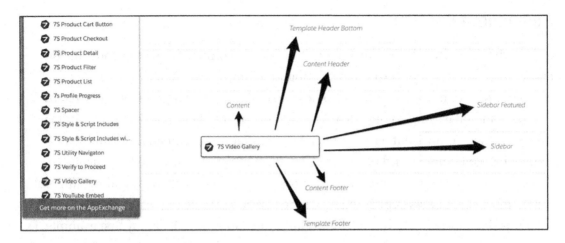

Figure 6-20. *Many potential choices exist for component placement*

I want to make sure that these factors are considered before a component is placed onto a page:

- What are the use cases, capabilities, and/or functions that the component will enable?

- What other components will reside on the page?

- What is the available "experience real estate," and how will the component be used in conjunction with other components?

- How will the component play a role in the expected user experience on the page?

- Is the component suitable for different page sections (i.e., has it been built to satisfactorily display in a single, full-width column on a desktop)?

It is quite easy to fall into the trap of going drag-and-drop crazy and letting user experience and context slip to the back of one's mind during a site build; site builders must fight against that potential slip and ensure that components are placed purposefully and intentionally within a specific page. If one asks these questions, successful positioning of the components will be much more likely.

Component Configuration

Even with the perfect placement and positioning of a component within your site, the component could render zero value if configured improperly. While this may seem obvious, a site administrator needs to know their Lightning components very well. By that, I mean that it's important to learn most, if not all, of the available configurations for a particular component. First, knowing the configurations means knowing the underlying functionality and not missing out on some potential value for your site. Second, it's all about the context. Many components are contextual, providing different functions or capabilities depending on where they are placed.

Consider context with the Headline component, for example. In my first example, I have the component on the Home page and simply set the Title property to "Welcome!". See Figure 6-21.

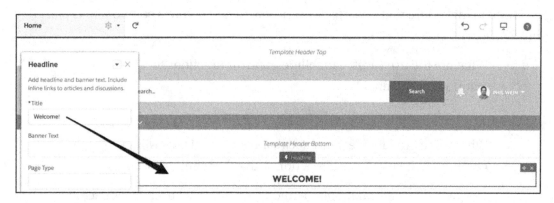

Figure 6-21. *Headline component on the Home page*

Now, I'll place the same component, configured similarly, on the Topic Detail page. I'll leave "Welcome!" as the title, but I'll make one change: setting the Page Type property to "topic" as shown in Figure 6-22.

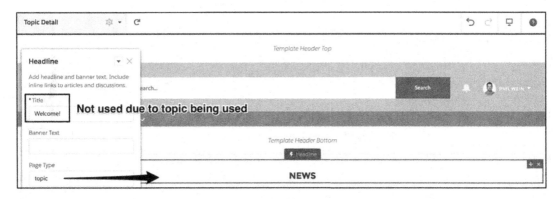

Figure 6-22. *Headline component on the Topic Detail page*

Notice that, although the Title attribute is set to the same value as it was on the Home page, "Welcome!" no longer appears. That has to do with the context and other settings. This is the Topic Detail page, so I want to show the name of the topic within the Headline component, not a static value that would show up on all topic pages. Once I set Page Type to "topic," the title "Welcome!" no longer shows up. The takeaway here is that site builders need to understand each of the properties available for their components, as well as how properties overlap and/or work together.

Progressive Rendering

You can take your page of components a bit further by turning on progressive rendering to load the components in a desired order. Let me be the first to say that you should only use this if you have a noticeable issue with the sequence of components loading on your pages (i.e., if it ain't broke, don't fix it). However, if you are seeing components that are lower on the page loading before the components above them, causing the higher components to abruptly "push" the lower components down, you'll want to consider progressive. It is enabled in Settings ➤ Advanced ➤ Progressive Rendering. See Figure 6-23.

Figure 6-23. *Enable progressive rendering, if warranted*

Once you enable it, you may then configure the priority of your components. By default, all components are set to "neutral" priority. In other words, enabling progressive rendering doesn't initially change anything. However, once you start assigning components to one of the two other levels ("High" and "Highest"), you will see a change. As you'd expect, components set to "Highest" are loaded first and those set to "Neutral" (or left alone) are loaded last. See Figure 6-24 for how to navigate to a component's progressive rendering settings.

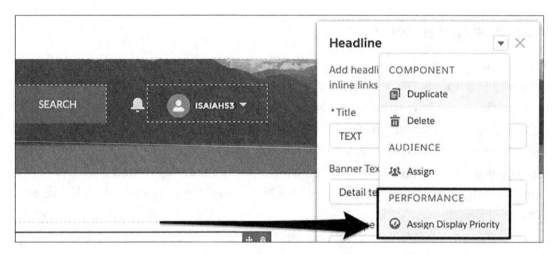

Figure 6-24. *Assign Display Priority*

After clicking "Assign Display Priority," a modal will appear and an admin can select the desired priority. See Figure 6-25.

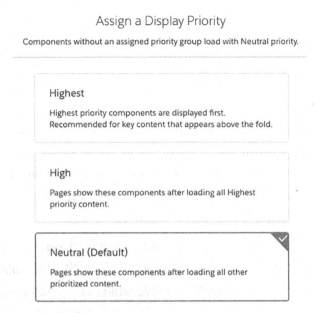

Figure 6-25. *Available rendering priorities*

Note   Please plan your rendering settings with extreme care and planning. Haphazard configuration of progressive rendering settings could have a detrimental impact to user experience.

A Real-World Example

For the majority of standard (Salesforce-created) site templates, numerous standard components are available (over 50 on just the Home page). As a result, it's not feasible for me to review all, or even most, of the available standard components available for communities. Instead, I will take a handful of components and use them as examples, walking through this select group to show possible configurations, and explain the different options and why one would select certain settings over others. I will leverage the following components:

- Headline
- Rich Content Editor

- Tabs

- Tile Menu

- Record List

- Create Case Form

These are not necessarily the most commonly used components for sites, but they are utilized fairly often. To best bring all of this to life, I'll start with a new standard page. From there, I will add, position, and configure components to create a site experience. I'll use the "Flexible Layout" page layout, as shown in Figure 6-26.

Note   While most standard components are available in standard (Salesforce-provided) site templates, they are not all available in each. The following Salesforce help page outlines which components are available in each template: `https://help.salesforce.com/articleView?id=rss_component_reference_table.htm`.

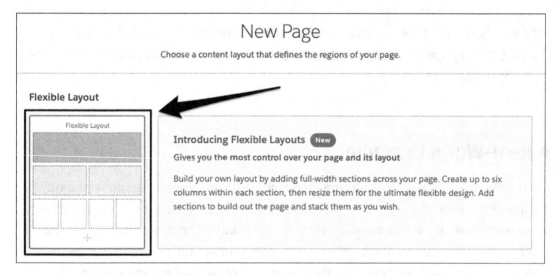

Figure 6-26. *The "Flexible Layout" page will be used for this example*

Figure 6-27 shows the blank canvas before the layout is modified or any components are placed.

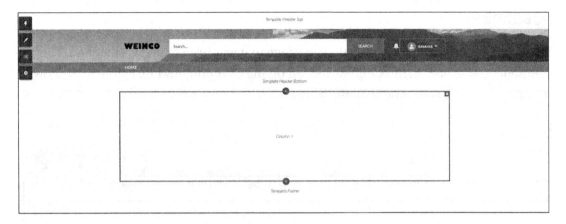

Figure 6-27. *Blank page, prior to the positioning of any components*

I made some basic changes to the Flexible Layout, including dividing the existing section into two columns and adding one additional section. See Figure 6-28 for a look at the page before components are added.

Figure 6-28. *Updated page layout*

Headline

The first component I'll drop onto the new page that was just created is Headline. This component is located in the Content section on the Components tab. Figure 6-29 shows step 1 (placing the component on the page).

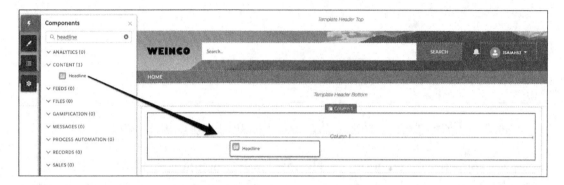

Figure 6-29. *Positioning the Headline component*

Headline is a fairly simple component that is useful for providing a text-based content header on a given page. The component configurations include the following:

- Title

- Banner Text

- Page Type

- Unique Name or ID

- Banner Text with Articles and Discussions

- Banner Text with Discussions

- Show Subtopics

The last five configuration settings here have to do with knowledge articles, topics, and discussions. This page won't include any of those, so the first two settings are the only two that require attention. I'll keep it simple and add explanatory text for each: "Chapter 6 Example Page" for Title and "Practical Guide to Salesforce Communities" for Banner Text. Figure 6-30 shows the configured component, after being placed in the Content Header section of the page.

Figure 6-30. *Configuring the Headline component*

Rich Content Editor

Next, I'll focus on Rich Content Editor. See Figure 6-31 for the initial placement.

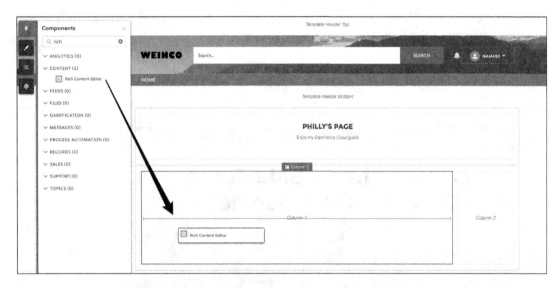

Figure 6-31. *The Rich Content Editor component is placed onto a page*

Similar to the Headline component, this component allows for emphasized text; however, it handles much more. An admin can feature images, videos, links, and formatted text with Rich Content Editor. Also, unlike most other components, standard configuration settings do not exist; instead, a rich text/content editor is provided (see Figure 6-32).

Figure 6-32. *Configuring the Rich Content Editor component*

For this page, I will use the Video option, which is the rightmost button in the editor shown in Figure 6-32. Figure 6-33 shows the component settings and the page after the update, as placed in the Sidebar section.

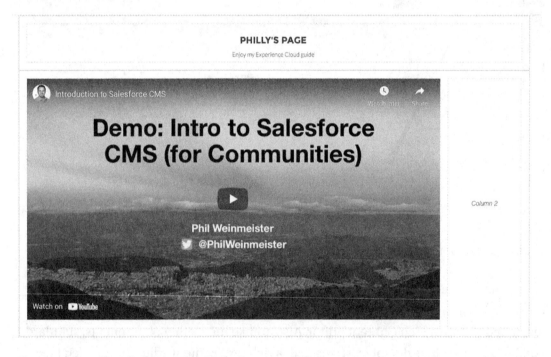

Figure 6-33. *Configuring the Rich Content Editor component to show a video*

Tabs

The Tabs component is simple yet extremely useful. In the case that a site admin wants to support a significant amount of content or functionality on a single page without cluttering up the experience, tabs will allow for the content to be spread across "subpages" that keep the in-focus display simple. The options with the Tabs component

158

are limited because it is basically a placeholder for other content; an admin can create, label, and sequence tabs. In addition, they can determine whether a tab will display on a public page (a page not requiring authentication). For the example page, I need to first place the component in the Content section (Figure 6-34).

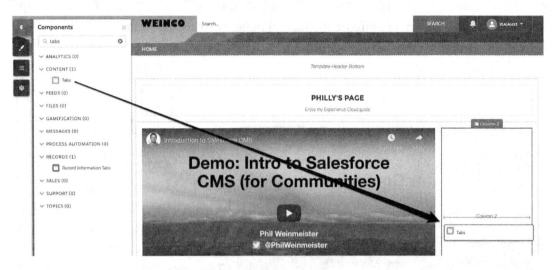

Figure 6-34. *Positioning the Tabs component*

To support the three remaining components for my example, I will configure the Tabs component accordingly; see Figure 6-35.

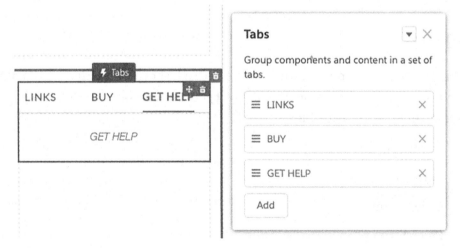

Figure 6-35. *Creating three tabs using the Tabs component*

Tile Menu

The Tile Menu component allows for branded/stylized links to other pages or content. For my example page, I'll use it to point to various site-focused pages in the Salesforce ecosystem. First, I need to place it in the first tab within the Tabs component I just set up. For each tile menu item, I configure the label, image, and destination URL. Figure 6-36 shows the settings for the first of the four tile menu items.

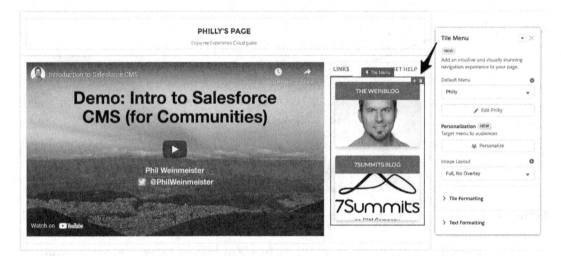

Figure 6-36. *Configuring the Tile Menu component*

Record List

Record List is a staple component within any site that leverages underlying CRM data. I would not say that is highly configurable, but it gets the job done. The following configuration options are available:

- Number of Records

- Layouts

- Object Name

- Filter Name

For this example, I will use a filter called Master List for the product object. I will select the Standard layout to provide a less-cluttered look within the tab. See Figure 6-37 for a look at this component, as configured for this example page.

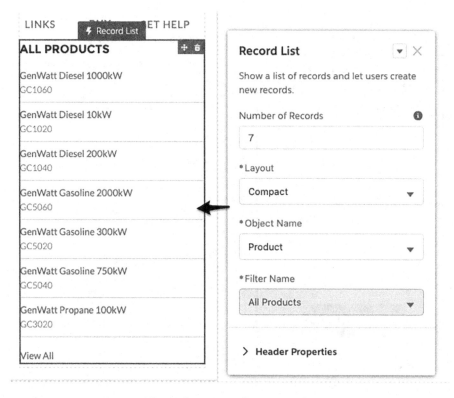

Figure 6-37. Positioning and configuring the Record List component

Create Case Form

If you need a simple way to submit a case, you can use the Create Case Form component. For this example page, I'll drop in the Create Case Form component (Figure 6-38) and configure it as needed.

Figure 6-38. Positioning the Create Case Form on the third tab

See Figure 6-39 for a look at a configured Create Case Form component.

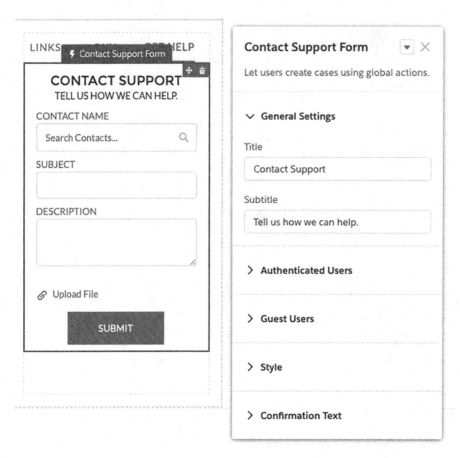

Figure 6-39. *Once an eligible action is specified, the Create Case Form comes to life*

Review

Now that the page has been configured, I don't want to neglect the best part: seeing the page in action. Figure 6-40 shows a standard desktop view of the new site page that has been set up.

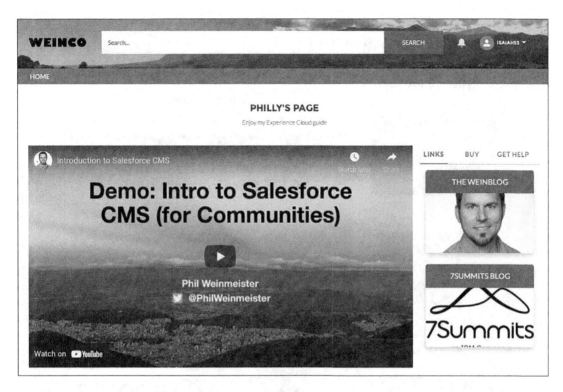

Figure 6-40. *Desktop layout of our new page*

Figure 6-41 shows the mobile and tablet views of the same page.

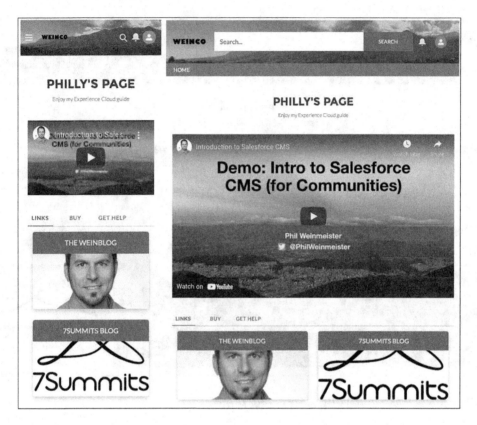

Figure 6-41. *Mobile and tablet layouts of our new page*

Recap

In this chapter, I transitioned from the Experience Builder tool in the previous chapter to the pages and components that it supports. I provided an overview of how site page creation and management works, along with the various options. I then dove into an example that featured a number of popular components, along with specific page placement and configuration, to provide a functional custom page within a site.

CHAPTER 7

Setup and Administration

While Experience Builder—and the pages and components it controls—is at the heart of all Lightning-based Experience Cloud sites, there's more to the full picture of what influences a site experience. In this chapter, I'll take a step back and look at the knobs and levers that drive sitewide settings for *all* sites, regardless of template type. I'll group these configurations into two buckets:

- Digital Experiences Settings (across all sites)
- Site Administration (per-site settings)

Digital Experiences Settings

When thinking about building the first site within a particular org, an admin will need to start at the Digital Experiences Settings menu. The settings here not only control key functional aspects of the sites but also enable sites altogether. One important aspect of these settings that is critical to understand is that they apply to the entire org, not an individual site. The Administration workspace, as I will cover later in this chapter, is site specific. Figure 7-1 shows the concept visually.

© Philip Weinmeister 2022
P. Weinmeister, *Practical Guide to Salesforce Experience Cloud*, https://doi.org/10.1007/978-1-4842-8132-1_7

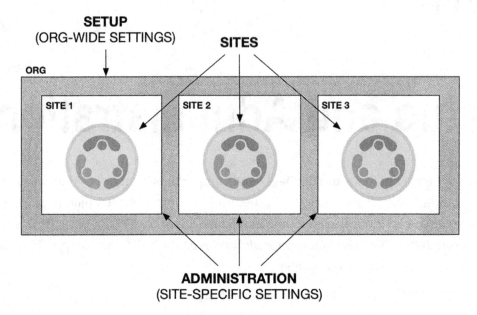

Figure 7-1. *The Digital Experiences Settings page (Setup) affects all sites; administration impacts a specific, individual site*

Initial Setup

The initial setup of sites within an org involves a few steps. Search for "digi" in the Quick Find search box to filter down to a few choices and then select "Settings" in the "Digital Experiences" section. See Figure 7-2 for a look.

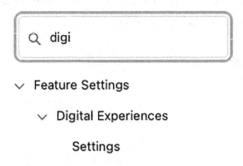

Figure 7-2. *Finding Digital Experiences Settings*

The first step is simply to enable sites within an org. Figure 7-3 shows the corresponding checkbox.

Experiences

Build pixel-perfect websites, portals, communities, and forums with Experience Cloud. Learn More

To get started with digital experiences, you must first enable it and select a domain. If enhanced domains are enabled, your org's My Domain name is the subdomain for any site you create.

Save

Enable Digital Experiences

| = Required Information

After you enable digital experiences in your org, you must still create, configure, customize, and then activate a site before it's live and available to users.

☐ Enable Digital Experiences

Save

Figure 7-3. *Enable Digital Experiences to allow the creation of a new site within an org*

Before saving and actually enabling sites for the org, an additional setting must be configured: selecting a domain name. This domain name will serve as the base/domain URL for all sites in the org. So, for example, if "bunkerjones" was selected, the domain in production would be https://bunkerjones.force.com/s for a site without a directory and https://bunkerjones.force.com/support/s for a site with a directory of support. Note that these examples assume a production org; the URL is different in trial or sandbox orgs. See Figure 7-4 for a view of the "Select a domain name" section once sites are enabled.

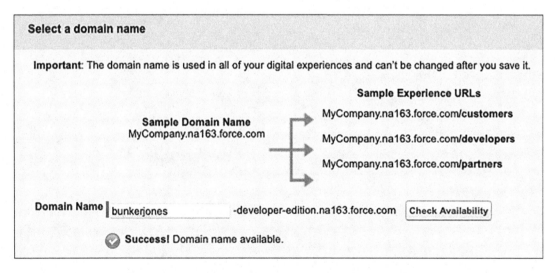

Select a domain name

Important: The domain name is used in all of your digital experiences and can't be changed after you save it.

Sample Experience URLs

Sample Domain Name
MyCompany.na163.force.com

MyCompany.na163.force.com/**customers**

MyCompany.na163.force.com/**developers**

MyCompany.na163.force.com/**partners**

Domain Name | bunkerjones   -developer-edition.na163.force.com   [Check Availability]

✓ **Success!** Domain name available.

Figure 7-4. *A domain name must be selected when enabling sites*

While it is strongly advisable to select a domain name with permanence in mind, it can potentially be modified later. Although Salesforce doesn't allow an administrator to modify it directly, it is possible that Salesforce support will change it if a support case is submitted for that request.

Note   Before a Partner Central site can be enabled, one or more valid Partner site licenses must be present within the org. However, in Enterprise, Performance, and Unlimited orgs, up to 100 active sites can be maintained without a license (although only guest and internal users will be able to access the site).

Additional Site Settings

Once sites are enabled and a domain name is selected, a number of additional settings are exposed. See Figure 7-5 for these settings.

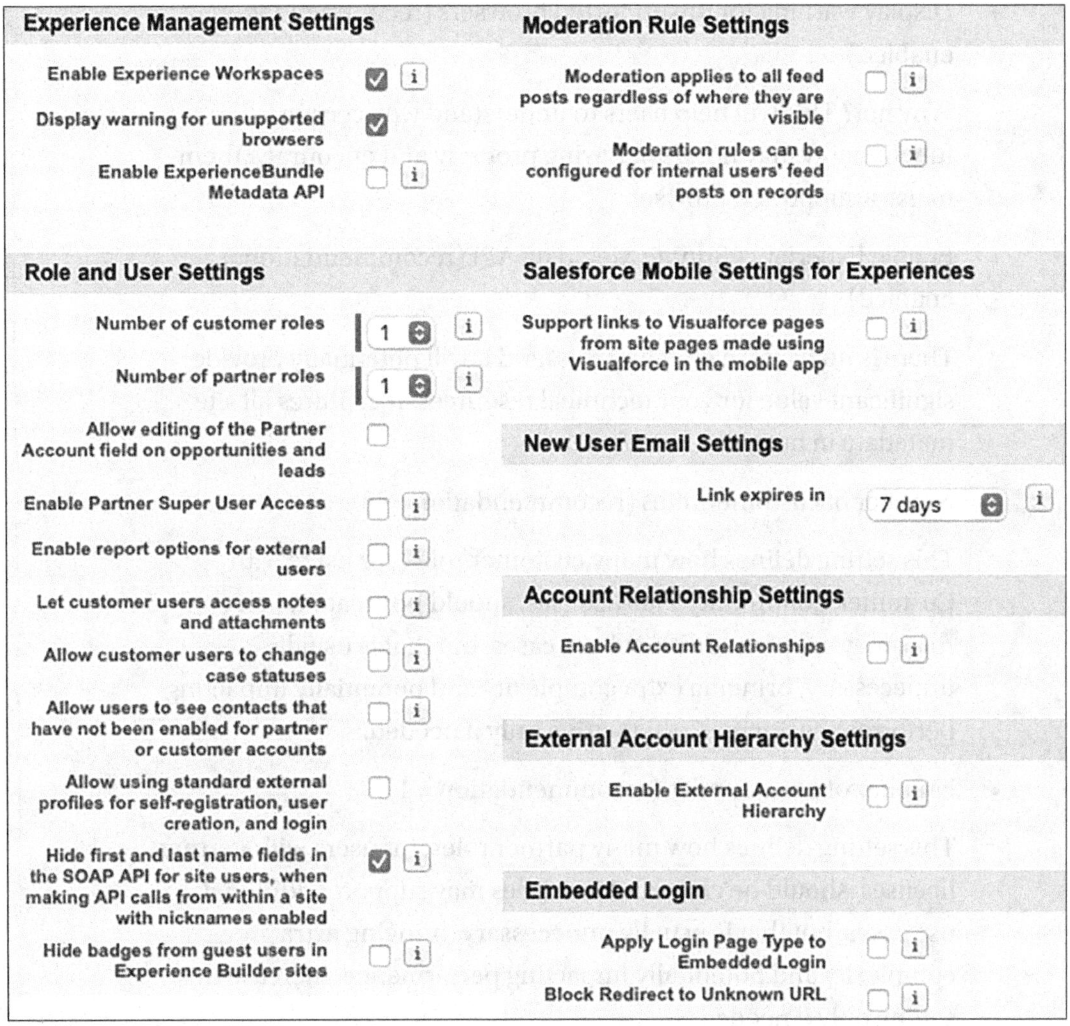

Experience Management Settings

Enable Experience Workspaces ☑ ⓘ

Display warning for unsupported browsers ☑

Enable ExperienceBundle Metadata API ☐ ⓘ

Role and User Settings

Number of customer roles `1 ⬍` ⓘ

Number of partner roles `1 ⬍` ⓘ

Allow editing of the Partner Account field on opportunities and leads ☐

Enable Partner Super User Access ☐ ⓘ

Enable report options for external users ☐ ⓘ

Let customer users access notes and attachments ☐ ⓘ

Allow customer users to change case statuses ☐ ⓘ

Allow users to see contacts that have not been enabled for partner or customer accounts ☐ ⓘ

Allow using standard external profiles for self-registration, user creation, and login ☐

Hide first and last name fields in the SOAP API for site users, when making API calls from within a site with nicknames enabled ☑ ⓘ

Hide badges from guest users in Experience Builder sites ☐ ⓘ

Moderation Rule Settings

Moderation applies to all feed posts regardless of where they are visible ☐ ⓘ

Moderation rules can be configured for internal users' feed posts on records ☐ ⓘ

Salesforce Mobile Settings for Experiences

Support links to Visualforce pages from site pages made using Visualforce in the mobile app ☐ ⓘ

New User Email Settings

Link expires in `7 days ⬍` ⓘ

Account Relationship Settings

Enable Account Relationships ☐ ⓘ

External Account Hierarchy Settings

Enable External Account Hierarchy ☐ ⓘ

Embedded Login

Apply Login Page Type to Embedded Login ☐ ⓘ

Block Redirect to Unknown URL ☐ ⓘ

Figure 7-5. *Additional site settings*

I will provide an overview of all of these settings, including my recommendation for the corresponding setting that works for most orgs:

- Enable Experience Workspaces (recommendation = enabled)

  This setting opens up a completely new site management interface. I highly recommend making the switch. There is no functionality lost, and it is the suggested approach moving forward, so get on board! Note that this is automatically enabled for new sites, as shown in Figure 7-6.

- Display warning for unsupported browsers (recommendation = enabled)

  Why not? This will help users to understand why certain functionality may not be behaving properly and encourage them to use a supported browser.

- Enable ExperienceBundle Metadata API (recommendation = enabled)

  There is no harm in enabling this, and it will potentially provide significant value for your technical resources. It captures all site metadata in human-readable text.

- Number of customer roles (recommendation = 1)

  This setting defines how many customer roles, for users with Customer Community Plus licenses, should be created. More roles may support additional use cases, but that is usually unnecessary, bringing extra complexity and potentially impacting performance. Increase this setting only if needed.

- Number of partner roles (recommendation = 1)

  This setting defines how many partner roles, for users with Partner licenses, should be created. More roles may support additional use cases, but that is usually unnecessary, bringing extra complexity and potentially impacting performance. Increase this setting only if needed.

- Allow editing of the Partner Account field on opportunities and leads (recommendation = disabled)

  This is an extra layer of protection to ensure that this relationship-defining field is not hastily updated. Of course, if your business process warrants editing, enable it, making sure that field-level security (FLS) is set properly.

- Enable Partner Super User Access (recommendation = disabled)

  This setting allows users individually identified as superusers to have visibility equal to other contacts on the same account. Truthfully, there is no immediate harm in enabling this setting. However, to be safe, leaving it disabled is probably ideal because it eliminates any risk of extraneous access being granted through this setting. Of course, if needed, use it.

- Enable report options for external users (recommendation = enabled)

  For site users who have the ability to run reports, this setting will also allow them to view and modify reports for the purpose of summarizing and filtering them.

- Let customer users access notes and attachments (recommendation = disabled)

  This option allows customer site users to access notes and attachments on contact and account records. I suggest defaulting this to disabled for security reasons, unless required.

- Allow customer users to change case statuses (recommendation = disabled)

  This allows users with Customer Community Plus licenses to modify the status on Case records. Enable this only if necessary and consider the consequences of that access.

- Allow users to see contacts that have not been enabled for partner or customer accounts (recommended = disabled)

  Keeping this setting as "disabled" means that your users will only be able to see contacts that have been enabled as customers or partners. This may be too restrictive for some; by all means, enable it if you want your users to see all contacts, regardless of their status as site members. My recommendation of the default simply provides additional protection over data, just in case.

- Allow using standard external profiles for self-registration, user creation, and login (recommendation = disabled)

  Salesforce implemented this with the unstated goal of forcing organizations to think more carefully about their external profiles vs. just using the off-the-shelf choices. It's a wise boundary. There really isn't a great reason to avoid setting up custom profiles for your external users, as it allows for much more granular control.

- Hide first and last name fields in the SOAP API for site users, when making API calls from within a site with nicknames enabled (recommendation = enabled)

  You won't really notice this one, but it does provide an additional level of data security.

- Hide badges from guest users in Experience Builder sites (recommendation = disabled)

  If you don't want guest users to see user badges, enable this one. Otherwise, it could be useful to expose achievements to a broader audience.

- Moderation applies to all feed settings regardless of where they are visible (recommendation = enabled)

  This option allows posts to be moderated across sites. Specifically, if a post exists in multiple sites, this setting would allow a moderator of any of the related sites to flag the post. Leaving this as disabled means that only site-specific posts can be moderated.

- Moderation rules can be configured for internal users' feed posts on records (recommendation = enabled)

  This is similar to the last rule but specific to internal users' posts. It allows those posts to be moderated in all corresponding sites where the post is visible.

- Support links to Visualforce pages from site pages made with Visualforce using the mobile app (recommendation = disabled)

  Enabling this setting will retain the Apex prefix on all site URLs to ensure that Visualforce pages will properly load using the mobile app. Enable if needed.

- Link expires in (recommendation = 7 or 180 days)

  Enabling this setting will set the site invitation link to expire in a certain number of days. The options are 1 day, 7 days, and 180 days.

- Enable Account Relationships (recommendation = depends)

  This should be disabled for organizations not using Account Relationships and, of course, enabled for those using them. Note: This setting cannot be undone and does impact sharing.

- Enable External Account Hierarchy (recommendation = depends)

  This should be disabled for organizations not using External Account Hierarchies and, of course, enabled for those using them. Note: This setting cannot be undone and does impact sharing.

- Apply Login Page Type to Embedded Login (recommendation = disabled)

  Most likely, this will not be needed. If you are using Embedded Login, enable it.

- Block Redirect to Unknown URL (recommendation = enabled)

  This setting will provide a level of security to prevent undesired redirects if Embedded Login is being used. Of course, if you understand the intricacies here and are comfortable with redirecting to an "unknown" URL, disable the setting.

Administration

I rarely access the Digital Experiences Settings menu once I enable sites and establish a domain. However, it's the exact opposite with administration, which is a different tool to control a site; it is critical to intimately know the corresponding configurations because they are guaranteed to come into play within your sites.

While the setup applies to *every* site in an org, the Administration menu is site specific. If it's not clear why both exist, one can make a parallel with page-specific components vs. a theme component. A theme component applies to the entire site and has settings that impact every page, while an individual component has settings that impact only that specific component.

Assuming workspaces are enabled (which I recommend), site administrators will find that "Administration" is one of the displayed workspaces. See Figure 7-6 for a view of the workspace.

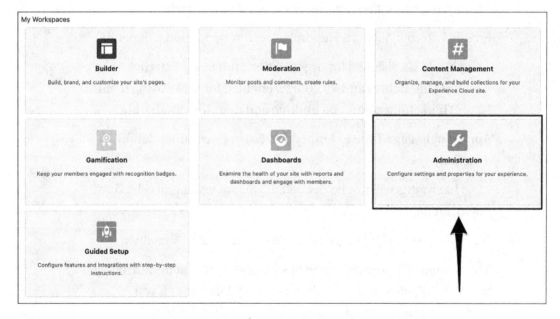

Figure 7-6. *Experience workspaces*

The following Administration sections exist:

- Settings

- Preferences

- Members

- Contributors

- Tabs

- Branding

- Login & Registration

- Emails

- Pages

- Reputation Levels

- Reputation Points

- Rich Publisher Apps

- URL Redirects

I'll walk through the settings of each of these sections.

Note   Some of these settings appear only in certain contexts. For example, the Tabs and Branding sections correspond only to Tabs + Visualforce sites.

Settings

In Settings, administrators can control three critical settings of a site:

- *Name*: The name of the site (network), as referenced within Salesforce. This is different from the site name, as configured in Experience Builder. The Experience Builder name setting impacts the name of the site, as displayed within a browser to site viewers.

- *Description*: The description of the site, as shown within Salesforce to internal users.

- *URL*: This is the site-specific part of the URL that follows the domain name that is used by all sites. For example, https://<site_domain>/<URL>.

See Figure 7-7 for a view of the Settings page.

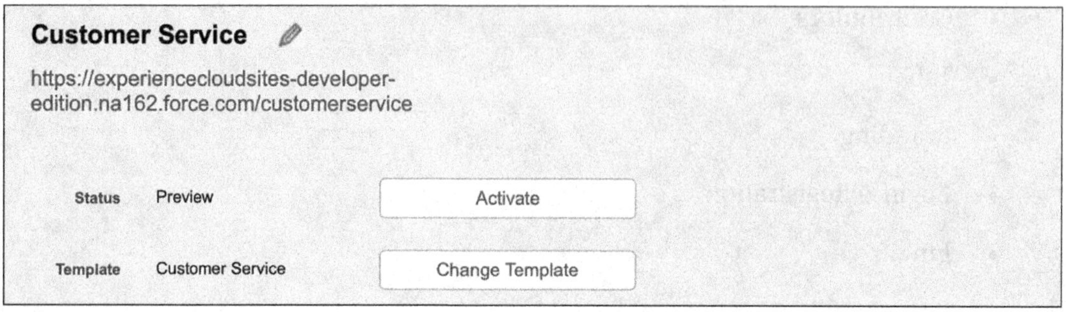

Customer Service 🖉

https://experiencecloudsites-developer-
edition.na162.force.com/customerservice

Status	Preview	Activate
Template	Customer Service	Change Template

Figure 7-7. *Administration Settings*

Preferences

The Preferences page of the Administration workspace provides a number of Boolean (on/off) settings that impact the associated site.

General

The General section in Preferences provides settings related to access, display, analytics, and more. Figure 7-8 shows the corresponding settings, which are described here:

- *Show nicknames*: Instead of displaying the user's first and last names within standard components, the value in the user's Nickname field will be displayed. Use this if you want to provide users with a visible identity without showing real names or if you want to allow users to self-identify by editing their own nicknames.

- *Optimize images for mobile devices*: Smaller images will be loaded on mobile devices, potentially decreasing page load time.

- *Give access to public API requests on Chatter*: Enabling this setting allows site administrators to display content in one or more public Chatter groups to guest (unauthenticated) users, along with any other public Chatter content that is served up.

- *Let guest users view asset files and CMS content available to the site*: This allows unauthenticated users to see certain resources (files and content) on corresponding pages within the site. An example of this setting's impact is the login page background image; that image will not be accessible by guest users if this setting is disabled, instead showing a background color without an image.

- *Enable direct messages*: This allows users to send direct messages to other site members. Note that direct messages differ from private messages. Direct messages are an older feature typically associated with customization.

- *Users can send and receive private messages*: This allows users to leverage the Messages inbox for private communication. I highly recommend enabling this when there is a need for private, one-to-one communication within a site.

- *Allow discussion threads*: This enables users to reply to answers and to previous replies.

- *See other members of this site*: Enabling this setting allows site members to view other site members within the site.

- *Let guest users see other members of this site*: Similar to the previous setting, this enables guest users to view site members within the site.

- *Use a profile-based layout for Lightning Knowledge search results*: This allows field-level control over article search results by profile.

- *Gather Customer Insights data*: This setting allows for the capture and propagation of data within the site to be exposed to internal users within Lightning Experience through the related standard component.

- *Use custom Visualforce error pages*: This setting replaces the standard (and ugly) error pages with custom-built, Visualforce error pages.

- *Show all settings in Workspaces*: While I don't recommend enabling this setting, it allows admins to "force" the display of all site settings, even if some of the settings are not relevant to their site.

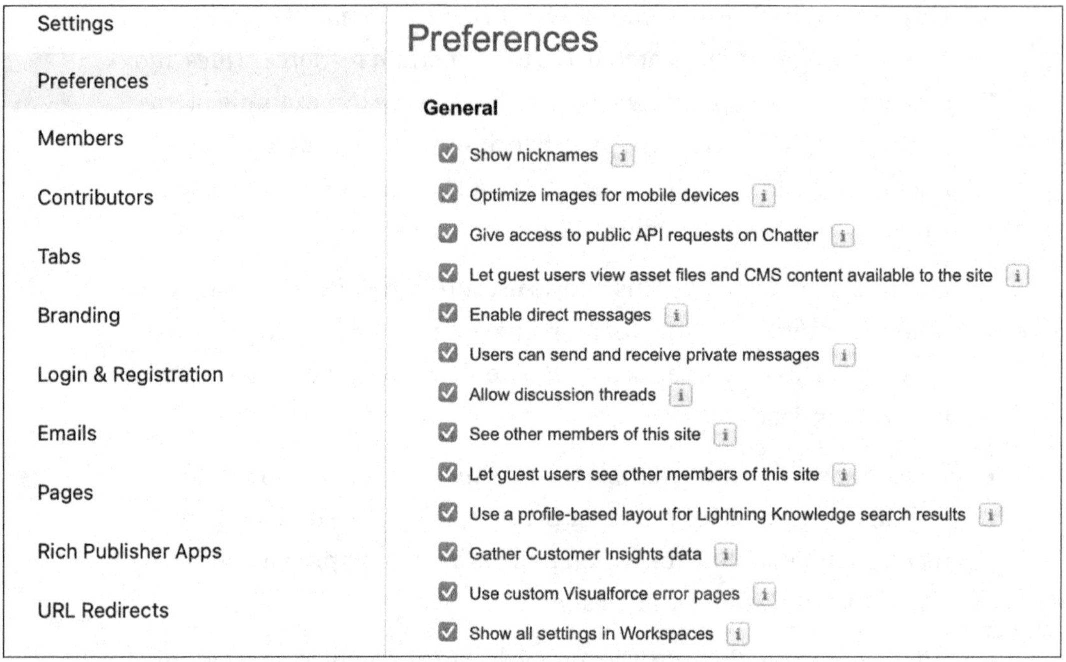

Figure 7-8. *General preferences. Note: "Show all settings in Workspaces" is enabled, causing a number of other normally hidden settings to appear*

Experience Management

The Experience Management section contains settings that directly impact a site member's experience or allowed functions. Figure 7-9 shows the corresponding settings, described here:

- *Allow members to flag content*: This setting enables members to flag content that they might consider to be inappropriate or a piece of spam. I recommended enabling this for sites with significant Chatter activity, but it is critical to understand that a resource must be available in the site to review the flagged content.

- *Allow members to upvote and downvote*: This setting, if enabled, will replace the Like button on questions and answers.

- *Enable setup and display of reputation levels*: This is a widely popular setting that essentially turns on gamification within a site. However, as the setting implies, reputation levels must be configured (i.e., set up) before they can be displayed.

- *Exclude contributions to records when counting points toward reputation levels*: In a site that includes significant operational activity via Chatter on records, the distribution of reputation points/levels can become extremely skewed based on those operational requirements. To center gamification around pure site activity, enable this setting.

- *Enable knowledgeable people on topics*: This setting allows users to identify users as "knowledgeable" on topics, enabling a self-managing expertise identification network. Admins should carefully assess the impact first, however; if users will not take the "nominations" seriously, the results may not be representative of true subject knowledge.

- *Override standard actions with a Lightning component*: This setting allows for standard actions (such as New and Edit) to be replaced with custom Lightning actions, configured in Object Manager.

- *Suggest topics in new site posts*: This setting will result in certain topics being suggested after a post is made; the suggested topics are derived from the post content itself.

- *Show number of people discussing suggested topics*: This setting shows a statement such as "100 people are discussing this topic" following a post that contains a topic. In a site with lighter traffic or a smaller user base, this may inadvertently discourage site members; think carefully before enabling this in a small site.

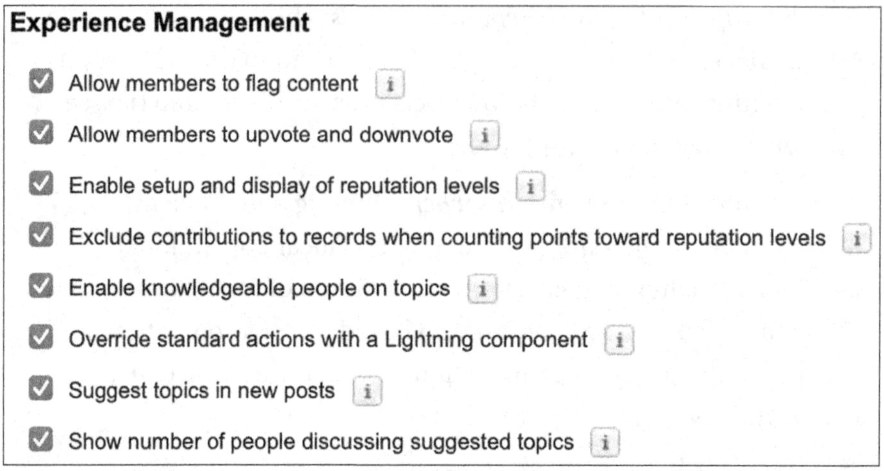

Experience Management

☑ Allow members to flag content [i]

☑ Allow members to upvote and downvote [i]

☑ Enable setup and display of reputation levels [i]

☑ Exclude contributions to records when counting points toward reputation levels [i]

☑ Enable knowledgeable people on topics [i]

☑ Override standard actions with a Lightning component [i]

☑ Suggest topics in new posts [i]

☑ Show number of people discussing suggested topics [i]

Figure 7-9. *Experience Management preferences*

Record Ownership

Once Salesforce made significant changes to guest user access within sites, certain settings were introduced to support these changes. Here, an administrator can identify a default owner of records created by guest users. See Figure 7-10 for a look at the setting.

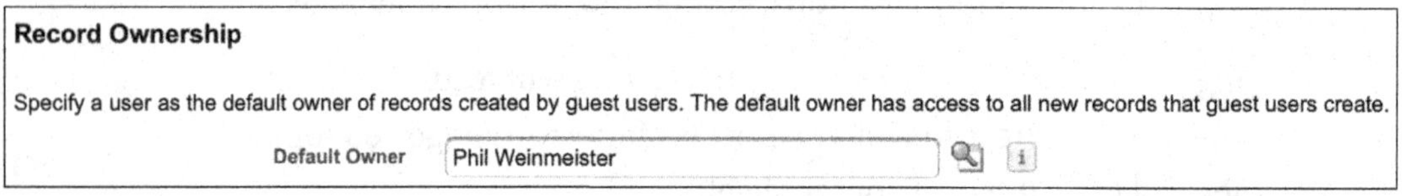

Record Ownership

Specify a user as the default owner of records created by guest users. The default owner has access to all new records that guest users create.

Default Owner   [Phil Weinmeister]   🔍 [i]

Figure 7-10. *Record Ownership preferences*

Files

While not discussed heavily, this section is quite handy. Administrators can limit the types of files allowed for Chatter upload, as well as the maximum file size allowed. It is a great thing that Salesforce allows such large files via Chatter, but a scenario may arise (i.e., limited storage space) in which a reduced maximum file size would be beneficial. The maximum file size must be between 3 MB and 2048 MB. See Figure 7-11.

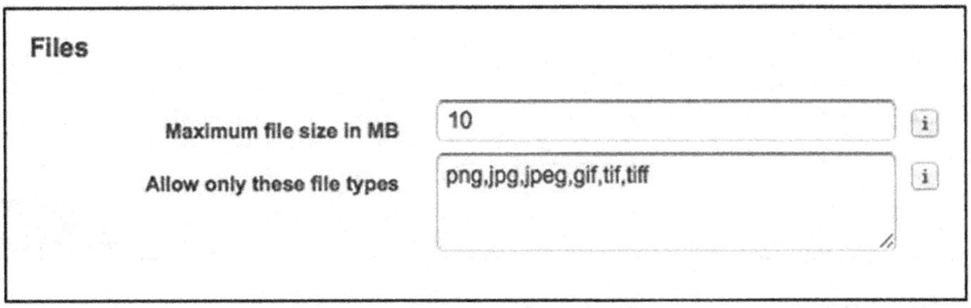

Files

Maximum file size in MB: `10`

Allow only these file types: `png,jpg,jpeg,gif,tif,tiff`

Figure 7-11. *Limit the file size and type of files that can be uploaded in a site*

Figures 7-12 and 7-13 show the result of each of these settings as they appear to end users.

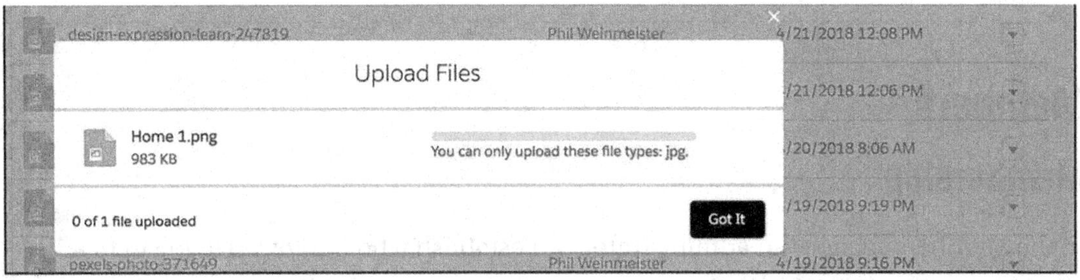

Upload Files

Home 1.png
983 KB

You can only upload these file types: jpg,

0 of 1 file uploaded   Got It

Figure 7-12. *A .png file is blocked when allowed file types are limited to .jpg files*

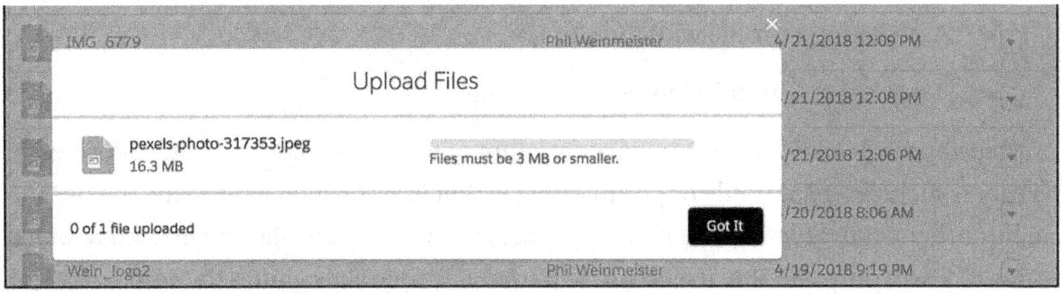

Upload Files

pexels-photo-317353.jpeg
16.3 MB

Files must be 3 MB or smaller.

0 of 1 file uploaded   Got It

Figure 7-13. *A 16.3 MB file is blocked when the maximum size is set to 3 MB*

Uploading a file via Chatter takes these limits into consideration as well, although the reason for the blocked file is not displayed. See Figure 7-14.

181

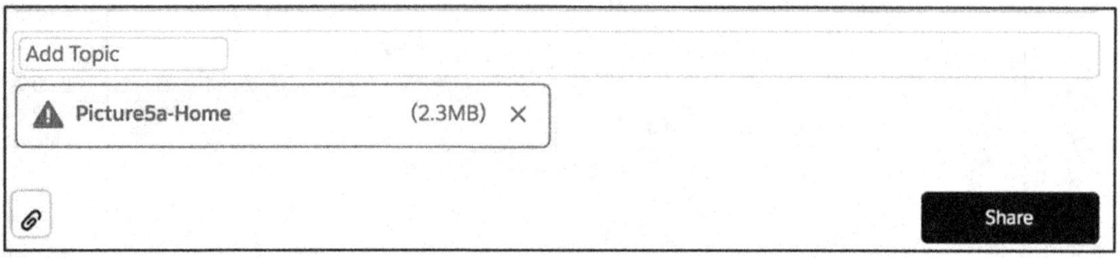

Figure 7-14. *Blocked file through Chatter*

Note   The Files settings do not impact standard attachments; they are specific to files.

Members

Membership

In the Members section, an administrator can establish who is allowed to log in to a specific site. Specifying "log in" vs. access is important, as a public site or Lightning page technically allows anyone access to the public portions of the site. Member access is granted in these two ways:

- Associating a profile with the site

- Associating a permission set with the site

This approach allows for a significant amount of flexibility for both users and sites. If a user is included in a profile or permission set that is associated with a site, the user can be authenticated for it. Since neither profiles nor permission sets are limited to being associated with only one site, users can be part of multiple sites within the same org. The permission sets allow for extremely granular access, even down to an individual user.

Additionally, on the site side, sites can be associated with multiple profiles and permission sets, allowing administrators to configure the authorized site audience with ease. Figure 7-15 provides a visual of how access might work within an org that has multiple sites, profiles, and permission sets.

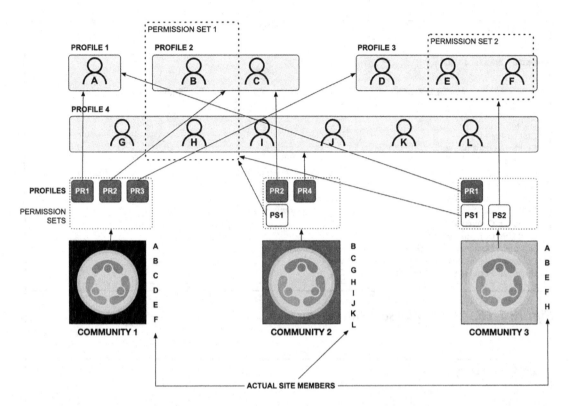

Figure 7-15. *An example of how access could be granted using profiles and permission sets*

Figure 7-16 shows the profile selection menu, and Figure 7-17 shows the permission set selection menu.

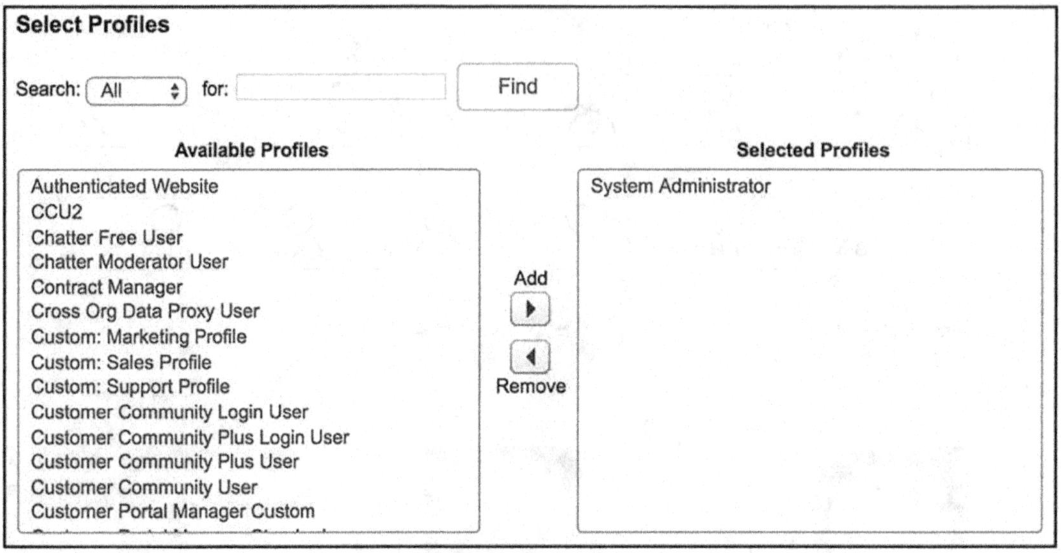

Select Profiles

Search: [All ⟷] for: [   ]   [Find]

Available Profiles	Selected Profiles
Authenticated Website	System Administrator
CCU2	
Chatter Free User	
Chatter Moderator User	
Contract Manager	
Cross Org Data Proxy User	
Custom: Marketing Profile	
Custom: Sales Profile	
Custom: Support Profile	
Customer Community Login User	
Customer Community Plus Login User	
Customer Community Plus User	
Customer Community User	
Customer Portal Manager Custom	

Add [▶]

[◀] Remove

Figure 7-16. *Site profile selection menu*

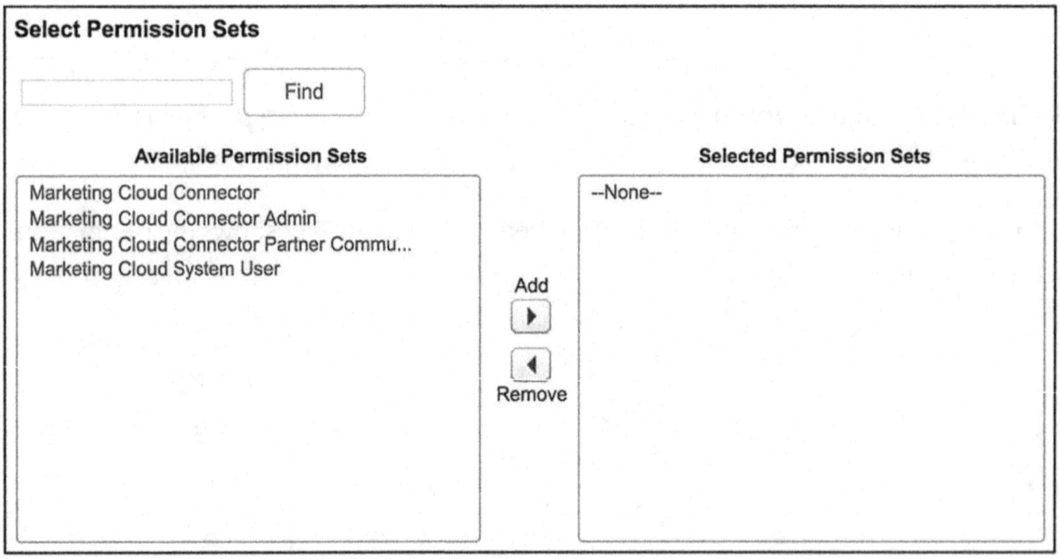

Select Permission Sets

[   ]   [Find]

Available Permission Sets	Selected Permission Sets
Marketing Cloud Connector	--None--
Marketing Cloud Connector Admin	
Marketing Cloud Connector Partner Commu...	
Marketing Cloud System User	

Add [▶]

[◀] Remove

Figure 7-17. *Permission set selection menu*

Site Role Labels

If an organization wants to refer to a member of a certain audience type (e.g., Customer, Partner, or Employee) with a nonstandard label, it can be configured here. See Figure 7-18 for an example.

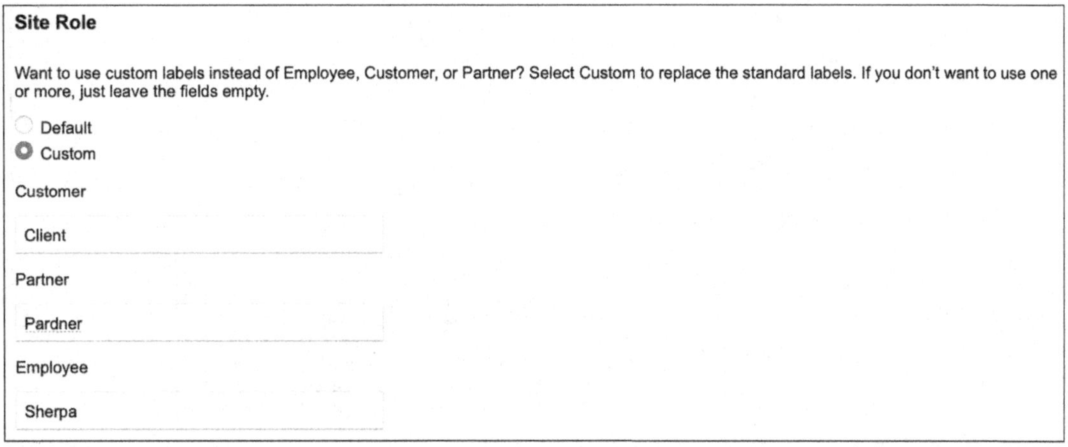

Site Role

Want to use custom labels instead of Employee, Customer, or Partner? Select Custom to replace the standard labels. If you don't want to use one or more, just leave the fields empty.

○ Default
● Custom

Customer

Client

Partner

Pardner

Employee

Sherpa

Figure 7-18. *Site role settings*

Contributors

Contributors is a relatively recent addition to Site Administration and allows for access to be granted in the areas of site creation and management. Four settings are available:

- *Viewer*: Read-only access to the workspace

- *Builder*: Full access to the workspace

- *Publisher*: Full access to the workspace and can publish the site

- *Experience Admin*: Full access to the workspace, can publish the site, and can manage contributors

See Figure 7-19 for a look at the wizard that allows these settings to be applied.

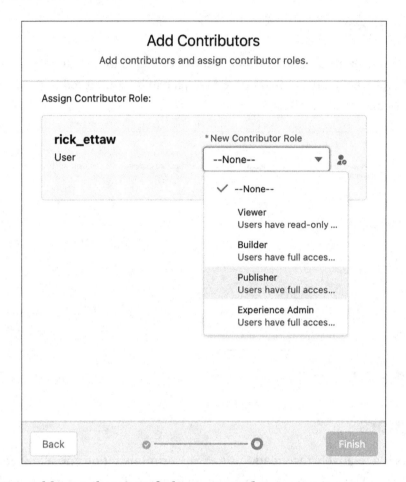

Figure 7-19. *Add contributors to help create and manage sites*

Tabs

Tabs is a straightforward administration area. This menu allows site administrators to add tabs to a site, causing them to appear in a Tabs + Visualforce site. Also, this panel will impact the objects that appear in the Salesforce mobile app (even if within a Lightning site). See Figure 7-20 for a look at the settings, and see Figure 7-21 for the result.

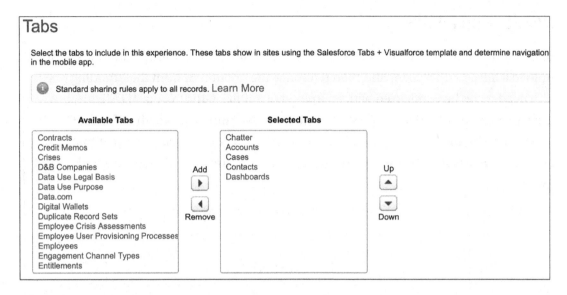

Figure 7-20. *Tabs settings*

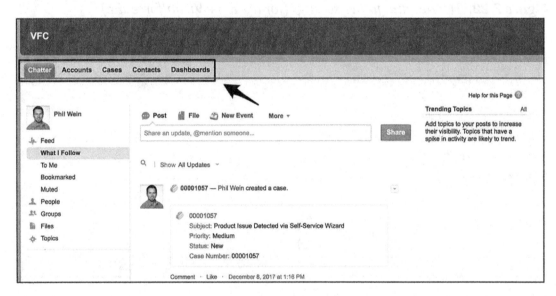

Figure 7-21. *Displayed tabs, as configured in Figure 7-20*

Branding

For Tabs + Visualforce sites, which do not use Experience Builder, defining the branding colors is done within the Branding page of the Administration workspace.

Header and Footer

In this subsection, the site header and footer are defined. An administrator must first upload a file as a document and then reference the document from the Branding page. The header can be configured with an upload of a JPEG, GIF, PNG, or HTML file, but the footer can be HTML only. Also, administrators should be aware that if the HTML file is uploaded for the header, they will need to include a custom search field within that HTML file. See Figure 7-22 for the settings, and see Figure 7-23 for the impacted area of the site.

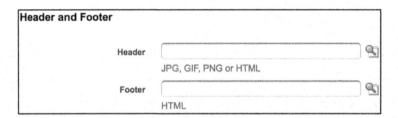

Figure 7-22. *Header and footer settings (for a Tabs + Visualforce site)*

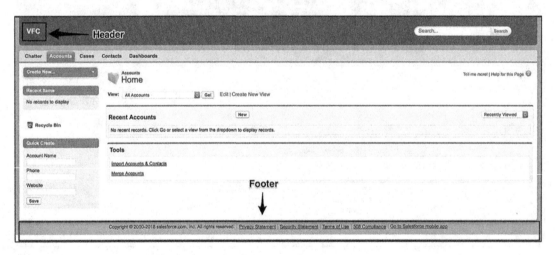

Figure 7-23. *The page areas impacted by the header and footer settings*

Colors

Site administrators of a Tabs + Visualforce site can control branding colors. See Figure 7-24 for the different settings.

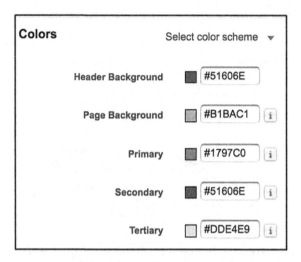

Figure 7-24. Branding color settings for a Tabs + Visualforce site

Login & Registration

The Login & Registration settings provide administrators with the ability to configure how users authenticate and register within a site.

Branding Options

Logo

The Logo section houses the settings to configure a site logo. This logo will be used on the login page, whether the site is Tabs + Visualforce or Lightning based. An administrator will first need to determine the logo type. That setting will determine the second setting. If File is selected for Logo Type, the administrator will click Browse to upload a file from the local computer. See Figure 7-25.

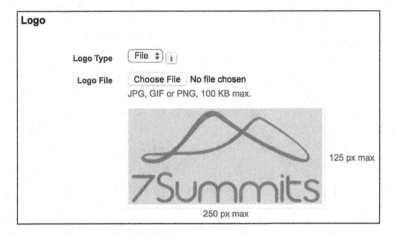

Figure 7-25. *A file or URL can be used to display a logo on the login page*

If URL is selected, a URL-based image can be used for the logo on the login page. One little-used feature is dynamic branding on the login page, set up by entering a dynamic URL. Search for *Dynamic Branding with Login Pages* to learn more. With this feature, an organization can show different login logos based on an audience.

Colors, Right Frame URL, and Footer Text

The following settings will further allow configuration of the login page:

- *Colors*: Configure the background color or the button color on the login page.

- *Right Frame URL*: This is a way to configure an image on the right half of the login. To add personalization, apply a dynamic URL to change the logo based on a particular audience.

- *Footer text*: Footer text on the login page.

See Figure 7-26 for an example of these settings, and see Figure 7-27 for what a login page might look like.

Figure 7-26. *Login page settings*

Figure 7-27. *A login page with configured right-side content*

Login Page Setup

The login page settings, while typically fairly straightforward, are critical to site success and can require some focused attention. In total, there are four login settings:

- Login page type

- Login page

- Direct site login for internal users

- Login options

The first setting is the configured login page type. Four login page types are available:

- Default Page

- Login Discovery Page

- Experience Builder Page

- Visualforce Page

See Figure 7-28 for a view of the login page options.

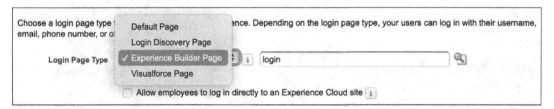

Figure 7-28. *Login page options*

These are my suggestions for various desired scenarios and the corresponding settings that should be selected:

- *Experience Builder site/standard login page*: Select Experience Builder Page and "login."

- *Experience Builder site/custom Experience Builder login page*: Select Experience Builder Page and then select a Lightning page.

- *Experience Builder site/custom Visualforce login page*: Select Visualforce Page and then select a Visualforce page.

- *Tabs + Visualforce site/standard login page*: Select Default Page.

- *Tabs + Visualforce site/custom Visualforce login page*: Select Visualforce Page and then select a Visualforce page.

"Login Discovery Page" allows for the use of a phone number or a custom identifier in addition to email and opens up the following additional options:

- *Login Prompt*: Label displayed above the login field

- *Login Discovery Handler*: Associated Apex class that handles the login discovery logic

- *Execute Login As*: The user that runs the Login Discovery Handler

A site admin will then decide whether internal users should be allowed to log in directly to the site. This is typically turned off, encouraging internal users to log in to the "standard" Salesforce org before toggling to the site. However, there is no inherent issue with enabling this setting. It's important to make sure that the login process aligns with company procedures and rules, but it's a legitimate option, especially if users exist who rarely log in to the main org. See Figure 7-29.

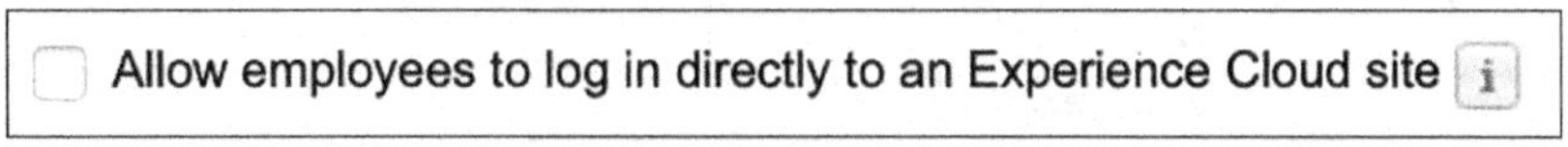

Allow employees to log in directly to an Experience Cloud site ⓘ

Figure 7-29. *Allow users to log in to the site without first logging in to the "internal" org*

The final login option involves single sign-on settings and authentication providers. Simply put, this is where an administrator would configure access to authenticate using something other than the standard site username and password. The first option, and often the only option selected, is the standard login method using the username and password. However, many sites require additional options. I won't go into detail on how to set up authentication providers, but I will show an example of how an administrator might set these up to drive site login options. See Figure 7-30 for a look at some configured providers.

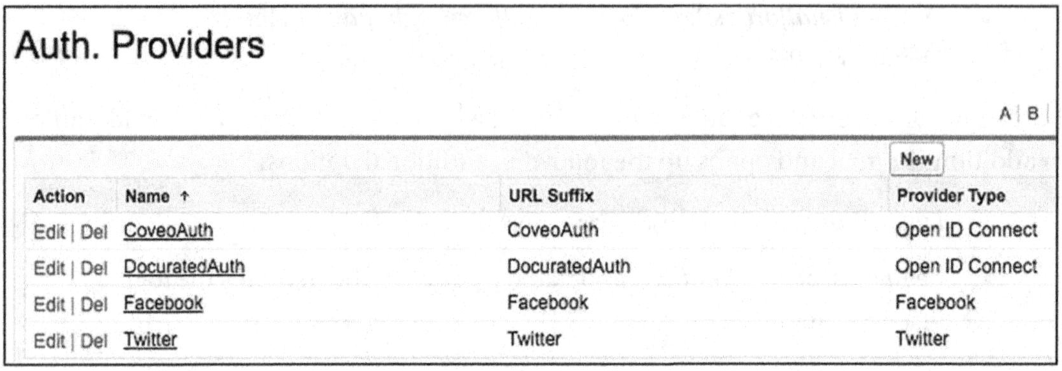

Auth. Providers

A | B

			New
Action	**Name** ↑	**URL Suffix**	**Provider Type**
Edit	Del	CoveoAuth	CoveoAuth	Open ID Connect
Edit	Del	DocuratedAuth	DocuratedAuth	Open ID Connect
Edit	Del	Facebook	Facebook	Facebook
Edit	Del	Twitter	Twitter	Twitter

Figure 7-30. *Configured authentication providers*

In Figure 7-31, the four configured authentication providers now appear in the Login section.

Select which login options to display [i]

☑ Capricorn Consulting username and password
☑ Facebook
☑ Twitter
☐ DocuratedAuth
☐ CoveoAuth

To configure more login options, go to Single Sign-On Settings or Auth. Providers. [i]

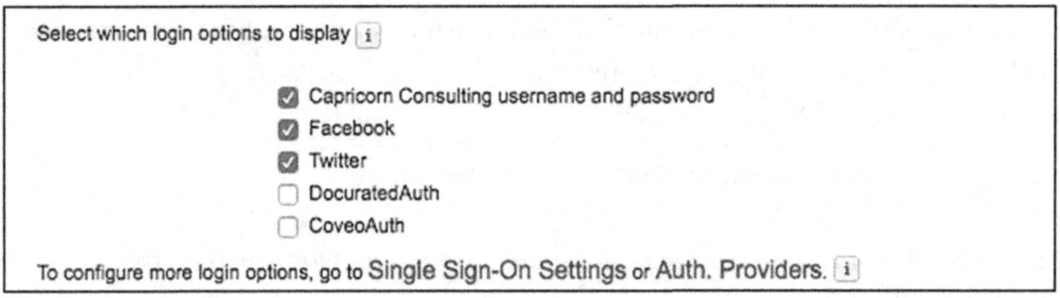

Figure 7-31. *The authentication providers from Figure 7-30 appear in the Login section on the Login & Registration page*

In this case, Facebook and Twitter are configured. Figure 7-32 shows the result of this on the actual site login page.

Figure 7-32. *A login page with Facebook and Twitter configured as login options*

Out-of-the-box authentication providers include

- Apple

- Facebook

- GitHub

- Google

- Janrain

- LinkedIn

- Microsoft Access Control Service

- OpenID Connect

- Salesforce

- Twitter

Logout Page URL

Salesforce provides one option for customizing the page that is displayed following a logout by a site member: the URL of the desired page. Even if an administrator wants to point to an Experience Builder page or a Visualforce page, the full URL needs to be configured. See Figure 7-33 for the Logout settings.

Figure 7-33. *An admin can enter a URL for the desired post-logout page*

Password Pages

While I recommend using the default pages, if possible, Salesforce sites support custom pages to communicate a forgotten password and to reset a password. The options are as follows:

- Forgot Password

- Default Page

- Experience Builder Page

- Visualforce Page

- Reset Password

See Figure 7-34 for a view of these options.

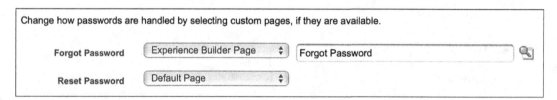

Figure 7-34. *Site settings for password-related pages*

Registration

Thankfully, Salesforce provides the ability to enable self-registration within sites. This is most relevant to customer sites since partners and employees will most commonly be identified as users by the organization that owns the site. Figure 7-35 shows the top-level self-registration settings.

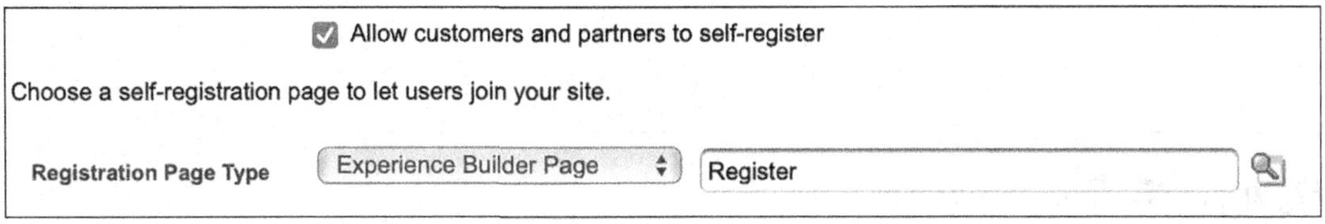

Figure 7-35. Self-registration settings

Users can be auto-assigned to a profile and account. See Figure 7-36 for an example.

Figure 7-36. Profile and account for auto-assignment

The first step in establishing self-registration within a site is enabling the "Allow customers and partners to self-register" setting. This opens up a few additional settings, including the registration page. Select an existing (standard) page or point to a custom-built registration page, as needed. Also, a profile and account need to be configured since users will not determine their own profile or account.

Emails

Sender

The display name and email address of the email sender should be configured. By default, "From Name" is "Customer Service" and email address is the email address of the user that first set up the org. If you want to change the email address, you'll need to verify it first. See Figure 7-37 for a look at the email sender settings.

Sender

* From Name	Customer Service
* Email Address	phil.weinmeister@7summitsinc.com

Requested new email address **philweinmeister@yahoo.com** isn't valid until verified.

Resend verification email

Figure 7-37. *Sender settings*

Chatter Email Branding

Chatter emails are handled differently from non-Chatter emails. With Chatter emails, the general look and feel and the content are set. However, you can configure the logo and footer text of Chatter emails; see Figure 7-38.

Chatter Email Branding

Logo	Salesforce Chatter logo

150 x 50 pixels or less on a transparent background is best.

Footer Text	salesforce.com, inc. The Landmark @ One Marke

We strongly recommend including your company's physical address to comply with applicable anti-spam laws.

Preview

Figure 7-38. *Chatter Email Branding settings*

Email Templates

Although standard email functionality (templates, alerts) within the classic or Lightning Experience interface is absolutely compatible with sites, some site-specific email settings are critical. Those settings are stored in the Emails section of the Administration workspace (see Figure 7-39).

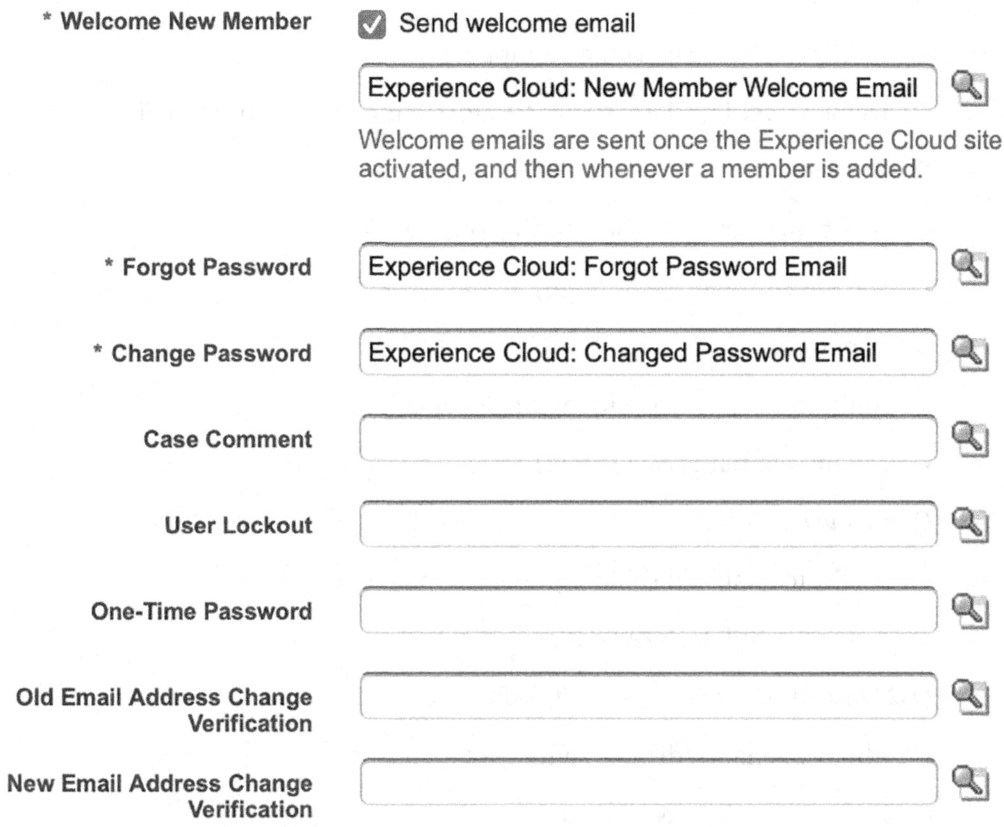

* **Welcome New Member**   ☑ Send welcome email

Experience Cloud: New Member Welcome Email   🔍

Welcome emails are sent once the Experience Cloud site is activated, and then whenever a member is added.

* **Forgot Password**   Experience Cloud: Forgot Password Email   🔍

* **Change Password**   Experience Cloud: Changed Password Email   🔍

Case Comment   🔍

User Lockout   🔍

One-Time Password   🔍

Old Email Address Change Verification   🔍

New Email Address Change Verification   🔍

Figure 7-39. *Email settings for sites*

The following configurable site email templates exist:

- *Welcome New Member*

  - Ability to disable this email template: Yes

  - Default template: Experience Cloud: New Member Welcome Email

- *Forgot Password*

  - Ability to disable this email template: No

  - Default template: Experience Cloud: Forgot Password Email

- *Change Password*

  - Ability to disable this email template: No

  - Default template: Experience Cloud: Changed Password Email

- *Case Comment*

  - Ability to enable/disable sending of email: Yes

  - Default template: N/A (none)

- *User Lockout*

  - Ability to enable/disable sending of email: Yes

  - Default template: N/A (none)

- *One-Time Password*

  - Ability to enable/disable sending of email: Yes

  - Default template: N/A (none)

- *Old Email Address Change Verification*

  - Ability to enable/disable sending of email: Yes

  - Default template: N/A (none)

- *New Email Address Change Verification*

  - Ability to enable/disable sending of email: Yes

  - Default template: N/A (none)

It is absolutely supported to change any or all of these emails to add branding or modify content. However, an admin should check all available merge fields carefully to ensure that no functionality is lost when transitioning to a different email alert.

Note   For admins working on a site who want to absolutely ensure that no emails are inadvertently sent out to potential members of the site, I recommend temporarily unchecking the "Send welcome email" checkbox. It's easy to reenable and can save some major headaches.

Pages

The Pages section is probably the least straightforward or self-explanatory of all Administration sections. Yes, it does relate to pages, but that doesn't exactly provide the full picture. See Figure 7-40 for a view of the Pages section.

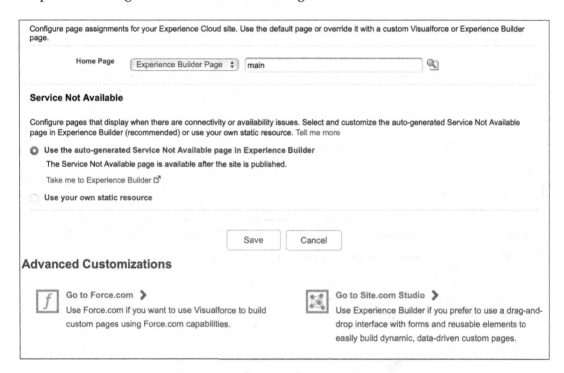

Figure 7-40. *The Pages section of the Administration menu*

Home Page and Service Not Available both allow a site administrator to override standard pages with a custom page. However, the greatest value on this page is found within Advanced Customizations, namely, the "Go to Force.com" link. Numerous settings exist that allow custom Visualforce pages to be swapped in to replace certain standard site pages. Quietly residing on the Force.com page are Guest User Profile controls. From here, an admin can configure exactly what guest users have access to. Note that this is just like any profile, allowing configuration of object access, field access, and much more.

Also on the Force.com page are certain related list sections, such as available
Visualforce pages. These sections allow Visualforce pages, Apex classes, and more to
be made available within the site. This is useful to apply when all users need the same
level of access to a specific element within the site. See Figure 7-41 for an overview of the
Force.com Pages menu.

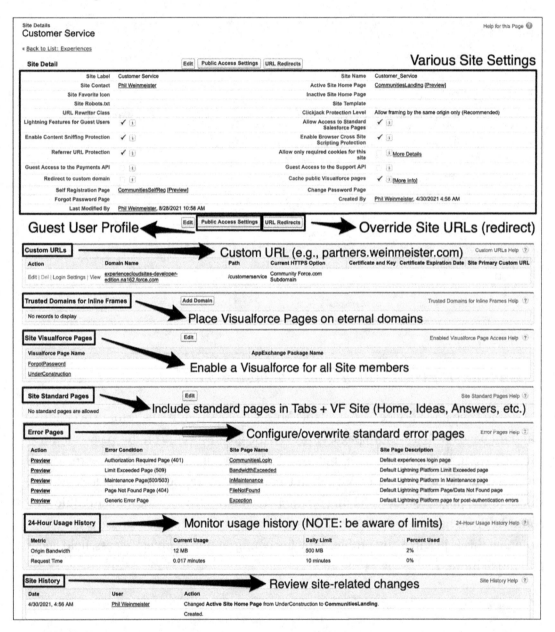

Figure 7-41. *Force.com Pages screen*

Reputation Levels

Once the setup of reputation levels and points has been enabled, an administrator can configure both of those new sections. See Figure 7-42 for a look at the Reputation Levels section.

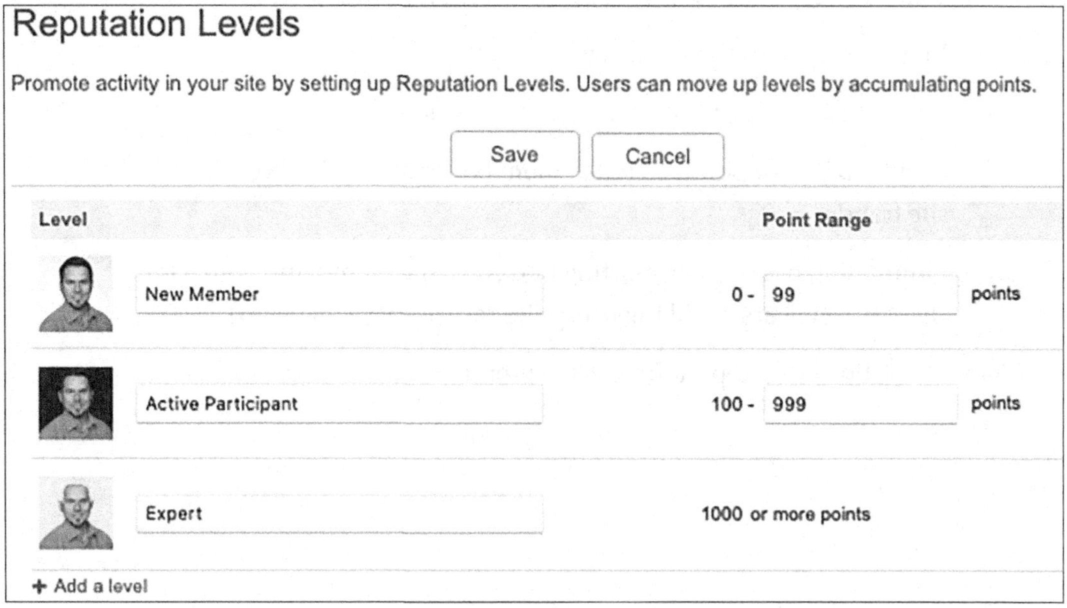

Figure 7-42. *Reputation Levels settings*

There are four steps to setting up reputation levels, shown here:

1. Determine the desired number of levels. The default number is ten, but this should be tailored to the needs of each site. To remove levels, an administrator can click the X icon by the last level until reaching the desired number of levels. To add levels, an administrator can click the "+Add a row" link and repeat until complete.

2. Configure the point range for each level. I recommend starting at level 1 and working up from there.

3. Name each level. A site administrator will want to know the audience to determine whether to come up with fun names or more serious/professional ones.

4. Upload a badge/level icon for each level.

Reputation Points

Reputation points directly relate to reputation levels, as each level is bound by a range of points. The number of points per contributing activity can be modified. It is critical to understand what might warrant a change in the number of points configured for a specific activity. I suggest the following as valid reasons, among others:

- Increased emphasis on particular activities

- Decreased emphasis on particular activities

- "Right-sizing" of points to make them better align with overall site trends

- Elimination of spam-supporting behavior (e.g., removing points for a "like" when users are liking every site record they can get to)

Figure 7-43 shows the Reputation Points menu.

Event	Points
ENGAGEMENT	
Write a post	+ 1
Write a comment	+ 1
Receive a comment	+ 5
Like something	+ 1
Receive a like	+ 5
Share a post	+ 1
Someone shares your post	+ 5
Mention someone	+ 1
Receive a mention	+ 5
QUESTIONS AND ANSWERS	
Ask a question	+ 1
Answer a question	+ 5
Receive an answer	+ 5
Mark an answer as best	+ 5
Your answer is marked as best	+ 20
KNOWLEDGE	
Endorsing someone for knowledge on a topic	+ 5
Being endorsed for knowledge on a topic	+ 20

Figure 7-43. *Reputation Points settings screen*

Figure 7-44 shows an example of the standard Leaderboard component once reputation levels and points have been configured.

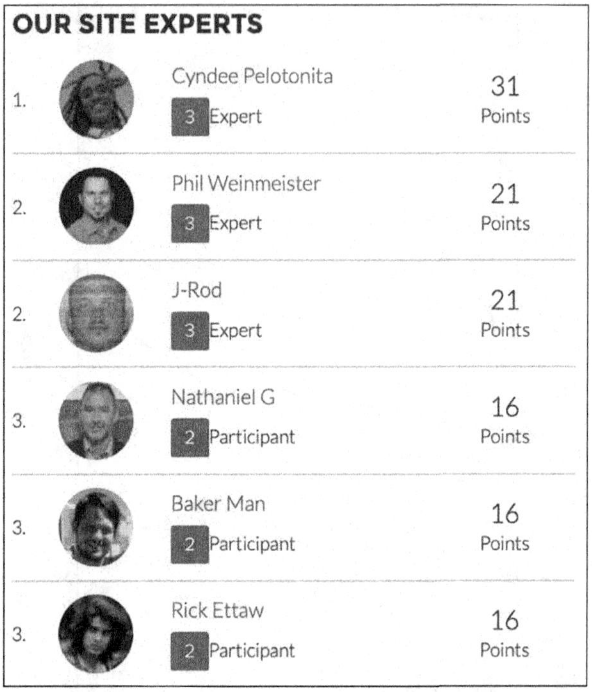

OUR SITE EXPERTS

1.		Cyndee Pelotonita 3 Expert	31 Points
2.		Phil Weinmeister 3 Expert	21 Points
2.		J-Rod 3 Expert	21 Points
3.		Nathaniel G 2 Participant	16 Points
3.		Baker Man 2 Participant	16 Points
3.		Rick Ettaw 2 Participant	16 Points

Figure 7-44. *Leaderboard component with reputation levels and points configured*

Rich Publisher Apps

Rich publisher apps are a newer feature that can be used within sites. These apps allow for a payload to be accessed from and associated with a specific Chatter post within the site. Once the Lightning components (Composition and Render) and the Chatter extension that are part of the rich publisher app have been created, the app can be associated with a site (see Figure 7-45).

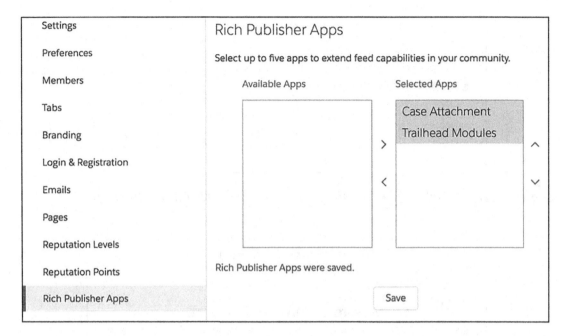

Figure 7-45. *Move publisher apps to Selected Apps to enable them within a site*

Once apps are enabled within a site, the icons will show up within the Feed Publisher component (see Figure 7-46).

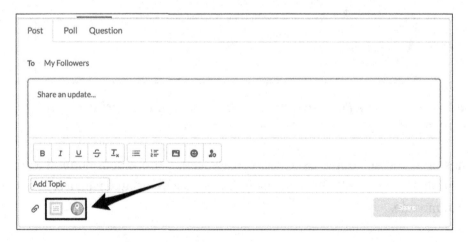

Figure 7-46. *Two rich publisher apps within the Feed Publisher component*

These apps allow for the selection of cases and Trailhead modules, respectively. See Figures 7-47 and 7-48 for the presented modals when each of the icons is clicked.

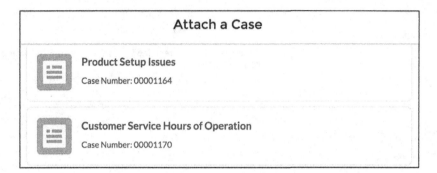

Figure 7-47. *Attach a case to a site feed item using a rich publisher app*

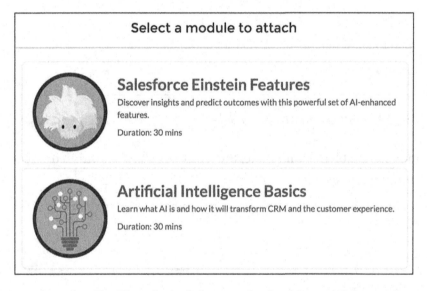

Figure 7-48. *Attach a Trailhead module to a site feed item using a rich publisher app*

When all is said and done, a site user can associate various data/content with a post within the site. See Figure 7-49 for an example of a post associated with a case and a Trailhead module.

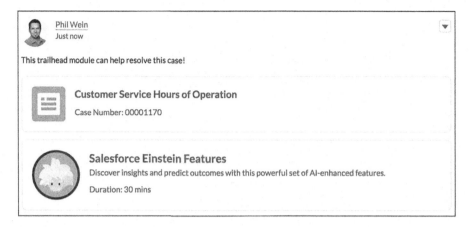

Figure 7-49. *View of a feed with an associated case and Trailhead module*

Recap

While I wouldn't exactly call the world of setup and administration glamorous or exhilarating, it is an absolute necessity on the path to success with a Salesforce site. In this chapter, I walked through each of the separate site settings and Administration menus (and explained the difference between the two), covering areas such as preferences, email, login, registration, reputation, and more.

CHAPTER 8

Access, Sharing, and Visibility

I assume all airlines list safety as their first corporate priority. The customer experience, while important, does not equate to the criticality of customer health. In the technology world filled with 1s and 0s, data security takes on a role analogous to that of airline passenger safety. Anyone would agree that user functionality and experience are of extremely high importance to Salesforce users; yet, the corresponding satisfaction from those factors will never outweigh the need for a secure system that provides access to those in need and prevents access from those who should be excluded. In other words, it's a great thing to have a powerful, useful application at one's fingertips, but, if that application does not appropriately guard private or confidential data, its added value is significantly diminished.

Just as access, sharing, and visibility are key considerations in Sales Cloud and Service Cloud, they are critical factors to consider when building an Experience Cloud site. I will walk through each area that I consider a key factor in establishing a foundation for appropriate access, sharing, and visibility within a site. I will not rehash the entire Salesforce security model, however, since there are security-related areas outside of sites that might warrant a completely separate book. Check out Trailhead for some relevant modules or my other book, *Practical Salesforce Development Without Code*, to learn more about sharing capabilities for the platform as a whole. I will focus on the following specific areas in this chapter:

- Site authentication and access
- Object and field access
- Record sharing
  - Organization-wide sharing (customer site vs. other user types, external sharing model, sites sharing settings)

P. Weinmeister, *Practical Guide to Salesforce Experience Cloud*, https://doi.org/10.1007/978-1-4842-8132-1_8

- Sharing sets/share groups

- Guest user access

Site Authentication and Access

Before anything else is discussed about a particular user's object access in a site or the visibility of a record on a site page, a site administrator must decide who should even be able to access the site. This is a two-part process, involving authentication and access settings.

Authentication (Private vs. Public)

By default, sites are private, meaning that authentication is initially required for any and all access to a site. However, that access can be opened up rather easily in one of two ways:

- Sitewide publicity

- Page-specific publicity

To modify the default setting, navigate to Settings ➤ General within Site Builder and select the checkbox shown in Figure 8-1.

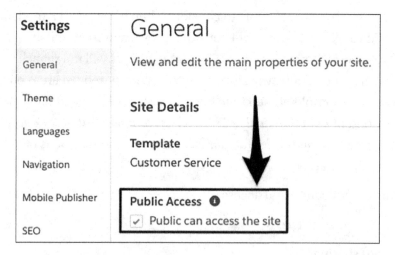

Figure 8-1. *Sitewide Public Access setting*

All page-level default settings are inherited from here. In other words, if this is set to Public, then each page would, by default, be set to Public unless manually updated in Page Access, as shown in Figure 8-2.

Figure 8-2. *The sitewide setting drives the Page Access values*

To make the picture clearer, I will step back and look at multiple sites that are configured differently. Take a look at Figure 8-3. In this diagram, I lay out three sites:

- *Site 1*: Private, with page settings all set to default

- *Site 2*: Private, with some pages manually set to public

- *Site 3*: Public, with some pages manually set to private

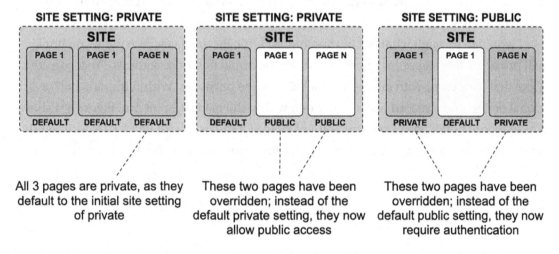

Figure 8-3. *Three scenarios involving sitewide publicity setting and different page-specific settings*

Site Member Access

To access any authenticated page (or functionality) within a site, a user must be provided access through the provisioning of a user profile or a permission set. I described the process in detail in Chapter 7 and won't repeat all of that, but this is a basic premise that needs to be understood when establishing site access; regardless of the scope of access and permissions individual users have through their profiles or a permission set, they will only be considered guest users (i.e., allowing consumption of public content only) without being added to the site. This goes for system administrators, too; be careful with removing that profile from a site.

Object and Field Access

The next critical area when establishing the proper security model for a site is the corresponding object and field access. The great news here is that this is a standard platform activity; there's nothing site specific to learn. For those who happen to have a copy of *Practical Salesforce Development Without Code*, a chapter is dedicated to this topic in detail.

I won't go through what is a fairly standard topic for the Salesforce platform, but I will provide a few examples to help illustrate the impact of these settings. First, consider a site that uses cases with customers for self-service purposes. Within the site, both a global action and a record list are provided within the navigation menu. Figure 8-4 shows a case record detail page from the point of view of a site user with Read, Create, and Edit access to cases and field-level security (FLS) visibility to all case fields.

Figure 8-4. *View of a case for a user with full case object access*

There are four aspects to note in Figure 8-4:

- A case global action in the navigation menu

- A case list in the navigation menu

- A displayed case page

- Three available actions at the top right: Edit, Change Owner, and Clone

If this user no longer has Create or Edit access, the available actions immediately disappear, as shown in Figure 8-5.

Figure 8-5. *Users may no longer see certain actions at the top right if they do not have Create or Edit access*

In Figure 8-6, I have served up the same page for a user with no case access.

Invalid Page

Figure 8-6. *A user without any case access sees neither the case record nor the case-related tabs in the navigation menu*

In Figure 8-6, I show the following conditions:

- The case global action does not appear in the navigation menu.

- The case list does not appear in the navigation menu.

- The case page does not load.

This is valuable because it's built completely on the existing Salesforce security model; administrators can set up the access for site users as they do for internal users, and all of the object and field permissions will carry through to the site fluidly.

Record Sharing

Object and field permissions are pretty straightforward (e.g., whether or not a particular user can edit/update case records). Record sharing, however, isn't so black and white. Record sharing is essentially the determination of who can see which records and in what capacity. In some orgs, it can get pretty complex. I'll cover a few areas specific to record sharing to help explain how to approach the subject for sites.

To get started, take a look at Figure 8-7. This shows how the layers discussed in this chapter so far provide access and visibility within a site.

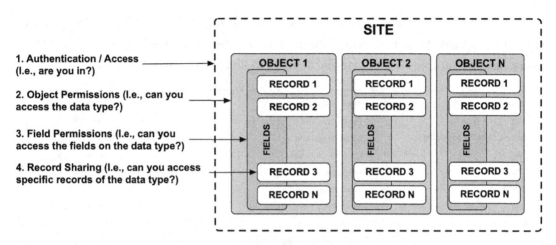

Figure 8-7. *A view of multiple visibility-related settings*

Like some of the other security-related areas, sharing is a general construct of the Salesforce platform. Still, although it's not specific to sites, there are some site-specific aspects of sharing to consider.

Organization-Wide Sharing and External Users

Just as with an "internal" Salesforce implementation, organization-wide sharing settings are critical to consider in a site implementation. These settings determine the base-level visibility to records of different object types. Three settings are available:

- *Public Read/Write*: All records are shared with all users and can be viewed and/or edited by those with proper object access.

- *Public Read Only*: All records are shared with all users and can be viewed by those with proper object access. The records can be edited based on additional sharing means.

- *Private*: Records are not automatically shared with all users. The records can be viewed and/or edited based on additional sharing means, depending on User object access.

Initially, within a Salesforce org, one setting per applicable object exists. However, an external sharing model can be enabled, allowing more granular sharing capabilities. Admins should note that access granted to external users cannot exceed that which is granted to internal users. So, for example, if the User object is shared as Public Read

Only internally, it can only be shared as Public Read Only or Private; Public Read/Write cannot be selected because it would grant external users more visibility than internal users. See an example view of external settings in Figure 8-8.

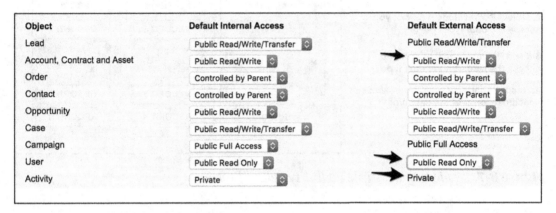

Figure 8-8. *External sharing (organization-wide sharing settings)*

It is important to understand that sharing visibility through these settings only goes as far as an individual user has access. Take accounts from Figure 8-7, for example. They are Public Read/Write. That does not mean all users can necessarily edit all accounts in the system; each user must have the appropriate object and field-level access to make that happen. See Figure 8-9 for a diagram of how this works.

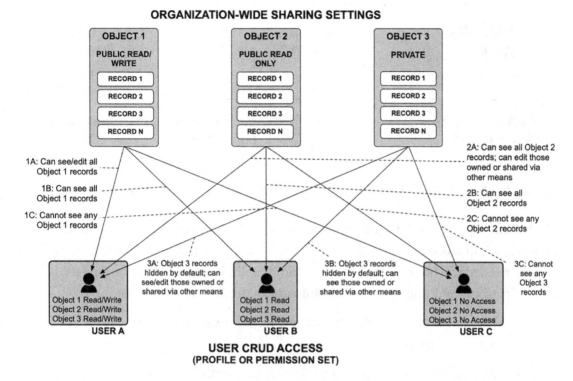

Figure 8-9. *A scenario with three users with varying object access and how sharing settings impact each of their access/visibility*

Customer Community vs. Other Site Licenses

As far as sharing goes, there is really only one site license type that one needs to be aware of: Customer Community (whether login or named user). Why? Because that type is considered "high volume" and does *not* use the standard sharing model (see Figure 8-10). That's a major consideration for building a site solution; do users need full record sharing or not?

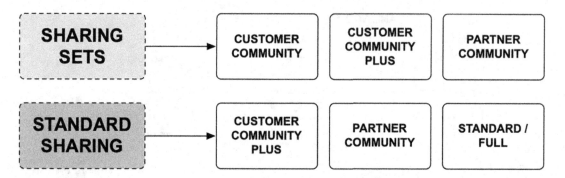

Figure 8-10. *Customer Community users do not use standard Salesforce sharing*

The concept here is that "high-volume" users will typically have very transactional needs that fit into one or a few narrow use cases (i.e., their activity and the corresponding records needed will be fairly predictable). Additionally, it assumes that the data the Customer Community license uses falls into one of the following buckets:

- It is shared directly with the user and no other external users (e.g., the user is the owner).

- It is shared with the user's organization (account).

- It is public read-only or read-write; all users can access it.

If a solution requires anything more complex for the group of users assigned to the Customer Community license, a reassessment of the chosen license types needs to be performed.

Sharing Sets

So, what exactly are sharing sets? I'll provide an overview and then dive into some examples.

Overview

To help explain sharing sets, let me first provide a hypothetical scenario for reference as I walk through the configuration options:

- License type of site users (Customer Community).

- The site includes the Case object.

- A customer-created case is always assigned to an internal user.

- The customer who created a case is set as the contact on the case.

- All contacts from the same account should be able to edit any case submitted by a colleague.

The first area to address here is organization-wide defaults. Organization-wide defaults do apply to customer site users. Whether an object's default is set to Private, Public Read Only, or Public Read/Write, that sharing model will extend to customers. Of course, some level of create/read/update/delete (CRUD) access to the object will need to be provided for it to be relevant; if a user cannot access an object, a sharing default of Private vs. Public Read/Write will have no bearing on that user.

In theory, Public access could be granted to everyone for Cases and Contacts. However, doing that would almost never make sense for an organization. Think about it—that would provide each customer with visibility into all contact and case records for all other customers. Assume the organization-wide default for both objects to be private. See Figure 8-11 for these settings.

Default Sharing Settings			
Organization-Wide Defaults	Edit		Organization-Wide Defaults Help ?
Object	**Default Internal Access**	**Default External Access**	**Grant Access Using Hierarchies**
Lead	Public Read/Write/Transfer	Private	✓
Account, Contract and Asset	Public Read/Write	Private	✓
Contact	Controlled by Parent	Controlled by Parent	✓
Order	Controlled by Parent	Controlled by Parent	✓
Opportunity	Public Read/Write	Private	✓
Case	Public Read/Write/Transfer	Private	✓

Figure 8-11. *Organization-wide settings*

In an internal org, an administrator can easily create a custom sharing rule based on ownership or defined criteria to extend the ability to view or edit records to additional users or groups of users (see Figure 8-12). This is available in sites with Customer Community Plus or Partner licenses.

Step 4: Select the users to share with	
Share with	✓ Public Groups
	Roles
	Roles and Internal Subordinates
Step 5: Select the level	Roles, Internal and Portal Subordinates

Figure 8-12. *Standard sharing (not available for Customer Community users)*

However, the administrator cannot create sharing rules in a Customer Community. Users with Customer Community licenses do not have roles and cannot be added to public groups. This results in an incompatibility between sharing rules and customer site users.

To mitigate the deliberate but potentially debilitating gap in the sharing functionality between customer and partner sites, admins can create one or more sharing sets. The first key piece to understand about how sharing sets work is that no more than one sharing set can be created for each available profile. An administrator cannot create multiple sharing sets that provide different access and apply both to the same profile.

Once admins set the label and description for a sharing set, they will select one or more applicable profiles for this sharing set. Navigate to Digital Experiences ➤ Settings ➤ Sharing Sets ➤ New to see the screen shown in Figure 8-13.

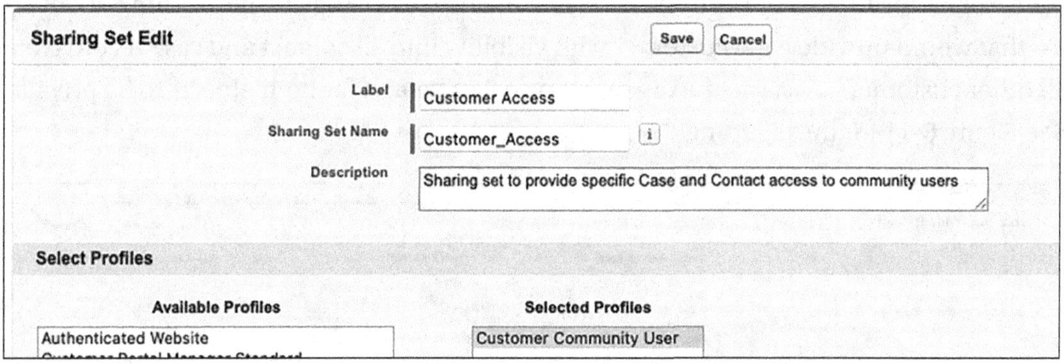

Figure 8-13. *Sharing sets can be created for Customer Community users*

On to the fun part. Here, the administrator will need to select the applicable object. In this case, the administrator will want to select Case and move it to Selected Objects. Once the admin has clicked Set Up next to Case, the access mapping for that object will appear. See Figure 8-14 for a look at Access Mapping for Case.

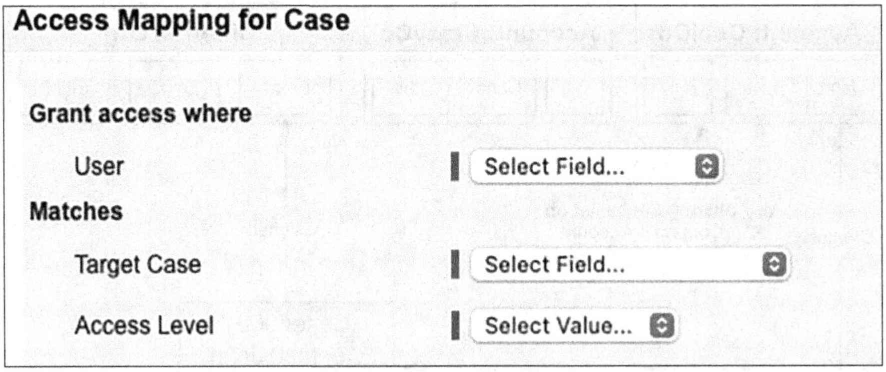

Access Mapping for Case

Grant access where

User	Select Field...
Matches	
Target Case	Select Field...
Access Level	Select Value...

Figure 8-14. *Access mapping (part of sharing sets)*

As I stated earlier, the assumption is that the admin wants to provide read-write access to all of the submitting contact's colleagues. To do this, the admin will want to share the cases to which all contacts on the submitting user's account have access. In other words, the administrator will provide access to all contacts where User.Contact. Account = Case.Account. See the configuration in Figure 8-15.

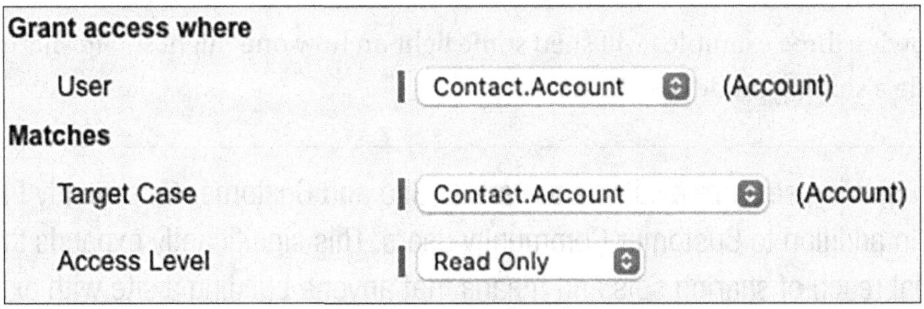

Grant access where

User	Contact.Account	(Account)
Matches		
Target Case	Contact.Account	(Account)
Access Level	Read Only	

Figure 8-15. *Sharing users from an account with all other users on that account*

Figure 8-16 provides a diagram of the finished product.

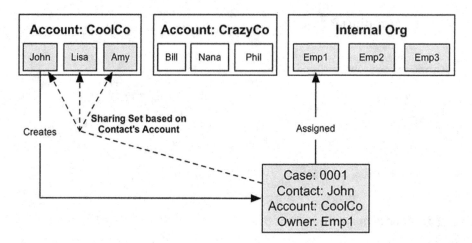

Figure 8-16. *This sharing set allows all external users associated with CoolCo to see the case created by John*

Success! We can see that this sharing set provides access to all of John's colleagues.

Examples

The following three examples will shed some light on how one might set up sharing sets to provide a sharing model for site users.

Note   Sharing sets are available to Partner Site and Customer Community Plus users, in addition to Customer Community users. This significantly expands the potential reach of sharing sets and means that anyone building a site with external users should be familiar with this tool/feature. The examples that follow will assume a Customer Community user.

Example 1: Sharing a Custom Object

Here are the scenario details:

- *Object*: Project (custom object)
- *Sharing settings*: Private
- *Owner*: Customer user associated with an account

- *Sharing requirement*: Share with all other users who are on the same account

See Figure 8-17.

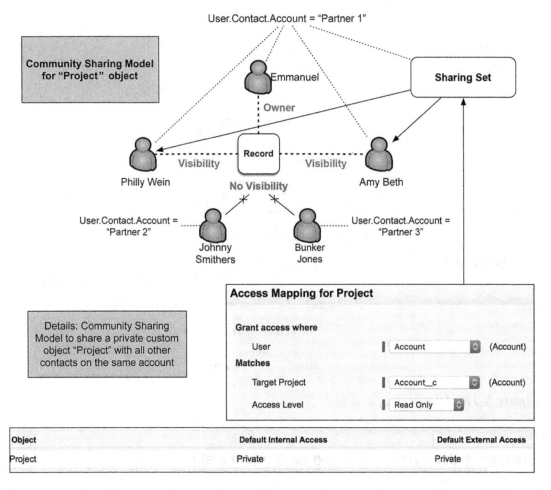

Figure 8-17. *Diagram of example 1*

Example 2: User Visibility Based on Account

Here are the scenario details:

- *Object*: User

- *Sharing settings*: Private

- *Sharing requirement*: Allow all users on the same account to see each other (i.e., have access to each other's user records)

See Figure 8-18.

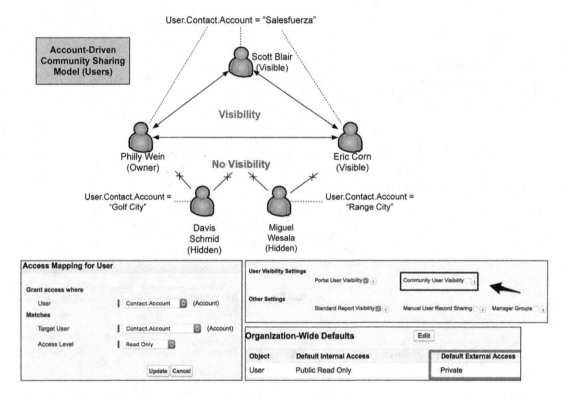

Figure 8-18.   *Diagram of example 2*

Example 3: User Visibility Based on Custom Field

Here are the scenario details:

- *Object*: User

- *Sharing settings*: Private

- *Sharing requirement*: Allow all designated/flagged users to see each other (i.e., have access to each other's user records); do not use the standard account field, as each user has a different account

See Figure 8-19.

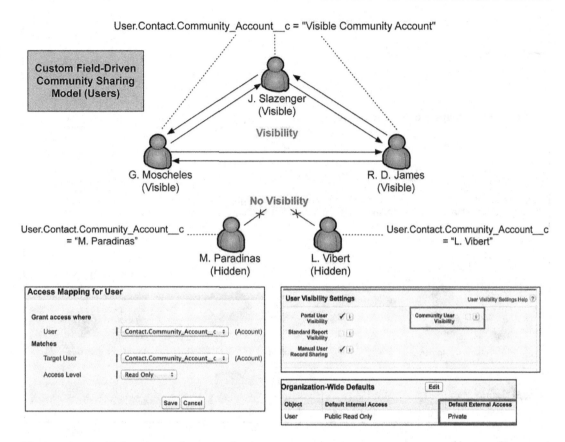

Figure 8-19. *Diagram of example 3*

Share Groups

Since Customer Community users do not use the standard Salesforce sharing model, they can't be accessed when building a sharing rule. For example, an administrator would not be able to create a rule to share a record owned by a customer site user with a role or group associated with users are assigned full licenses.

This scenario is why Salesforce created share groups, which automatically share all records owned by high-volume portal users (e.g., Customer Community users) with specified users who are not of the same (e.g., Partner users, full internal users, etc.). To set up a share group, one must first create a sharing set. Once that is complete, a Share Group Settings tab appears on the Sharing Set page (see Figure 8-20).

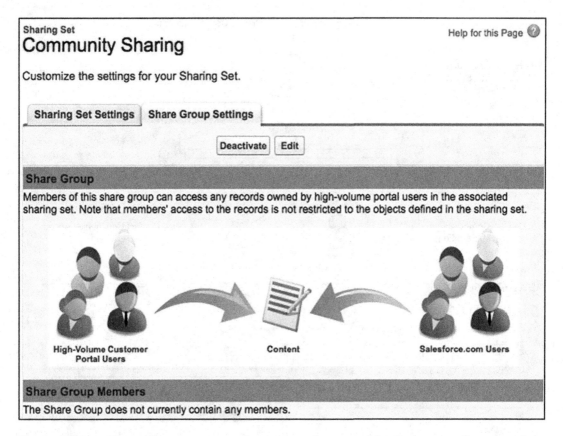

Figure 8-20. *Use a share group to share records owned by Customer Community users with internal users*

To add members, an administrator clicks the Edit button and moves the available members to Selected Members (use the Search drop-down to change the user type). See Figure 8-21.

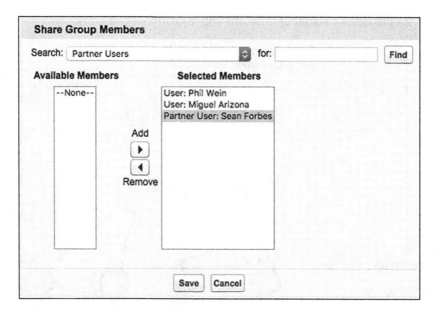

Figure 8-21. *Add users to a share group*

Upon adding the desired members, the users to whom records owned by the corresponding Customer Community users will be listed (see Figure 8-22).

Share Group Members	
Action	**Name**
Remove	User: Miguel Arizona
Remove	User: Phil Wein
Remove	Partner User: Edge Communications: Sean Forbes

Figure 8-22. *Share group members*

Let's wrap up the share group discussion by looking at an example. Here's the scenario:

- *Customer Community with two profiles*: WeinCo Customer and MeisterCo Customer

- *Requirement*: Share records owned by users with the WeinCo Customer profile with the following:

- *Partner user*: R. D. James

- *Public group*: Super Clique

Figure 8-23 provides a visual of how this share group would work.

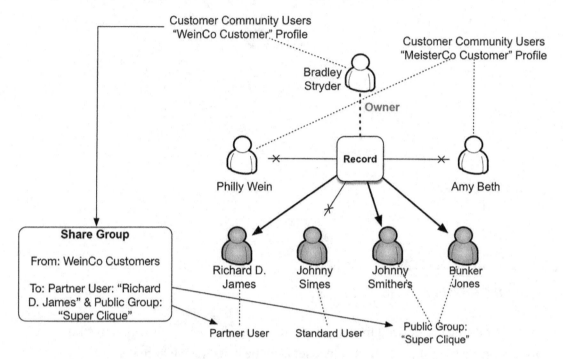

Figure 8-23. *A look at a share group*

Guest User Access

Salesforce previously had a fairly large issue on their hands that impacted a large number of sites worldwide: guest users often had more control than was desired or even necessary. Not only was the maximum access often in excess what was ever sensible, the default access levels gave too much control to this group of users. And, if it's not abundantly clear who "guest users" are, let me clarify: the world! Yes, guest users equate to the public, or, essentially, anyone with Internet access in the world. Hopefully, you can see why this is a critical area to cover.

In this section, I'll call out some of the critical guest user access policies that any site admin should be aware of:

- Org-wide defaults are always set to private for guest users. You can't automatically grant access to records via org-wide defaults.

- Guest users cannot edit records (they can't have more than read access to data). Note that "system mode" can be used to edit or delete data as a result of a guest user activity; this requires customization.

- Guest users can't be members of public groups or queues.

- Manual sharing no longer exists for guest users (you can't share a one-off record with the public).

- View All and Modify All are not available for guest users.

- Guest users cannot be owners of newly created records; ownership will transfer to a default, configured owner.

- Records *can* be shared with guest users via sharing rules. Make sure to think about which objects your guest users need access to and set up sharing rules, accordingly.

The bottom line here is that you'll need to be a lot more thoughtful about what access the public should have to data in your site. Fortunately, Salesforce has plugged some potentially dangerous holes to ensure that you don't inadvertently share your data with the world. Now, the burden to establish correct sharing with the public is yours.

Recap

In this chapter, I examined some key considerations for sites that impact security, access, and visibility. While a significant portion of the security model for sites leverages standard Salesforce platform mechanisms (e.g., object/field access), some aspects are specific to sites themselves (e.g., authentication, site membership, sharing sets, share groups, etc.). Make sure to thoroughly review and test your site for security requirements before launching to make sure that all users who need access have appropriate access and any users who should not have access are correspondingly restricted.

CHAPTER 9

Topics in Experience Cloud

Topics are quite interesting entities in Salesforce. While they have been around for years, they aren't extensively used in "internal" Salesforce (e.g., classic or Lightning Experience) outside of Chatter. In Chatter, users can associate topics with feed items to tag posts, polls, questions, and more; this helps users to quickly find related discussions. Figure 9-1 shows a view of a Chatter post with topics in Lightning Experience.

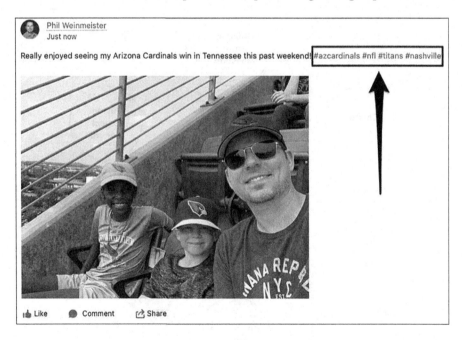

Figure 9-1. *Topics in Lightning Experience*

In Experience Cloud sites, however, topics take on a much more central role in the lives of administrators, site members, and internal users. While not every site leverages discussion-style chatting, topics apply to a number of other areas, including questions,

© Philip Weinmeister 2022
P. Weinmeister, *Practical Guide to Salesforce Experience Cloud*, https://doi.org/10.1007/978-1-4842-8132-1_9

articles, and contextually driven experiences. In this chapter, I will cover the following as related to topics within sites:

- Overview/purpose

- Topic types (standard, navigational, featured)

- Internal vs. site topics

- Other considerations for topics within sites

Overview/Purpose of Topics in Sites

As I said in the introduction, topics apply broadly to sites and can serve as a central element in overall site interactions. I like to describe topics as the "glue" in sites because they introduce cohesion between different entities that would otherwise be disparate, disconnected items. Figure 9-2 shows how this happens, conceptually.

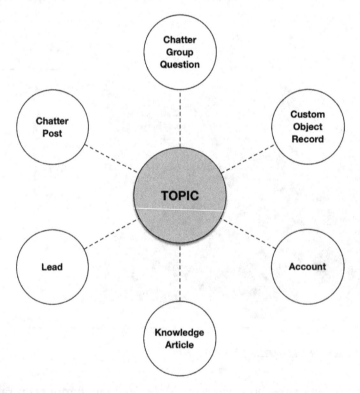

Figure 9-2. Topics are the "hub" to join unrelated items (the "spokes")

At their core, topics are all about context. As shown in Figure 9-2, it is a topic that allows for a connection between an account and an article, a Chatter group question and a link posted to a lead record, a custom object record and a Chatter post, and so on. For a closer look at how this works, I will need to dive into the data model.

Topic Data Model

At the center of a fairly simple data model that drives topics sits the Topic Assignment object. The Topic Assignment object is a junction object between the Topic and Target objects (see Figure 9-3).

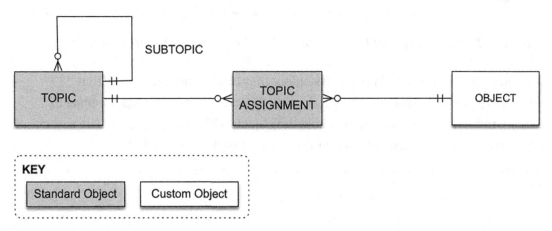

Figure 9-3. *Topic data model*

Let's take this a step further and make it specific with a real-life scenario. A few years ago, I helped to design a Salesforce site for a church. Custom objects were used to capture data such as sermons and church events. In this example, I'll show how topics can be intertwined with that data to create context and useful associations within the site. See Figure 9-4 for a visual representation of the following bullet points:

- Site (online church site/website)

- Topic (grace)

- Objects for which grace-related records exist: Sermon (custom), Event (standard), News (custom)

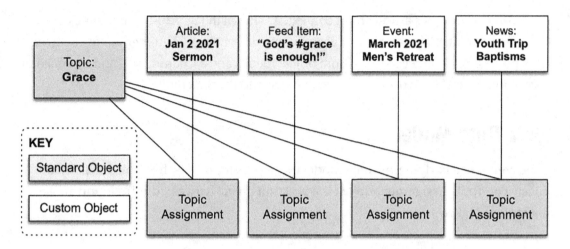

Figure 9-4. An example of how a topic might be used in an online church site

Topics must be enabled for objects before they can be associated with that object (whether standard or custom). In the Setup menu, under Topics for Objects, administrators must make sure to enable the objects with which topics will be associated within their sites. See Figure 9-5 for a look at where topics are enabled.

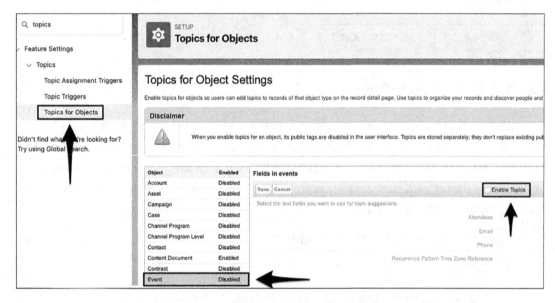

Figure 9-5. Enabling topics is handled via the "Topics for Objects" menu

Topic Presentation/UI

Within sites, a dynamic topic page exists that allows for related records (via topic assignments) to be displayed. On this page, two object types are displayed out of the box: discussions (feed items) and knowledge articles. Other object types can be displayed, but custom components are required. Figure 9-6 shows a topic detail page with related records from custom objects (via custom Lightning components), along with a feed item that shares the topic.

Figure 9-6. *Custom components on a topic page showing related content*

Figure 9-7 shows another example of how topics can be applied. In this instance, topics are used for filtering and categorizing custom records.

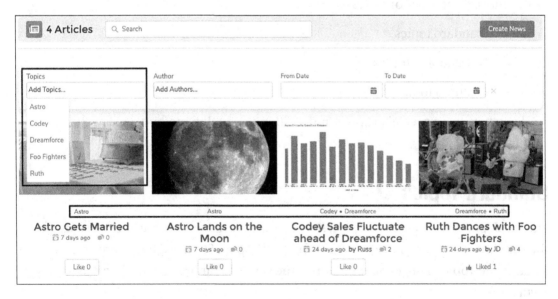

Figure 9-7. *Topics, as featured within custom components*

Figure 9-8 shows a record detail page with a custom component that references a topic.

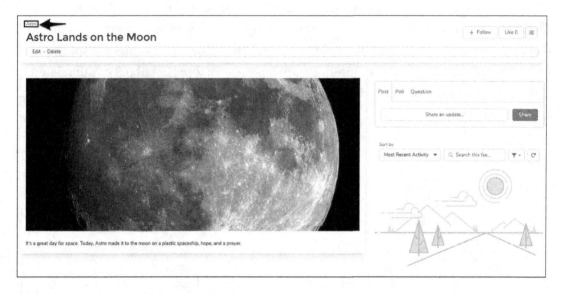

Figure 9-8. *Topics, as featured within custom components on the detail page*

Topic Types

Within sites, three types of topics exist:

- Standard topics

- Navigational topics

- Featured topics

Each type has a special purpose and a different creation method. I will walk through each.

Standard Topics

Standard topics are really just topics; *standard* is a word I am adding to emphasize that they are not referencing navigational or featured topics. Standard topics are created through the Topic Management section of the Content Targeting workspace, as shown in Figure 9-9.

Figure 9-9. *Topic Management menu within Content Targeting*

Here, administrators can create a new topic or merge topics. To allow the topic to be used with content, "Enable for Content" needs to be selected. For this example, I will create a new topic, as shown in Figure 9-10.

Figure 9-10. *New topic creation*

Creation is fairly straightforward. If an existing topic is too close to the new topic to warrant distinction, the two topics can be merged. In this case, I am going to merge the topic Cody with my existing topic, Codey. Any feed item or record with the topic Cody will now show Codey. See Figure 9-11.

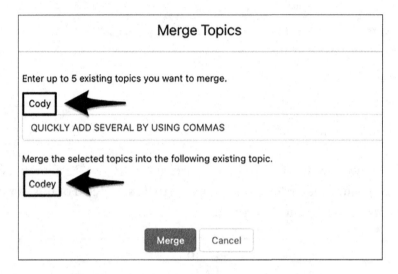

Figure 9-11. *Merge Topics page*

Once the new topic is created, I will see it as an option (depending on my permissions) when creating a new feed item. See Figure 9-12.

Figure 9-12. *Adding an existing topic to a feed item*

Navigational Topics

Navigational topics have additional, separate purposes on top of what standard topics bring to the table. First, navigational topics are, as one might expect, a part of the navigation menu. The Topics tab is, by default, included in the navigation menu and displays all navigational topics. See Figure 9-13 for an example of a site that has Products and Services as navigational topics.

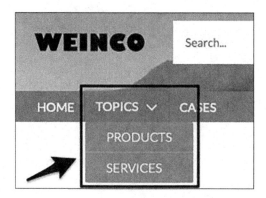

Figure 9-13. *Navigational topics in the navigation menu*

Additionally, when a user is leveraging topics and does not find the desired or expected content, Salesforce provides a standard component through which the user can ask a question using navigational topics. See Figure 9-14.

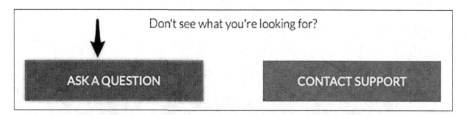

Figure 9-14. *Asking the site will leverage navigational topics*

Upon clicking "ASK A QUESTION," the site member will have to select one of the available navigational topics when the question is submitted. See Figure 9-15.

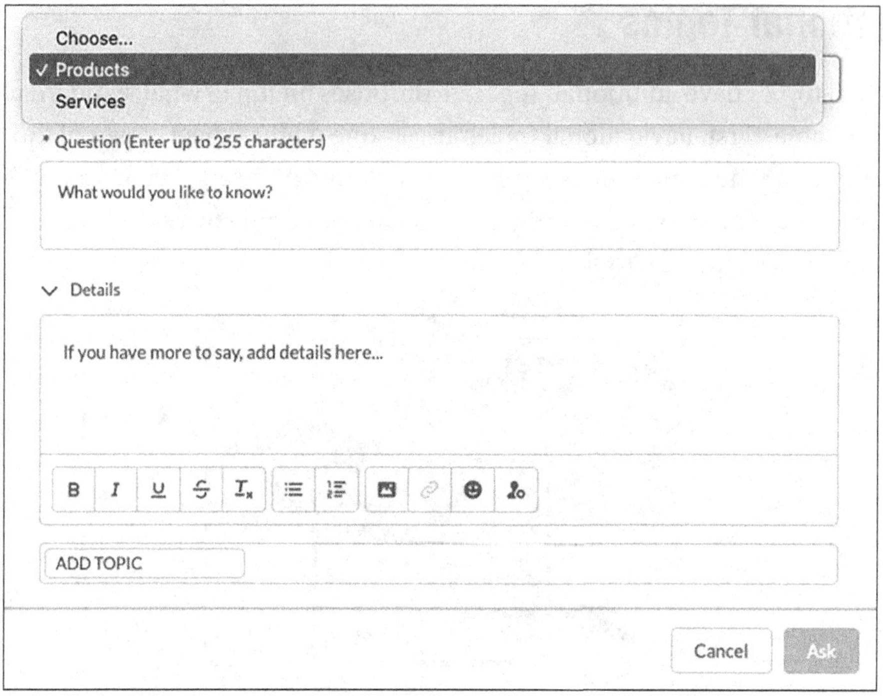
Choose...
✓ Products
Services
* Question (Enter up to 255 characters)
What would you like to know?
Details
If you have more to say, add details here...
ADD TOPIC
Cancel
Ask

***Figure 9-15.** Navigational topics within the "Ask a Question" modal*

With navigational topics, site administrators can configure a different header image to be displayed. Administrators can click to upload an image, as shown in Figure 9-16.

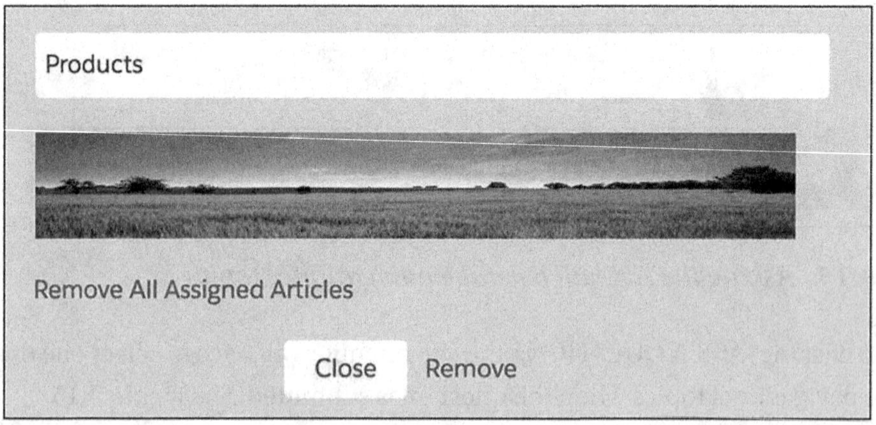
Products
Remove All Assigned Articles
Close
Remove

***Figure 9-16.** Adding an image to a navigational topic*

Figure 9-17 shows what the updated topic page looks like.

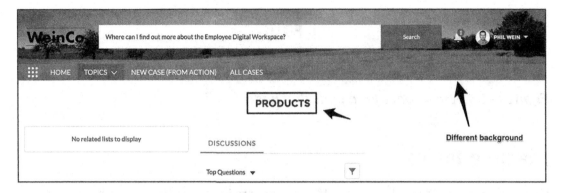

Figure 9-17. *Navigational topic page with a background image*

Navigational topics can go to an even deeper level with subtopics. This allows for a robust navigation experience based on areas of interest or relevance. I've put together an example of what a topic catalog might look like for a company that is building online sites products in Figure 9-18.

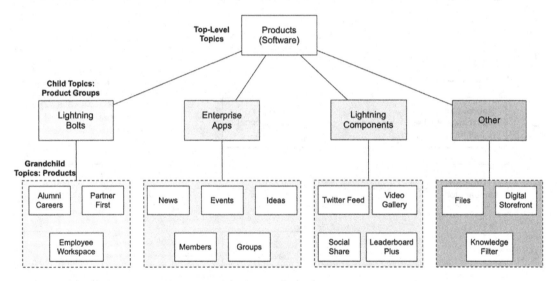

Figure 9-18. *A potential topic catalog design, with subtopics*

By creating subtopics, the overall site experience can be enhanced by guiding site users intuitively. See Figure 9-19 for an example of a topic that has subtopics associated with it.

FRUIT

ORANGE | BANANA | GRAPE | APPLE | PINEAPPLE

Figure 9-19. *A topic page for a topic that has subtopics*

Featured Topics

Featured topics are basically standard topics that are identified/flagged as highlighted. Once identified as featured, they can be dynamically showcased to site members to promote collaboration or interaction around those particular topics. To create a featured topic, an admin must first create a standard or navigational topic. See Figure 9-20 for an overview of topic creation prerequisites and dependencies.

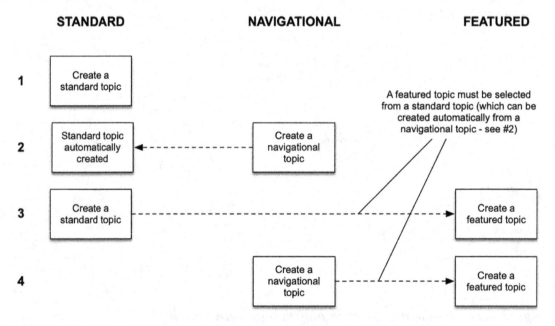

Figure 9-20. *An overview of topic creation dependencies and prerequisites*

Once a topic exists, it can be selected on the Featured Topics menu page during the creation process. In Figure 9-21, examples of existing topics are shown when a new featured topic is being configured.

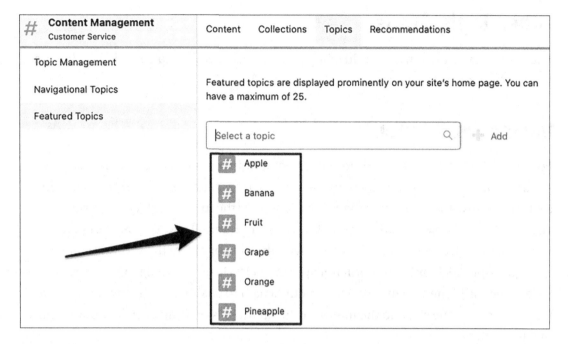

Figure 9-21. *Examples of existing topics when a new featured topic is being configured*

Similar to navigational topics, images can be associated with featured topics. However, instead of an image showing up in a header, it appears in the Featured Topics component that is available within Site Builder. Figure 9-22 shows the "Featured Topics & Feeds" component with all three featured topics having an associated image.

Figure 9-22. *"Featured Topics & Feeds" component*

Other Topic Areas

A few other areas exist in the world of topics that site administrators need to understand. I will walk through each at a high level.

Internal vs. Site Topics

For sites that expose records, it is important for administrators to understand that a topic applied to a record in classic or Lightning Experience is automatically exposed within a site that shows that record. Each topic assignment (the junction object between the Topic and Target objects) has a NetworkID field. For internal use, this field is blank. However, for a site, this field is populated with the network ID of the site; this creates a unique topic assignment that will not appear in classic or Lightning Experience. Sure, topic assignments can be cloned or duplicated to ensure that the same topics are leveraged across the site and the internal org, but there is nothing out of the box to make that happen.

In Figure 9-23, I provide an example where the same topic of Products is applied to an Account record in both a site and the internal org.

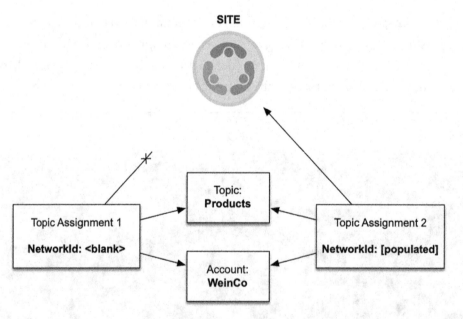

Figure 9-23. *Two topic assignments for the same topic; only one is associated with a site*

Unlisted Chatter Groups

Currently, topics are not supported within unlisted Chatter groups. The Salesforce platform does not currently have a way to handle topics for these ultra-secure collaboration groups that would not potentially expose some data to unauthorized users.

Topics and Articles

Articles and topics overlap within sites quite a bit. I will go into more detail on how topics work with articles in the next chapter.

Management Within Site Builder

There is an option to directly access Site Builder. Navigate to Settings (via the tabs on the left), click General, and scroll down. See Figure 9-24.

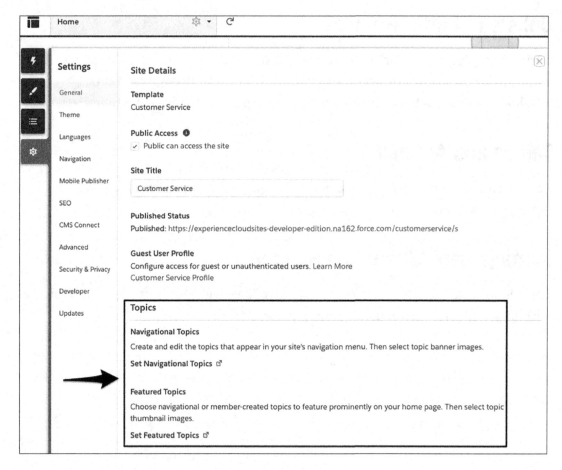

Figure 9-24. *Managing topics from Site Builder*

Recap

In this chapter, I focused on topics within sites and how they can be leveraged to enhance the site user experience. I dove into some of the nuances around topics that are critical for administrators to understand when managing a Salesforce site and explained the different types of topics—standard, navigational, and featured—and their purposes.

CHAPTER 10

Knowledge Articles in Experiences

Since the inception of Experience Cloud, Salesforce Knowledge has been a cornerstone in many of the sites that have been built on the Salesforce platform. Whether for customers looking for self-service troubleshooting help, partners needing documentation on a process, or employees seeking information on release notes for their own product, knowledge articles have often been the means to provide relevant information to site members.

For those who have managed an internal knowledge base in classic or Lightning Experience, much can be reapplied to sites. However, it is important to understand that articles do boast some site-specific functionality and capabilities (mostly around topics). In addition to covering those items, I will walk through the Salesforce Knowledge prerequisites and basic setup/administration to help developers, administrators, and managers get up and running with Salesforce Knowledge in their sites.

Prerequisites and General Setup

Before a site manager can work with Knowledge in a site, certain prerequisites must be satisfied, and Knowledge must be properly configured.

Licensing/Permissions

The first step in setting up Knowledge for sites is obtaining one or more Knowledge licenses for the org that houses the corresponding site. The Company Information section (in the Setup menu) shows the number of licenses for the org under Feature Licenses. See Figure 10-1.

© Philip Weinmeister 2022
P. Weinmeister, *Practical Guide to Salesforce Experience Cloud*, https://doi.org/10.1007/978-1-4842-8132-1_10

Feature Licenses				Feature Licenses Help ⓘ
Feature Type	Status	Total Licenses	Used Licenses	Remaining Licenses
Marketing User	Active	2	1	1
Apex Mobile User	Active	2	1	1
Offline User	Active	2	1	1
Knowledge User	Active	2	1	1
Service Cloud User	Active	2	1	1

Figure 10-1. *A Knowledge User license must be available for Knowledge to be enabled*

Once a Knowledge User license is provisioned, it must be applied to a specific user. Navigate to a user record and select the Knowledge User checkbox to allow a user to manage Knowledge. See Figure 10-2.

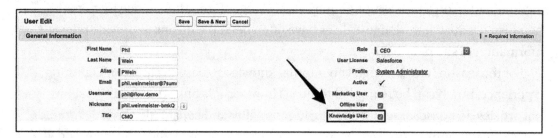

Figure 10-2. *A user who will manage Knowledge articles in any way (i.e., not simply viewing the articles) will require a Knowledge User license*

Once a user has been granted the Knowledge User license, the user can access the Knowledge-related settings within the Setup menu. The first step is enabling Knowledge, as shown in Figure 10-3.

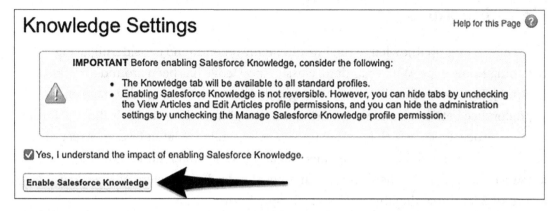

Figure 10-3. *Knowledge must be enabled before first use*

After enabling Knowledge, an administrator will see various settings that can be configured. Those are not specific to sites and should be examined as an organization rolls out Salesforce Knowledge. Figure 10-4 shows a sample of Knowledge settings that are available.

General Settings

☐ Allow users to create and edit articles from the Articles tab (Classic Only)
☐ Activate Validation Status field ⓘ
☐ Allow users to add external multimedia content to HTML in the standard editor (Classic Only) ⓘ

Lightning Knowledge Settings

☐ Enable Lightning Knowledge ⓘ
☐ Enable automatic loading of rich-text editor when editing an article ⓘ

Article Summaries

Show article summaries in article list views (Classic Only)

☐ Internal App
☐ Customer
☐ Partner

Figure 10-4. *Knowledge settings*

Lightning Knowledge

If you haven't set up Knowledge yet, I would highly recommend considering using Lightning Knowledge. While standard/classic Knowledge has been around for years, Lightning Knowledge has distinct advantages that are worth taking advantage of. The key difference between standard Knowledge and Lightning Knowledge is that the former employs article types (which are similar to objects), while the latter leverages record types (based on one object). This means that articles used in Lightning Knowledge follow a data model that aligns more with other standard and custom objects. See Figure 10-5 for the setting that enables Lightning Knowledge.

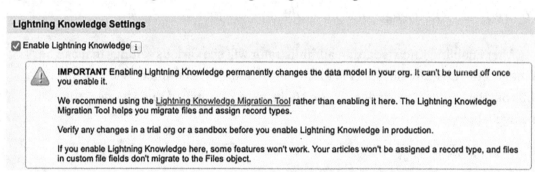

Figure 10-5. *Lightning Knowledge can be enabled from the standard Knowledge Settings screen*

Knowledge Administration

While not specific to sites, article types and data categories are critical to proper Knowledge administration. I will cover each at a high level to help site managers get the ball rolling.

Article and Record Types

Article types (classic Knowledge) and record types (Lightning Knowledge) help to distinguish knowledge that is fundamentally different in content and desired presentation. These are some examples of types:

- FAQ

- Troubleshooting Guide

- Tutorial

- Release Notes

- Product Manual

Each of these could have completely different fields and page layouts; as a result, they are solid candidates for article or record types. Note that, for classic, each org has an article type called Knowledge by default, which will suffice if only one article type is needed. See Figure 10-6.

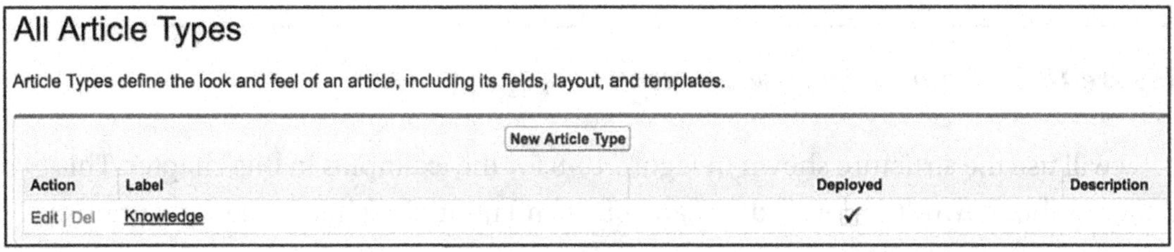

All Article Types

Article Types define the look and feel of an article, including its fields, layout, and templates.

New Article Type

Action	Label		Deployed	Description
Edit | Del	Knowledge		✓	

Figure 10-6. *The default Knowledge article type that exists upon enabling Knowledge*

Data Categories

Data categories are also critical within the world of Salesforce Knowledge. To best understand their purpose, it's probably easiest to think of data categories in the context of searching. When users want to find one or more articles, data categories will help users to categorize, group, or filter article search results. Data categories can be set up hierarchically, with child data categories; Figure 10-7 shows a data category called Location with two subcategories.

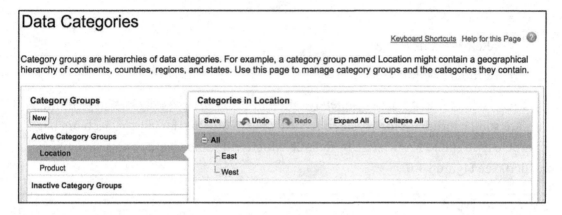

Figure 10-7. *Data category setup menu*

I will use the structure shown in Figure 10-8 for the examples in this chapter. This diagram shows two "top-level" data categories and multiple "child" data categories that roll up to the top-level categories.

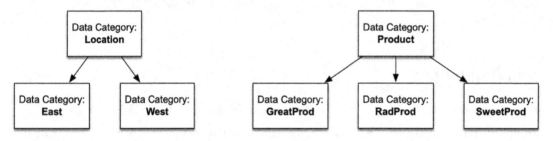

Figure 10-8. *An example of a data category setup*

Note   Profiles and permission sets can be used to control the visibility of articles based on data categories.

Articles in Sites

A few items must be considered within the context of sites regarding articles:

- Article visibility

- Articles and topics

- Articles in global search (for sites)

Article Visibility

When creating articles, a Knowledge manager or author can associate an article with zero to many channels. A channel determines whether the article is potentially visible at all for a particular group of users. The following are the available channels:

- Internal App

- Public Knowledge Base

- Customers

- Partners

Regardless of the permissions of users in these channels, they will not be able to see articles if the corresponding channel is not enabled. In Figure 10-9, an article is set to be visible to customers and partners.

Figure 10-9. *Channels are used to control the visibility of articles in sites*

While it may be fairly intuitive, it is critical to note which license types map to the applicable channels. Figure 10-10 shows the association between the two entities.

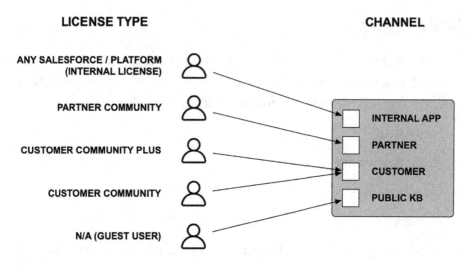

Figure 10-10. *Mapping of license type to Knowledge channel*

Articles and Topics

A key area for Knowledge managers to be aware of is the interplay between articles and topics. This overlap comes into play in a few ways, through standard components and relationships between articles and topics and between data categories and topics.

Topics for Articles

Before topics in sites can be used with articles, topics must be enabled for the applicable article types from the Topics for Objects settings within the Setup menu. Figure 10-11 shows the page from which topics are enabled for articles.

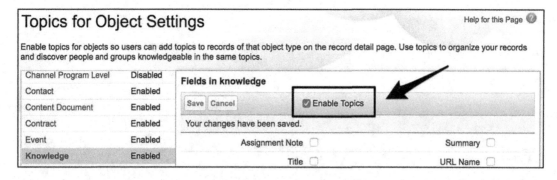

Figure 10-11. *Topics must be enabled on all applicable article types to allow for full usage of articles in a site*

Article Management in Sites

The first method to associate Knowledge articles with site topics is a direct association of an existing article with an existing topic. Figure 10-12 provides a view of what happens from a data model/schema perspective.

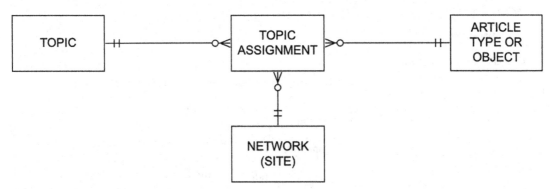

Figure 10-12. *Data model of articles and topics within sites*

Within the Content Targeting workspace, the Article Management menu allows articles to be selected for topic assignment. See Figure 10-13. In this example, an article is associated with three related topics.

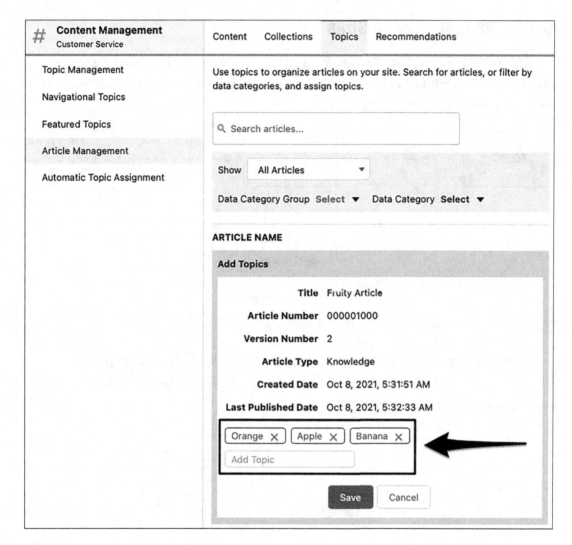

Figure 10-13. *Here, an article named "Fruity Article" is associated with fruit-related topics*

Note   While this feature absolutely has value in some scenarios, direct association of topics with articles is not dynamic and will require manual administration for any changes to corresponding topics.

Automatic Topic Assignment

Salesforce did us all a huge favor a few years ago when they introduced the ability to automatically associate topics with articles. This is done by identifying one or more topics that should be assigned to topics based on a data category. The function can apply to existing articles and will automatically associate any newly created article that has the applicable data category with the selected topics.

Figure 10-14 provides an example. Here, all articles with a parent data category group of Fruit and a data category of Orange are associated with the topic "Orange." Additionally, the "Add above topic(s) to all existing articles in the data category" setting means that any existing articles will be updated.

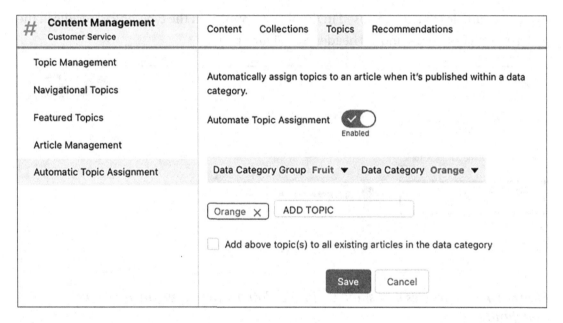

Figure 10-14. *Articles in sites can automatically be associated with topics, based on article data categories*

Article Display

Once everything is set up, a site manager can enjoy the display of articles related to a topic from a topic detail page. In Figure 10-15, one article is dynamically listed on the topic detail page for the topic "Orange."

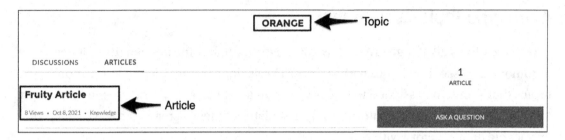

Figure 10-15. *A topic page showing a related article, based on an associated topic*

Articles in Global Search

By default, articles that are exposed in the site will appear in the type-ahead results in the global search from the standard header. See Figure 10-16.

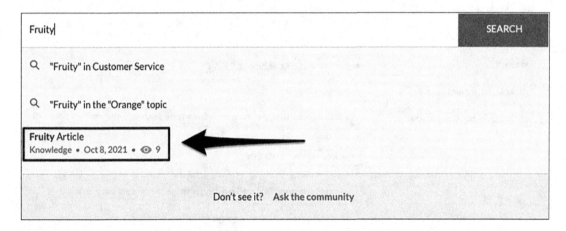

Figure 10-16. *Articles will show up in the global search type-ahead results by default*

The default setting is typically recommended, but there may be scenarios where an administrator wants to hide those results. To do so, access the property editor settings for the component and click the X next to Knowledge (or Articles, depending on your setup) in the "Objects in Autocomplete Results" section. See Figure 10-17.

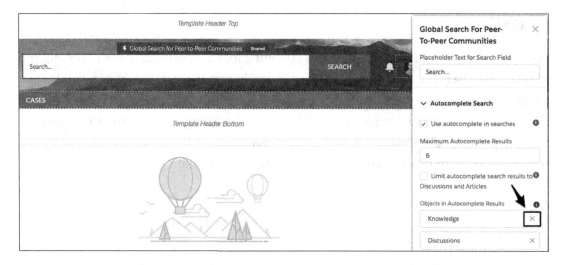

Figure 10-17. *Articles can be removed from autocomplete results*

Similarly, articles can be repositioned on the full search results page. However, this is a different setting. This can be accessed on the search page in Site Builder by clicking the Global Search Result component and modifying the appropriate settings in the property editor. See Figure 10-18.

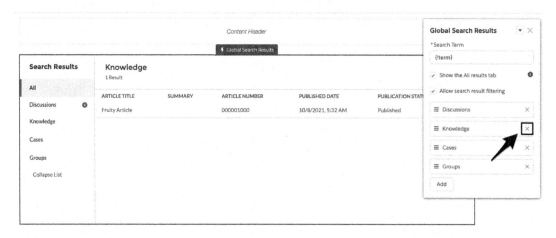

Figure 10-18. *Removing articles from the search results page*

Recap

Salesforce Knowledge is a large, platform-spanning topic. A plethora of documentation exists to help users become experts in Knowledge. In this chapter, I strictly focused on the intersection of articles and sites. I covered the basics of Knowledge setup, walking through prerequisites and "core" Knowledge administration (article types and data categories). Additionally, I dove into site-specific areas of Knowledge, including channels, topics for objects, article management, and automatic topic assignment.

CHAPTER 11

Audience Targeting and Personalization

Regardless of whether a site's audience is primarily made up of customers, partners, or employees, its members want to feel like they are known. Often, they desire a personalized experience that is tailored to them, cringing at the idea of a one-size-fits-all site (or even page) that fails to take their purpose and needs into consideration. Enter audience targeting functionality for sites from Salesforce.

In the past, any notion of a personalized experience in a Salesforce site had to be custom; there was just no way around that. Sure, some of the data would be dynamic, but the actual look and feel itself could not vary unless it was buried within Visualforce and Apex, far from the reach of nontechnical resources.

However, all that changed when audience targeting was first introduced to Lightning sites. Now, an array of weapons is available to declaratively manage unique experiences for specific site users, empowering administrators, business analysts, and site managers to get more involved and help drive this personalization. In this chapter, I'll cover the following audience targeting topics:

- Audience definition, management, and application

- Audience targeting types

  - Branding sets

  - Page variations

  - Component audiences

  - Navigation menus

  - Tile menus

  - CMS collections

263

© Philip Weinmeister 2022

P. Weinmeister, *Practical Guide to Salesforce Experience Cloud*, https://doi.org/10.1007/978-1-4842-8132-1_11

- Personalized components

- Targeting with record-based criteria

Overview

Before I dive into specific elements of audience targeting, I think it's important to ensure that the concept of personalization is clear. The premise for this chapter lies in the notion that users want to have unique, personalized experiences and the organization that owns the site wants to manage it without enduring an extreme burden in doing so (i.e., they want to avoid a time-consuming change that requires extremely technical resources). At the end of the day, it's as simple as what is shown in Figure 11-1; what one user sees may differ from what another sees.

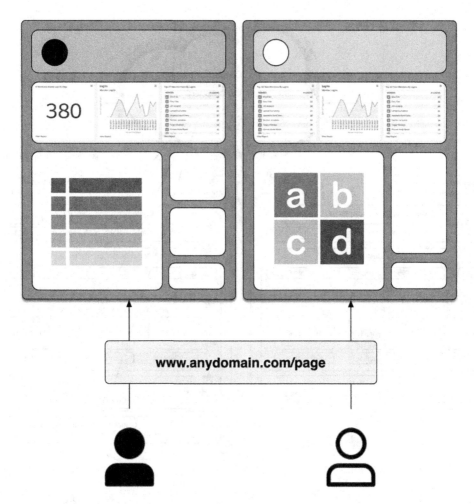

Figure 11-1. *One web page, two users, and two different experiences*

Everyone understands the basic concept of unique experiences; one can simply navigate to two different websites. However, there is much more to consider. First, the multiple Experience Cloud experiences I am talking about occur within the same site and sometimes even the page or same component. Additionally, the maintenance/management piece makes this scenario typically very tricky. With Salesforce sites, administrators can set up a site to provide personalization without using code or making frequent changes to keep everything functioning properly.

Figure 11-2 goes a bit deeper. In this example, I show an example of how a site page is represented to two unique audiences (differentiated by authentication) differently. The page contains additional content and is branded for the customer, while the guest version has a subset of the page content and is shown generically.

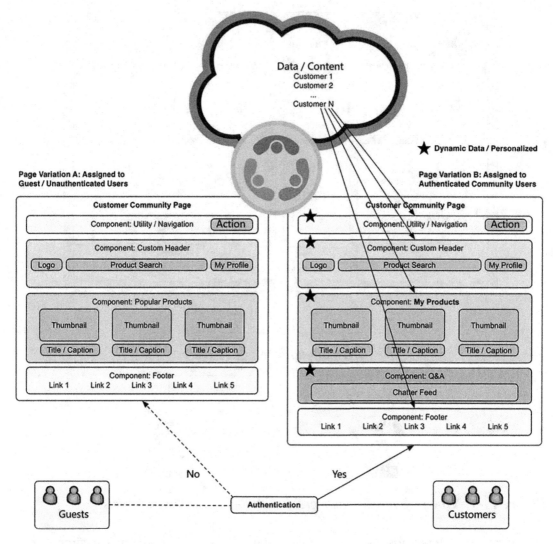

Figure 11-2. *Different audience-based experiences of the same page*

Audiences

Audience targeting within online sites is essentially a definition of *who* and *what*, as applied to a visual and functional experience. The first area to examine when one is looking at audience targeting is the *who*, or the audiences themselves. Fortunately for site administrators, Salesforce has created a logical system that allows for central management of audiences and application of experiences to those audiences.

Note   Audiences for audience targeting within Salesforce sites are completely separate from and not related to site "recommendation audiences" in any way.

The first priority when tackling audiences is to clearly understand the concept. At its most basic level, a site audience is simply the identification of a group of individuals that may be accessing the site. Figure 11-3 shows a simple example of two different audiences.

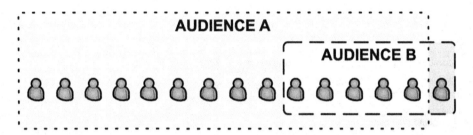

Figure 11-3. *Individuals can be a part of multiple audiences and those audiences can overlap*

After seeing Figure 11-3, the critical question must be asked: How is each audience constructed/defined? Within Salesforce sites, audiences can be defined by using one or more of the following as criteria:

- Profile

- Permission

- Location

- Domain

- User (fields; includes related objects)

- Record-based criteria

- Audience

Profile

One or more profiles can be assigned to an audience. See Figure 11-4 for a view of an audience with two selected profiles; note the drop-down list from which additional profiles can be selected.

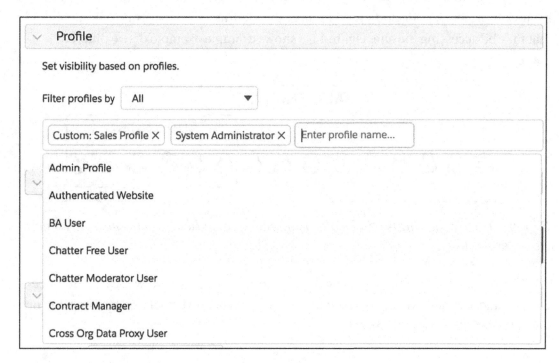

Figure 11-4. *Profiles can be added to an audience*

To expedite the profile search, profiles can be filtered; see Figure 11-5.

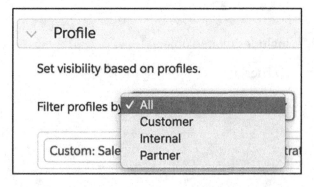

Figure 11-5. *Filter profiles by type to find the desired profile faster*

Permission

Similar to the idea of leveraging a profile for audience targeting, permissions can be used to determine who sees what within a site. Figure 11-6 shows what the selection of a permission looks like when configuring an audience.

Figure 11-6.   *Permissions can be used as part of audience criteria*

It's critical to understand the difference between associating an audience with a profile and doing so with a permission. A profile allows for quick audience targeting at scale. Profiles, of course, already exist, so an administrator can simply point a page or component at one or more profiles. It's simple and it's fast. However, do you *really* want every single user with a particular profile to see the same thing? If not, permissions allow for extreme granularity. Instead of grouping at the profile level, permissions allow you to bring the targeting down to the user level. You may need to create a (custom) permission, and you will need to assign that permission to relevant users, which may be a manual process for additional users over time. Weigh the costs and benefits carefully, and you should be able to make a wise decision between profiles and permissions as audience criteria.

Location

Locations can be added to an audience as well. A location is a user's physical location, determined by their IP address. An administrator can start to type in a city, state/subdivision, or country and select from a displayed list of results. See Figure 11-7 for an example of the search.

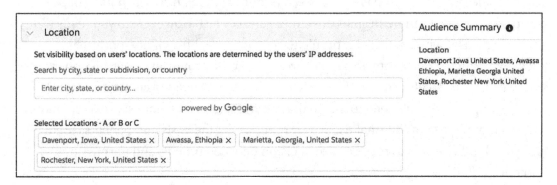

Figure 11-7. *Type-ahead feature to find city, state/subdivision, or country as a location within an audience*

Once all locations are selected, the list will be displayed below the search (and to the right, as well, as part of the overall summary). See Figure 11-8.

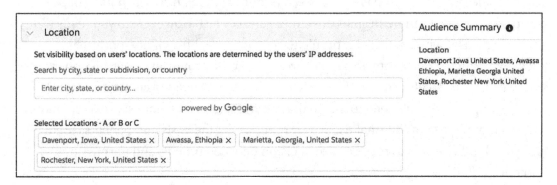

Figure 11-8. *Selected audience locations*

Domain

While not the most commonly applied criteria type, a domain can be valuable as a means to define an audience. Through the standard Salesforce setup, organizations can establish custom domains. Let's say an organization (WeinCo Industries) sets up the following domains for its partners:

- partner1.weinco-industries.com

- partner2.weinco-industries.com

- partner3.weinco-industries.com

These domains can then be used as part of the overall audience criteria definition to target users based on the domain they are accessing.

User Object

Permission, profile, and location have clear applications when it comes to audience targeting. However, the power and flexibility of the User object as audience criteria must not be ignored. While the scope of some other audience criteria is extremely straightforward (albeit limited), the User object opens up essentially limitless options for audience definition. Site administrators can leverage any text or picklist field of the following as part of the User object:

- User object

- Contact

- Account

- Profile

- Manager

- Role

- Many more standard lookups through the previous objects

- Other custom lookups

Note   The Contact and Account objects are identified via a lookup on a site member's user record (User.Contact.Account).

One subtle detail that requires the attention of every site builder is that custom fields can be used. That means an administrator can create a custom picklist and use that to define an audience. The administrator could even allow an end user to update the field themselves (e.g., via Flow)! Translation: With this functionality, a site could be configured to allow a user to change their own experience by giving a user access to a custom field that impacts the experience.

Figure 11-9 shows the view when creating User object criteria for an audience.

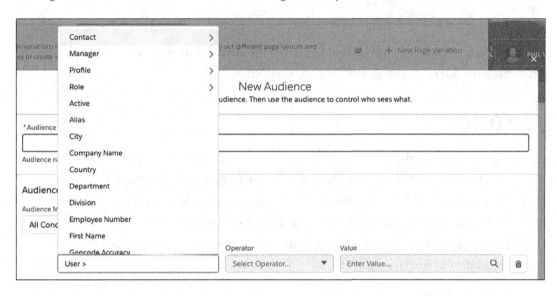

Figure 11-9. *User fields (including fields on lookup objects) can be added to an audience*

See Figure 11-10 for an audience with multiple criteria related to the User object, two based on object lookups.

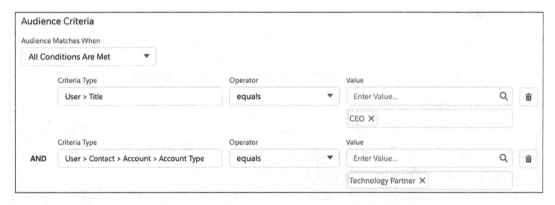

Figure 11-10. *This audience includes multiple fields from different objects related to (and including) the User object*

Record

Record-based criteria can also serve as a criteria type that can be used to determine an audience. An administrator can define record-based criteria to drive visibility for the audience. See Figure 11-11 for an audience that looks at the annual revenue for an Account record.

Figure 11-11. *Adding record-based criteria to an audience*

Why is record-based criteria considered advanced? They are inherently different from other audience criteria. Other audience criteria simply define the *who*; the record type inclusion also contributes to the *what*. In the example in Figure 11-12, two different audiences are each associated with a unique set of record-based criteria. This audience may impact the look, feel, and content of the page, just like all other audiences. However, because of the record criteria, the content layout is impacted as well.

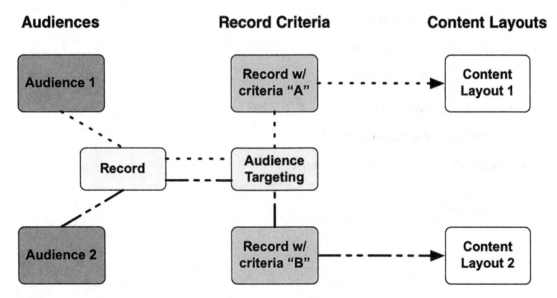

Figure 11-12. *Record-based criteria can impact the experience beyond what is possible with other criteria types*

The end result is that an admin can control which fields display for particular users by leveraging audiences with record criteria (of course, assuming that unique content layouts are properly configured).

Audience

Most recently, Salesforce added an additional criteria type that doesn't necessarily change overall audience creation capabilities, but significantly improves the administration experience. This new type is that of an audience itself. Now, an admin can use an audience *as criteria* within another audience. Brilliant! To bring the value of this one to life, an example is critical.

Let's say that an admin at Little Shop of Workflows (LSoW), a small consultancy, would like to create an audience for all Salesforce certified employees, as well as individual audiences for each relevant certification. This data is being tracked through checkbox fields on the User object, with a unique checkbox field mapped to each Salesforce certification. LSoW has only 20 employees total. Of those, the following employees are certified:

- *Cindita*: Administrator, Experience Cloud, Service Cloud

- *Kraggem*: Administrator, Service Cloud

- *Deverest*: Administrator, Experience Cloud

- *Yinzyall*: Administrator

- *Rickelle*: Administrator

- *Janny*: Service Cloud

- *Prunston*: Experience Cloud

Figure 11-13 shows these buckets of users.

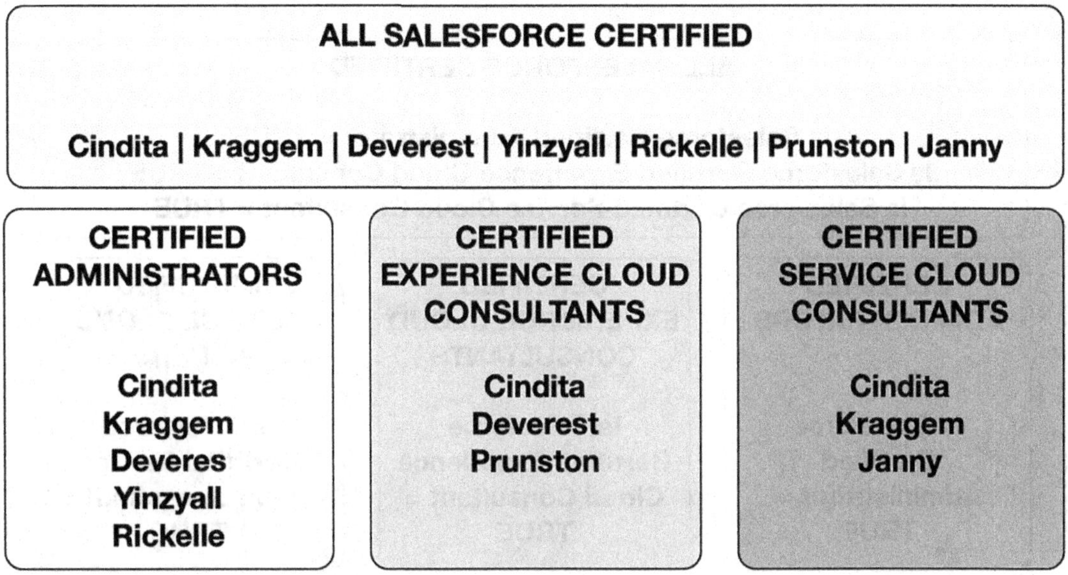

ALL SALESFORCE CERTIFIED

Cindita | Kraggem | Deverest | Yinzyall | Rickelle | Prunston | Janny

CERTIFIED ADMINISTRATORS	CERTIFIED EXPERIENCE CLOUD CONSULTANTS	CERTIFIED SERVICE CLOUD CONSULTANTS
Cindita Kraggem Deveres Yinzyall Rickelle	Cindita Deverest Prunston	Cindita Kraggem Janny

Figure 11-13. *Grouping of users by Salesforce certification at Little Shop of Workflows*

Before audience-in-audience capability existed, four distinct audiences containing each relevant set of criteria were needed. See Figure 11-14.

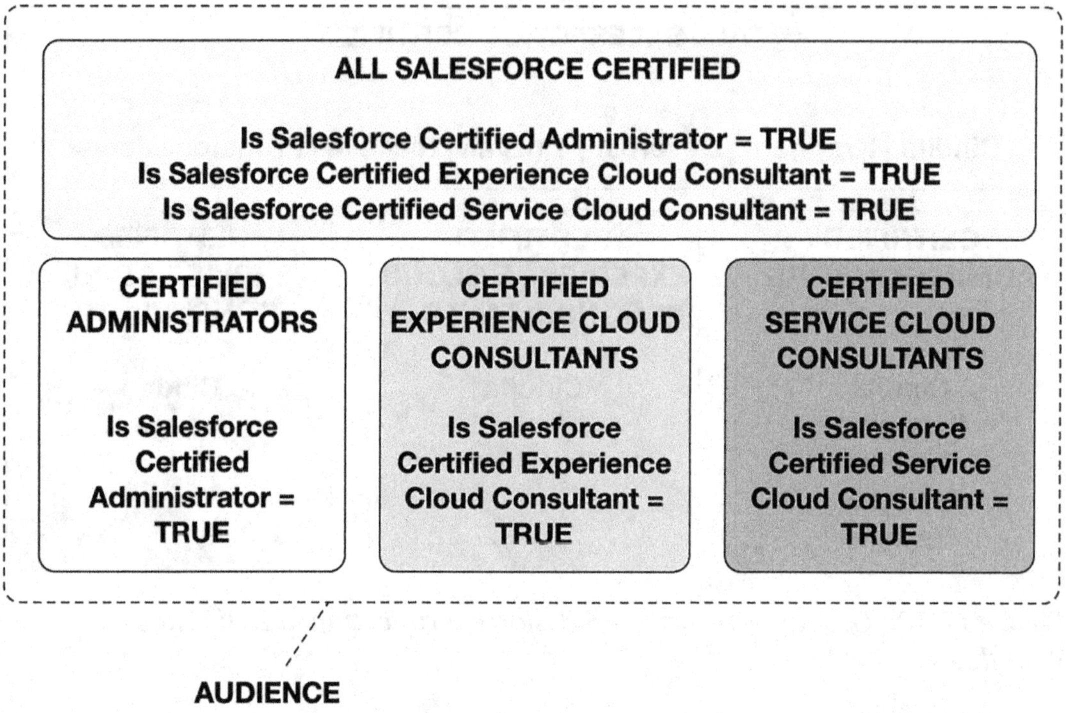

ALL SALESFORCE CERTIFIED

Is Salesforce Certified Administrator = TRUE
Is Salesforce Certified Experience Cloud Consultant = TRUE
Is Salesforce Certified Service Cloud Consultant = TRUE

CERTIFIED ADMINISTRATORS	CERTIFIED EXPERIENCE CLOUD CONSULTANTS	CERTIFIED SERVICE CLOUD CONSULTANTS
Is Salesforce Certified Administrator = TRUE	Is Salesforce Certified Experience Cloud Consultant = TRUE	Is Salesforce Certified Service Cloud Consultant = TRUE

AUDIENCE

Figure 11-14. *The old way of doing things required that a superset (e.g., "ALL SALESFORCE CERTIFIED") contained the combination of criteria found in the audience subsets*

However, with audiences allowing audiences as criteria, the redundancy is gone. An administrator can manage subset audiences and simply add them as criteria to the parent audience. See Figure 11-15 for how a new parent audience would be set up.

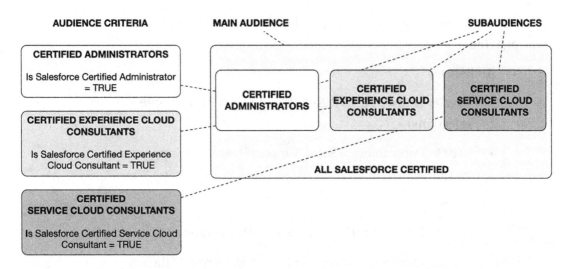

Figure 11-15. *The new way of doing things allows an audience to be added as criteria within a parent audience—making management of the parent audience much easier*

Audience Criteria Logic

The logic applied between audience criteria matches standard "filter logic" found on the Salesforce platform, providing three choices for site admins:

- All conditions are met (AND)

- Any condition is met (OR)

- Custom logic is met

However, it is critical to understand that the logic within one specific criteria is always that any condition is met ("OR"). So, to play this out, let's look at an example.

Example

We'll use the following logic and criteria:

- Logic = All conditions are met (AND)

- Criteria 1 = (Criteria 1A **OR** Criteria 1B)

- Criteria 2 = (Criteria 2A **OR** Criteria 2B)

Additionally, we'll use two hypothetical audiences and four users to bring this concept to life:

- Audience 1

    - User ➤ Title = SVP, EVP, AVP (SVP, EVP, AVP are unique selections)

    - User ➤ Department = Sales, Support (Sales and Support are unique selections)

- Audience 2

    - User ➤ Title = SVP, EVP (SVP and EVP are unique selections)

I'll consider a few users and convey whether a user is part of the audience or not:

- User 1

    - Title = VP

    - Department = Sales

    - Result: Not in either audience

- User 2

    - Title = SVP

    - Department = Marketing

    - Result: Audience 2

- User 3

    - Title = AVP

    - Department = Marketing

    - Result: Audience 1

- User 4

    - Title = SVP

    - Department = Sales

    - Result: Audience 1 and Audience 2*

Note   *User 4 in the previous example is part of Audience 1 and Audience 2. Which audience applies if each audience is associated with different elements (e.g., page variations)? The audience with the most criteria does; in this case, that would be Audience 1. If similar criteria exist, the criteria types themselves are assessed in this order of priority: profile, record type, and location (going from most specific to most general).

Bringing It Together

Once audience criteria have been established, a picture that can vary dramatically from Figure 11-3 (earlier in the chapter) comes into focus. Figure 11-16 shows a couple examples of how audiences could be constructed.

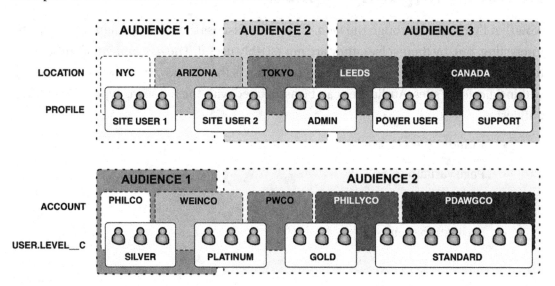

Figure 11-16. *Examples of possible audiences*

When I add in record types, it adds another layer of detail; see Figure 11-17. In this case, I will take a closer look at one of these users.

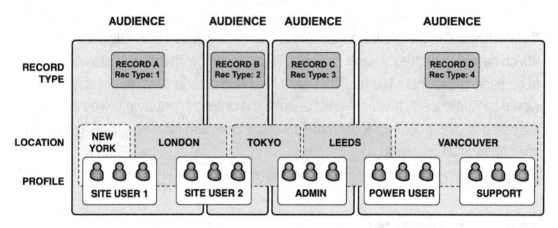

Figure 11-17. Audiences with record types, locations, and profiles

Audience Targeting Types

Now that I've walked through the *who*, it's time to discuss the *what*. Audiences are pretty interesting, but, by themselves, they are not terribly useful. The *assignment* of audiences to a particular experience to drive personalization is the real power of audience targeting within Salesforce sites. Audiences can be associated with the following types of targeting entities:

- Branding sets

- Page variations

- Component audiences

- Navigation menus

- Tile menus

- CMS collections

- Personalized components

I will walk through each in detail, provide an explanation of how each works, and provide an example of how it can be appropriately applied.

Branding Sets

With branding sets, site administrators and builders can tailor unique branding experiences to different audiences. Partner sites, in particular, are a great fit for this powerful feature because it allows an organization to present a unique experience for each partner. So, what exactly is a branding set? A branding set is a combination of the following:

- Site branding colors

- Header image

- Company logo

Figure 11-18 shows an example of multiple branding sets.

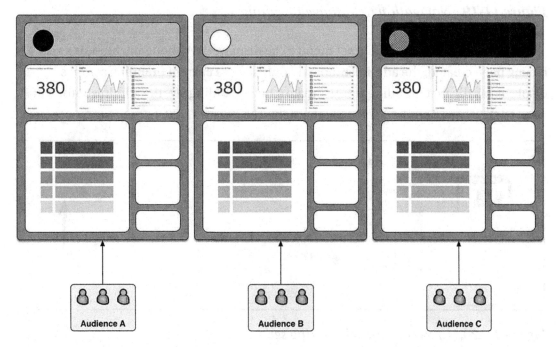

Figure 11-18. *With branding sets, an organization can display the same content and layout but a different header to multiple audiences*

To create a branding set, a site administrator clicks the Theme tab on the left, then the downward arrow at the top right, and finally Manage Branding Sets. See Figure 11-19.

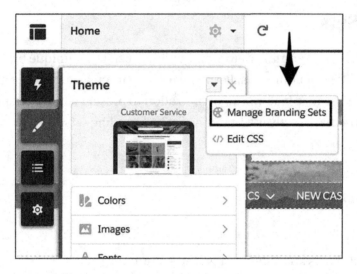

Figure 11-19. *Navigation to Manage Branding Sets*

This will cause the branding set menu to be displayed. Without any branding sets having been created, the administrator will only see the current branding settings displayed as the first branding set. To create a new branding set, the administrator will need to click New Branding Set at the top right; see Figure 11-20.

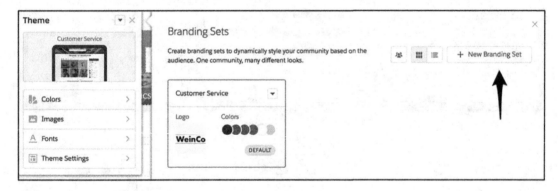

Figure 11-20. *Creating a new branding set*

In this scenario, I'll create two additional branding sets, one for Partner A and one for Partner B. See Figure 11-21.

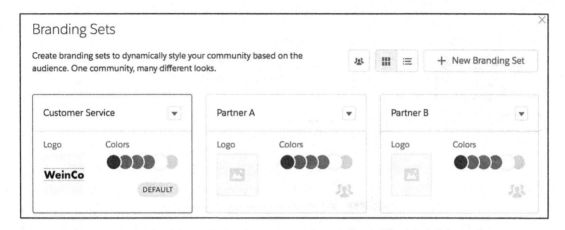

Figure 11-21. *Two additional branding sets, one for Partner A and one for Partner B (once completed, the logos and colors will differ for each)*

To edit a branding set, an administrator clicks the arrow at the top right of the applicable branding set and selects Edit; see Figure 11-22.

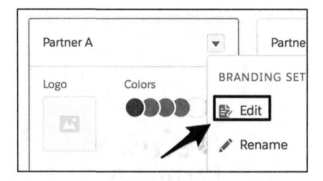

Figure 11-22. *Editing a branding set*

Once selected, an administrator can change the branding settings in the same way that the "original" branding was configured. See Figure 11-23.

Figure 11-23. *Making changes to a branding set*

In Figure 11-24, the branding set is configured for Partner A with a company logo and a header image. Figure 11-25 shows how this branding set and two others appear on a mobile device.

Figure 11-24. *The new Partner A branding set*

Figure 11-25. *Three branding sets for the same site (mobile view): WeinCo, WeinCo Partner A, WeinCo Partner B. Note the header and logo*

To create or apply an audience, an administrator can click the arrow to the right of Status and then select from the Audience section at the bottom. The options will vary depending on the context (e.g., Edit Audience will appear if an audience has already been assigned). See Figure 11-26.

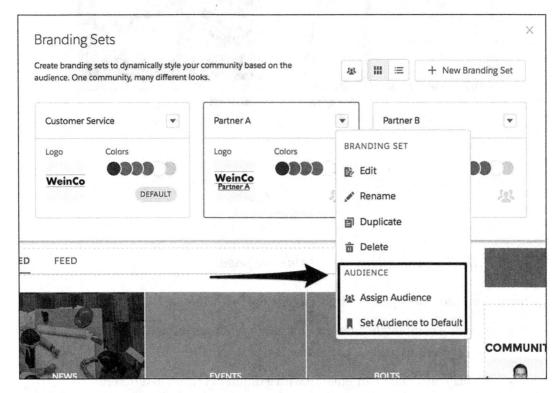

Figure 11-26. *Applying an audience to a branding set*

Page Variations

Page variations are the next step in audience targeting and allow site builders and administrators to create different experiences through the same page for different users. A page variation enables two different users to navigate to the same page and have a personalized view. See Figure 11-27.

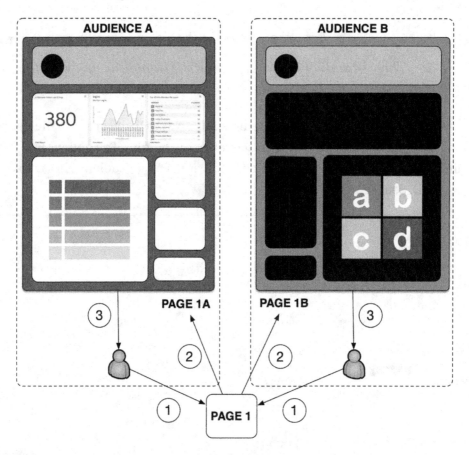

Figure 11-27. *Two variations of the same site page*

Some scenarios for page variations include the following:

- Showing completely different content to different audiences on the same common page (e.g., the Home page)

- Displaying similar content, but with a different layout, to different audiences

Note   If the desired variation is at the component level (e.g., show/hide one specific component), component audiences should be considered. I'll cover that next.

To create a page variation, an administrator must navigate to the page setup screen first. From there, New Page Variation can be selected. See Figure 11-28.

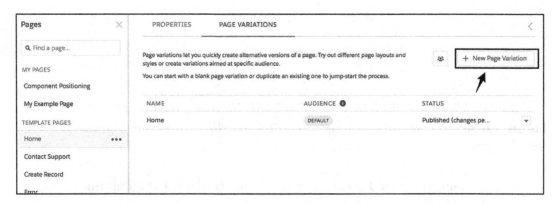

Figure 11-28. *Creating a new page variation*

When a new page is created, the administrator has the option to create a new page from scratch or to select an existing page (see Figure 11-29). To learn more about creating and exporting a page for reuse, check out Chapter 6. Here, I will go ahead and create a new page.

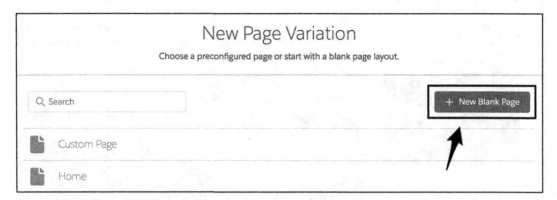

Figure 11-29. *A new page variation can be created from an existing page or made from a new blank page*

Next, the layout is selected; see Figure 11-30.

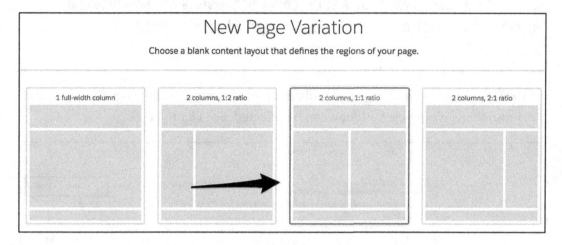

Figure 11-30. *The layout of a page variation can differ from the original page's layout*

Finally, a name is selected, and the page variation is all set. The administrator is pushed right to the new page, from which they can place and configure components, as desired. See Figures 11-31 and 11-32 for an example of Home page variations.

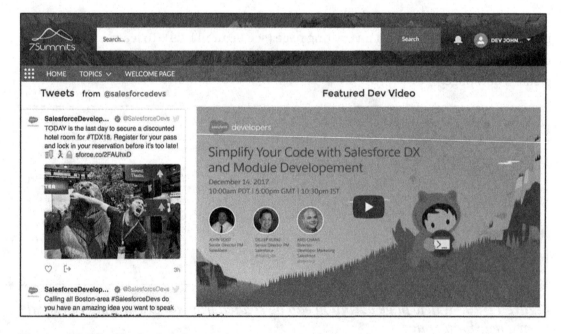

Figure 11-31. *Variation A*

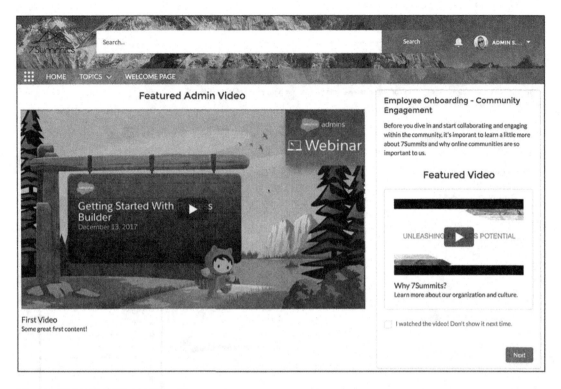

Figure 11-32. *Variation B*

To create or apply an audience, an administrator can click the arrow to the right of Status and then select from the Audience section at the bottom. The options will vary depending on the context (e.g., Assign Audience will appear if no audience has been assigned). See Figure 11-33.

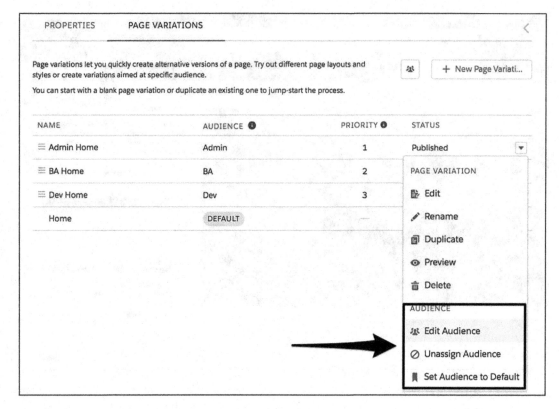

Figure 11-33. *Editing an audience of a page variation*

Page variation application can be fairly straightforward. See Figure 11-34.

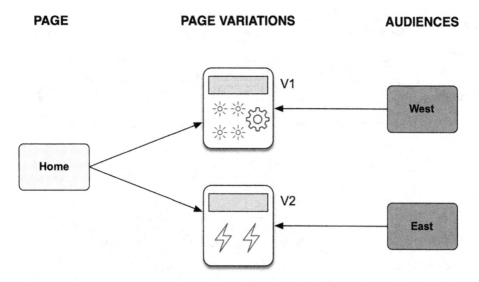

Figure 11-34. *Here, a single page is shown in two different ways to Audience 1 and Audience 2*

The complexity increases when record types are brought into the picture. Take a look at Figure 11-35.

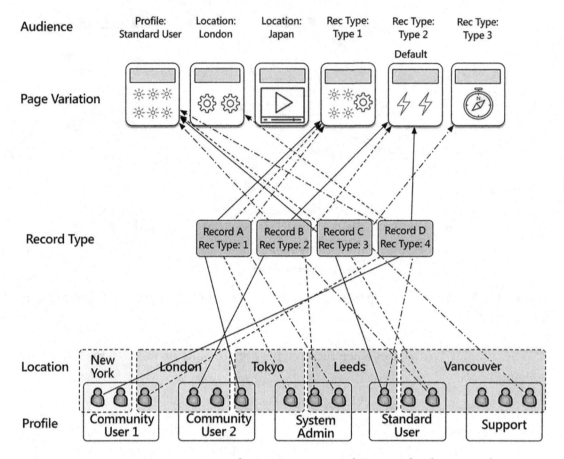

Figure 11-35. *Page variation application can get a bit complex because the number of variations, audiences, and audience criteria all grow*

Component Audiences

Component audiences allow an individual component to be configured per audience, so as to allow its display and function to vary by audience. This allows an administrator to avoid managing multiple page variations (which adds extra overhead), instead of allowing the management of the content at the component level. At a high level, there are a couple different approaches to this functionality:

- Show or hide a component for specific audiences

- Configure a nondynamic component uniquely per audience to drive dynamic-like experiences (i.e., show a component to multiple audiences but configure it differently)

Configuring component audiences is really all about the audience; the component aspect really doesn't change. An admin would place and configure the component as would be done for a non-audience-specific component, with a couple exceptions:

- The component for an audience needs to be configured for that specific audience.

- If the component will be shown to multiple audiences, the component needs to be placed and configured multiple times.

See Figure 11-36. Here, I've placed a custom 7S Banner component and configured it for three different audiences. Note that, as an admin, I see the component three times since, technically, three components are present on the page.

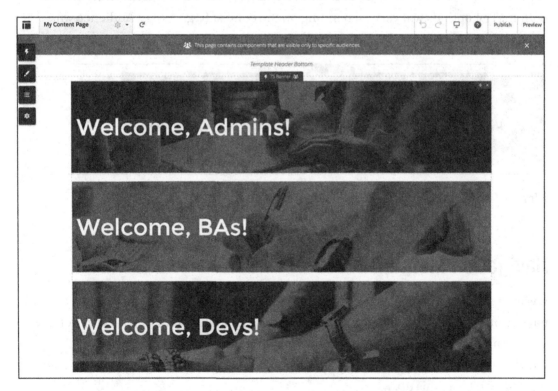

Figure 11-36. *Three versions of one audience-specific component*

When an audience member navigates to the page shown in Figure 11-36, the member will only see the component as configured for their specific audience. See Figure 11-37 to see what an audience member sees.

Figure 11-37. *Same page (not a page variation), but two users are not seeing the same thing; this is a result of component audiences*

To create or apply an audience to a component, an administrator can click the arrow at the top right of the property editor and then select from the Audience section at the bottom. The options will vary, depending on the context (e.g., Assign Audience will appear if no audience has been assigned). See Figure 11-38.

Figure 11-38. *Adding an audience to a component*

Navigation Menus

It was a great day when Salesforce delivered the ability to target audiences with navigation menus. While it's easy to overlook this capability, sometimes it is extremely important to show or hide a particular tab or submenu from a specific group of individuals. That's exactly what this allows an administrator to do. See Figure 11-39 for the first step to set this up.

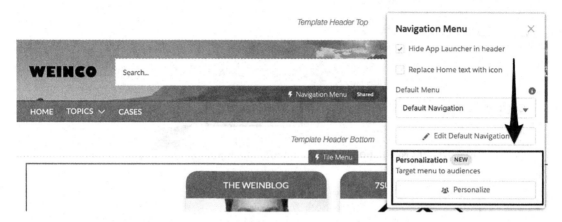

Figure 11-39. *To start personalizing a navigation menu, click the menu and, then, the "Personalize" button*

Once the personalize modal appears, an administrator will select the menu to be targeted (see Figure 11-40). Of course, this assumes that you have already created a custom menu. To do that, click Settings (Tab) ➤ Navigation within Experience Builder and set up a custom navigation menu.

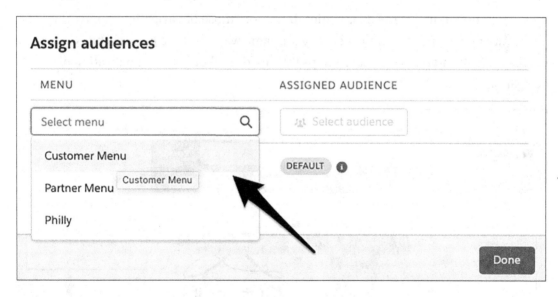

Figure 11-40. *Select a menu to be targeted*

For the final step, select an audience and assign it to the selected menu. See Figure 11-41 for a look at the modal after the audience is assigned.

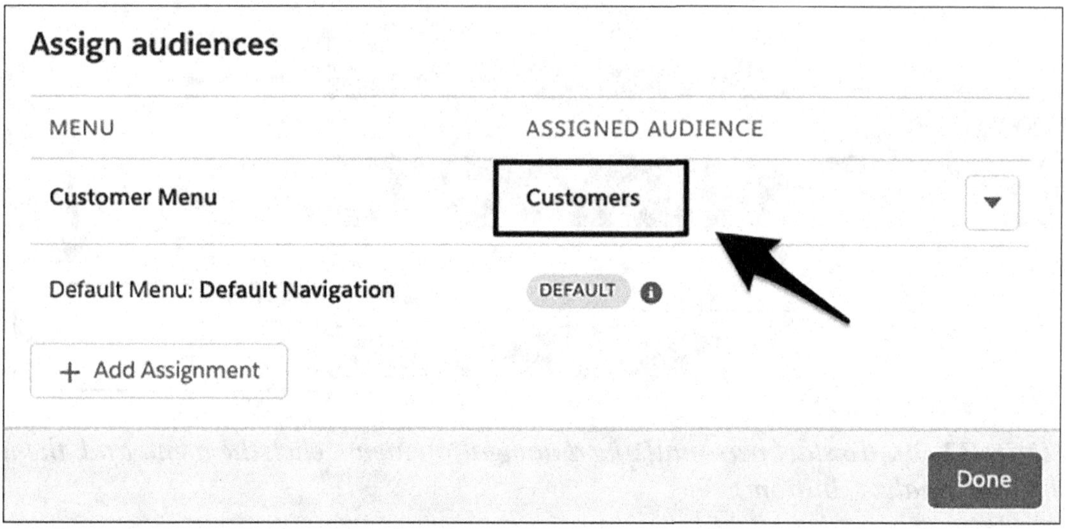

Figure 11-41. *Assign an audience to the menu*

Tile Menus

While their functionality and capabilities differ from those of navigation menus, tile menus are personalized in almost exactly the same way. Start the process that's shown in Figure 11-42 and follow the same steps that are described for personalization of a navigation menu.

Figure 11-42. *Personalize a tile menu with ease in Experience Builder*

CMS Collections

Similar to navigation and tile menus, CMS collections can be targeted as well. See Figure 11-43.

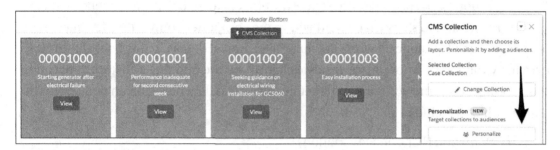

Figure 11-43. *CMS Collections can be targeted*

We'll focus on CMS in a dedicated chapter later. For now, understand that setup is simple and a collection of content can be displayed based on the viewing user. Do note, however, that the type of collection being targeted (e.g., Case, News, etc.) must match the type of the default collection in the component. In Figure 11-44, the collection selected is of type "Case"; therefore, any personalization of this component must be associated with a collection of that type.

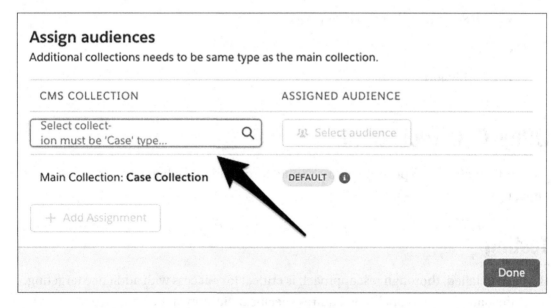

Figure 11-44. *Personalized collections must be of the same type as the main collection added to the CMS Collection component*

Personalization APIs

A lesser-known benefit of audience targeting is the ability to target records that are surfaced within custom Lightning components in Experience Cloud. The Personalization APIs from Salesforce allow developers to associate an audience with a specific record and to show that record within the component only if the viewing user is in the assigned audience. I won't get into the technical details in this book. I think it's extremely valuable to know, however, especially if you are building a custom application that leverages data and you want to target the displayed data based on an audience. The support objects include

- Variation (ExperienceVariation)
- Any custom object
- Navigation Menu (NavigationLinkSet)
- Topic
- Collaboration/Chatter Group
- Knowledge Article
- Files (ContentDocument)
- CMS Content (ManagedContent)
- Report
- Dashboard

Other Considerations

As a best practice, a couple other items should be considered when leveraging audience targeting for Salesforce sites.

Testing

Having a detailed, thorough test approach is critical for success with audience targeting. Since the nature of this capability requires specific definition of the audience, verifying expected functionality should not (and cannot) be properly executed by one logged-in user, even a system administrator. At a minimum, the following users should be created for effective testing:

- Users who correspond to each of the defined audiences

- Users who correspond to more than one audience (to verify priority)

- Users who do not correspond to any of the defined audiences (i.e., these users would be part of a default audience)

Additionally, consider audiences that include location-based criteria. Either an IP emulator will be needed or the location of users conducting tests will need to match the defined criteria, based on the IP address.

Suitability/Application

Audience targeting does not address all UX personalization scenarios that can be envisioned within a Salesforce site. Simply put, it is the wrong solution in some cases. I will capture those conditions next, along with a possible alternative approach:

- *Significant volume of audiences*: At a point, audiences will become unwieldy and hard to manage. I won't personally define a cutoff point (the threshold for each organization may differ), but audience targeting works best with a reasonable number of audiences. However, leveraging the Personalization API is definitely one way to address this, at least partially.

- *Frequently changing audience criteria*: The current UI and corresponding process to manage an audience makes this scenario less than ideal. Audience criteria should be relatively static.

- *Hybrid customization and configuration*: As of the Summer '18 release, a custom theme has limited options for being used with audience tools, specifically branding sets.

- *Extreme dynamic branding*: Branding sets have a fairly limited scope. While I wouldn't be shocked to see dynamic themes come out at some point, they are not available at this point.

So, what are the alternatives?

- *Dynamic custom components*: This is the best solution for creating personalized experiences when criteria are changing or audience volume is high. Build out the front end to handle back-end criteria/ logic to show different content or branding on the fly. As mentioned before, a hybrid approach that incorporates Personalization APIs may be beneficial in this scenario.

- *Dynamic theme components*: This is the same idea as the last bullet point but specifically applied to custom theme components.

- *Separate sites*: This doesn't solve a scenario with a large number of audiences, but it allows for extreme differences. A decision to consider separate sites, however, is much larger than just a personalization topic. This typically wouldn't be the first recommended option, although it is definitely an option.

Recap

Audience targeting is a key area of sites, and it's sure to expand further in future releases. In this chapter, I provided an overview of audiences, both conceptually and practically, and then explored the targeting types that can be used with audiences:

- Branding sets

- Page variations

- Components

- Navigation and Tile Menus

- CMS Collections

- Personalization APIs

With a solid understanding of how audiences work and the tools to configure them, site administrators can create dynamic, personalized experiences within a site.

CHAPTER 12

Experience Builder Templates (Lightning Bolts)

A significant—and often misunderstood—feature to come out of Experience Cloud in over the years is the ability to create and manage what are called Experience Builder templates, or "Lightning Bolts." With the introduction of templates, declarative app builders and programmatic developers alike have been empowered on the Salesforce platform. In this chapter, I will clearly explain what Lightning Bolts are and demonstrate how to build and distribute them.

Lightning Bolts equate to site templates; the terms are essentially interchangeable. As with a template, a bolt provides the means to define, deliver, and implement a specific starting point for a site that differs from one of the other, currently existing templates. See Figure 12-1 for a visual of this concept.

© Philip Weinmeister 2022
P. Weinmeister, *Practical Guide to Salesforce Experience Cloud*, https://doi.org/10.1007/978-1-4842-8132-1_12

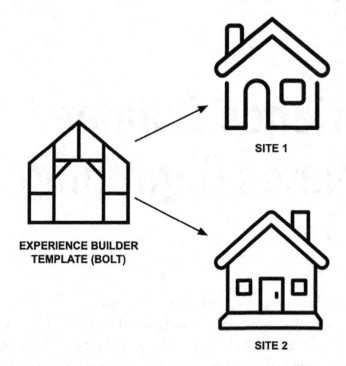

EXPERIENCE BUILDER TEMPLATE (BOLT)

SITE 1

SITE 2

Figure 12-1. *A Lightning Bolt serves as a starting point for a variety of different sites that have some overlapping requirements or use cases*

While this may evolve over time, a bolt currently has no specific scope; it could be a fairly simple, straightforward site use case or could entail a highly complex solution. Figure 12-2 shows a basic example of two templates. Template A has two pages, while Template B has three. The components on page 2 in both sites are laid out similarly, but the other pages are unique to each template.

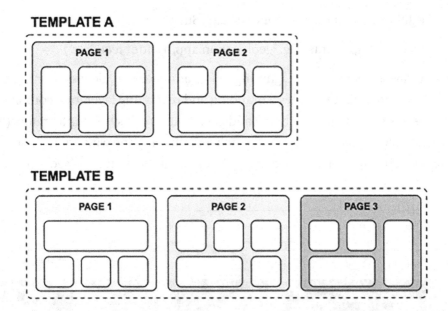

Figure 12-2. *Two different bolts, or templates, could include a different number of Lightning pages*

The pages and components in Figure 12-2 are for clarification but don't fully capture the complete contents of a bolt. A bolt contains a variety of site content and metadata to allow for a complete solution for the recipient on the installing end. See Figure 12-3 for a list of items that are included.

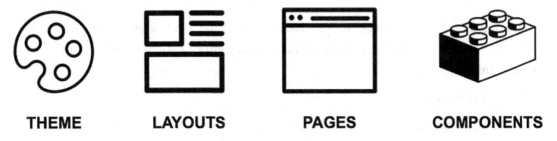

Figure 12-3. *Bolt elements range from sitewide to component specific*

To get more specific, here are the likely candidates for inclusion in a bolt:

- Custom theme (including configuration)

- Custom Lightning pages

- Custom content layouts (including application to certain pages)

- Additional standard components (e.g., Survey, Tile Menu, etc.)

- Custom components (e.g., geolocation app, Twitter feed, etc.)

The best way I can describe a Lightning Bolt is as a means to deliver a templated, packaged site solution that includes a branding and marketing layer for a complete picture of the business challenges being addressed. Although system integrators (SIs) in the Experience Cloud space are primed to deliver bolts, anyone with appropriate access can create one. The Salesforce AppExchange even has a Bolt Solutions section; see Figure 12-4.

Figure 12-4. *Bolt Solutions page within the Salesforce AppExchange*

From a Salesforce perspective, bolts are ideal ways to deliver foundations for specific horizontal or vertical solutions. Horizontally, broad solutions such as the following are prime candidates:

- Employee sites

- Partner sites

Additionally, a large number of vertical use cases lend themselves well to the bolt framework. Look for some of the following industries to have a series of bolts over the next few years:

- Healthcare and life sciences

- Manufacturing

- Retail

- Financial services

Building a Bolt

At a high level, the concept of building a bolt is pretty simple. An organization starts with, ironically, a bolt. It then builds a site through adding, removing, and modifying the initial bolt contents. Finally, the ultimate end state of the site is captured, becoming a new bolt. Figure 12-5 provides a basic overview of the process.

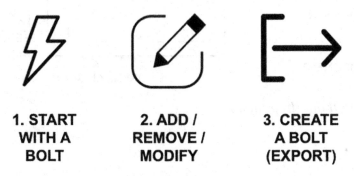

1. START WITH A BOLT   **2. ADD / REMOVE / MODIFY**   **3. CREATE A BOLT (EXPORT)**

Figure 12-5. *High-level overview of the bolt-building process*

To make sure the concept is clear, I'll walk through a more detailed theoretical example of the process. It's time to build a bolt!

Step 1

Creating a site from an available bolt is the starting point. In this case, the site has the following details:

- Page 1

  - Component 1

  - Component 2

- Page 2

  - Component 1

  - Component 3

- Page 3

  - Component 1

  - Component 4

Figure 12-6 shows this starting point.

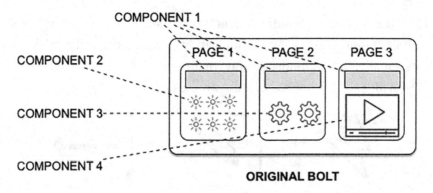

Figure 12-6. *Bolt building, step 1*

Step 2

In this step, the change process is initiated (see Figure 12-7). The following changes are made:

- The page 1 layout is changed.

- Page 2 is removed.

- The component 1 configuration is changed.

- Component 4 is removed.

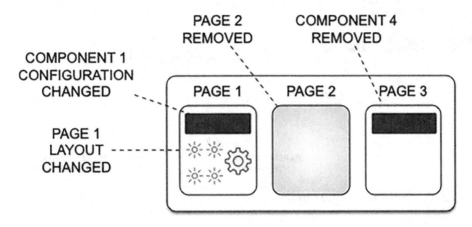

Figure 12-7. *Bolt building, step 2*

Step 3

Here, some additional components come into play (see Figure 12-8):

- Page 4 is added.

- Component 5 is added to page 4.

- Component 6 is added to page 3.

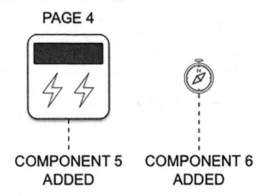

Figure 12-8. *Bolt building, step 3*

Step 4

Now that the new site is ready to go, it can be exported as a bolt. See Figure 12-9.

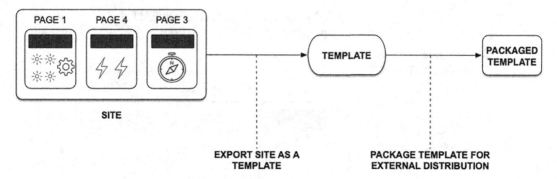

Figure 12-9. Bolt building, step 4

Bolt Creation in Experience Builder

While the conceptual understanding of bolt creation is important, administrators and site builders will also need to understand the specifics of how a bolt is actually constructed within Experience Builder. Once a site has been updated and is ready to be "stamped" as a bolt, the site administrator will navigate to the Settings tab on the left and then click Developer. See Figure 12-10.

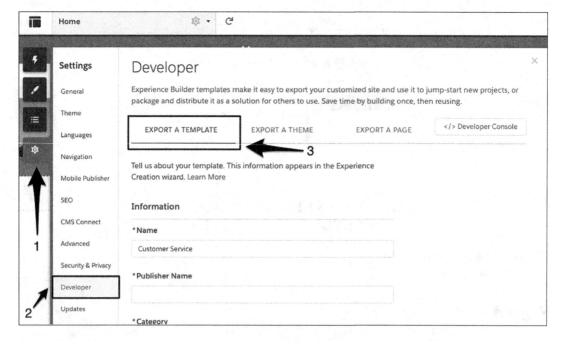

Figure 12-10. Developer page on the Experience Builder Settings tab

Once on the Developer page, Export a Template will be selected. This is where the branding and marketing layer is created for the bolt. The following will be needed:

- Name

- Category

- One to three images (recommended dimensions: 1260px × 820px)

- One to four features (including a feature title and feature description)

Figure 12-11 shows the first part of the creation screen with the required fields populated ("Features" section not shown).

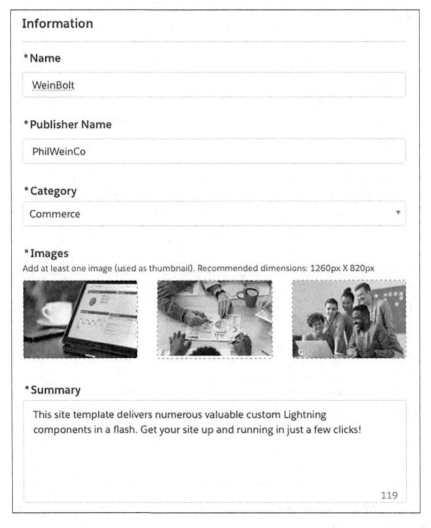

Figure 12-11. Bolt description/marketing page that appears during creation

Figure 12-12 shows the second part of the creation screen with the required fields populated ("Features" section only).

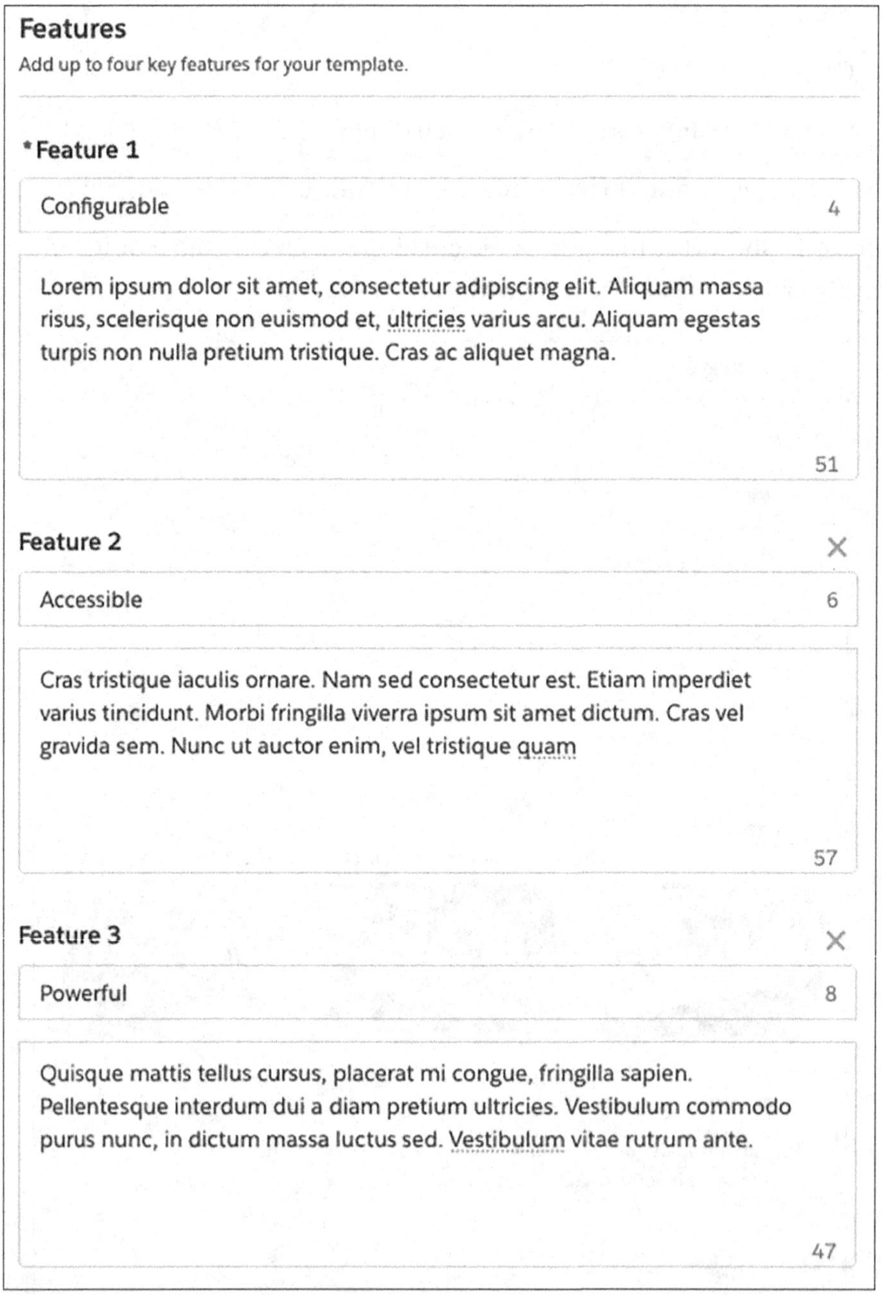

Features

Add up to four key features for your template.

---

* Feature 1

Configurable	4

Lorem ipsum dolor sit amet, consectetur adipiscing elit. Aliquam massa risus, scelerisque non euismod et, ultricies varius arcu. Aliquam egestas turpis non nulla pretium tristique. Cras ac aliquet magna.	
	51

Feature 2   ✕

Accessible	6

Cras tristique iaculis ornare. Nam sed consectetur est. Etiam imperdiet varius tincidunt. Morbi fringilla viverra ipsum sit amet dictum. Cras vel gravida sem. Nunc ut auctor enim, vel tristique quam	
	57

Feature 3   ✕

Powerful	8

Quisque mattis tellus cursus, placerat mi congue, fringilla sapien. Pellentesque interdum dui a diam pretium ultricies. Vestibulum commodo purus nunc, in dictum massa luctus sed. Vestibulum vitae rutrum ante.	
	47

Figure 12-12. *The Features section of the Bolt description/marketing page that appears during creation*

Click Export, and the bolt creation is finalized. See Figures 12-13, 12-14, and 12-15.

Figure 12-13. *Click the Export button to kick off the final bolt creation step*

Figure 12-14. *Wait for it...*

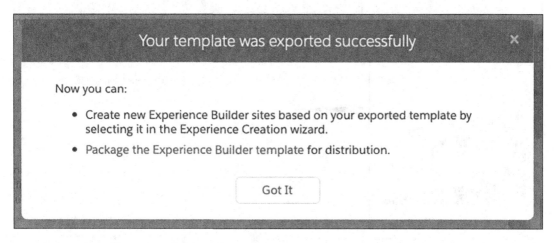

Figure 12-15. *Success! The template was exported successfully*

Bolt Installation

Are you curious what it looks like to walk through new site creation using the bolt from Figure 12-11? Figures 12-16 to 12-20 show the corresponding views from the bolt installation process.

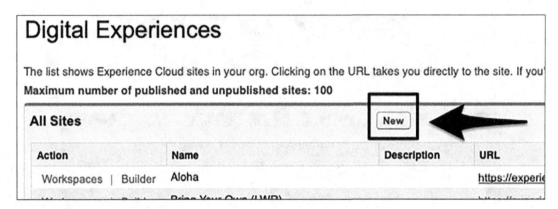

Figure 12-16. *Click "New" to start the site creation process*

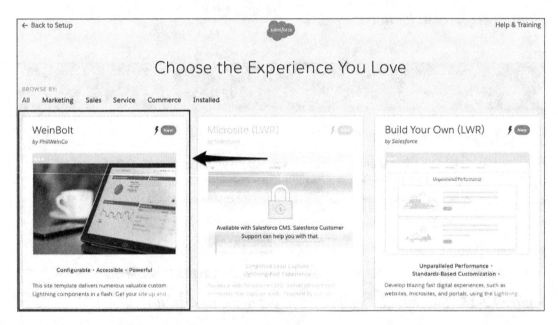

Figure 12-17. *Select the desired Lightning Bolt*

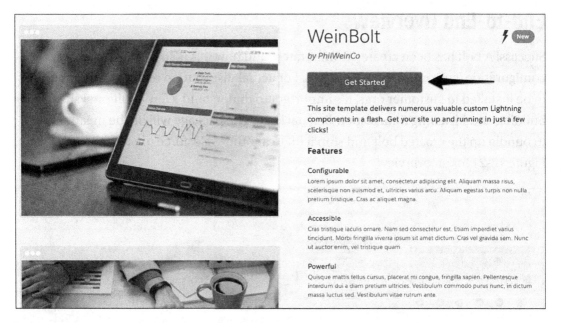

Figure 12-18. *Click Get Started*

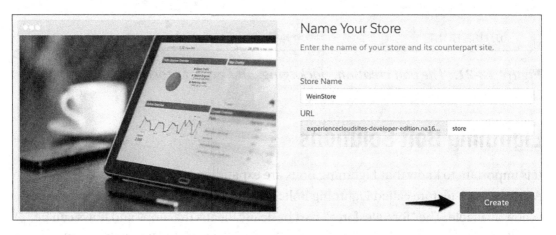

Figure 12-19. *Provide a name and URL. Click Create*

Figure 12-20. *Success! A new site has been created from a bolt*

End-to-End Overview

Success! A bolt has been created from scratch, and now it is ready for use (or further configuration/customization), if desired. For actual distribution of the exported bolt to be installed in customer orgs, it's important to understand a few additional steps: building and installing a corresponding package. The package will be the means to bundle up the created bolt and ship it off to another Salesforce org for use. See Figure 12-21 for an overview.

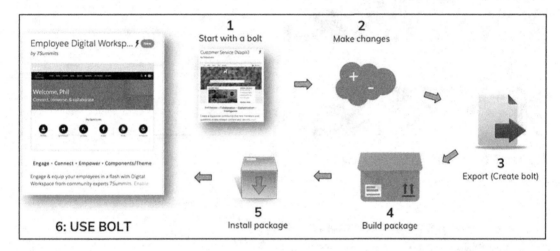

Figure 12-21. *The bolt creation, packaging, and export process*

Lightning Bolt Solutions

It is important to know that Lightning Bolts are expanding to other areas of the platform. A little-known feature called Lightning Bolt Solutions (or Lightning Bolt for Salesforce) is now available. The "for Salesforce" part basically means that apps and flows can be bundled with (or without) a site template to become a Lightning Bolt Solution. See Figures 12-22 to 12-25 for a walk-through of the process.

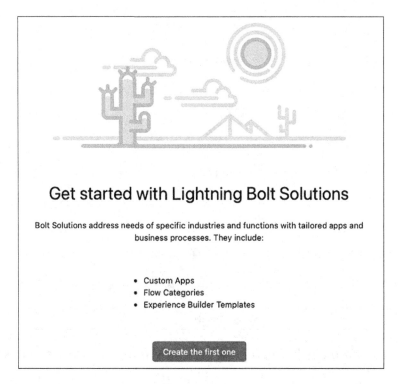

Figure 12-22. *Navigate to Lightning Bolt Solutions in the setup menu*

Figure 12-23. *Provide details about the solution*

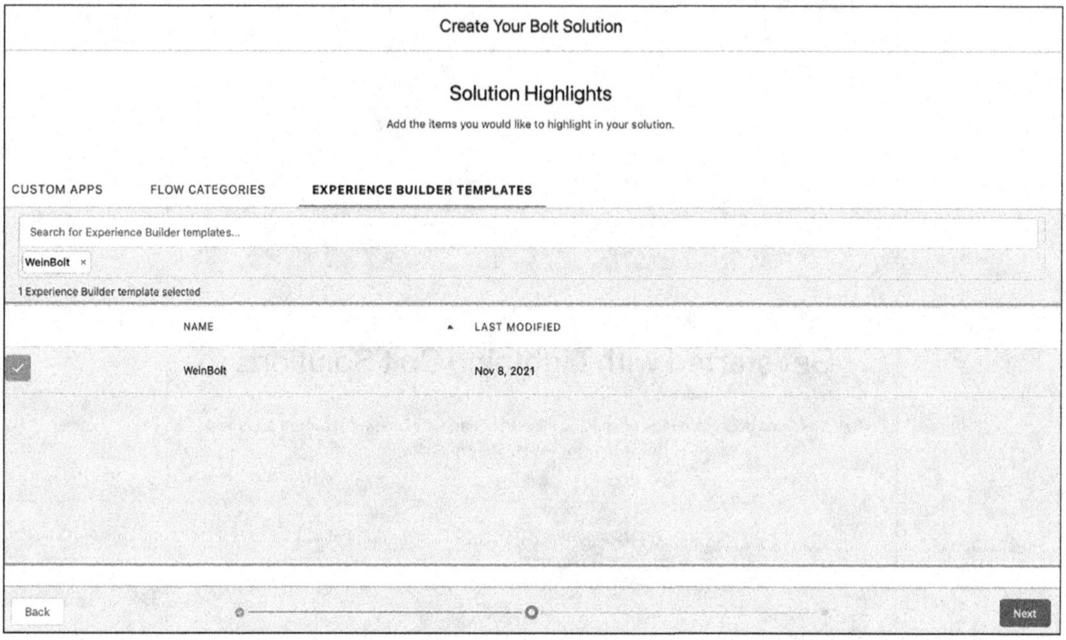

Figure 12-24. *Add the solution highlights (apps, flows, or site templates)*

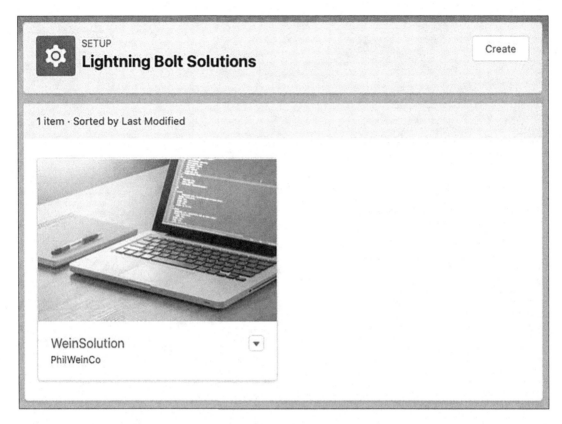

Figure 12-25. *Library of completed Lightning Bolt Solutions*

Recap

This chapter will arm any site administrator/builder with a solid foundation to become a bolt builder. In this chapter, I detailed the following:

- Definition of Lightning Bolts (site templates)

- Purposes and suitable use cases for bolts

- Bolt creation process

- Bolt packaging and installation process

- Lightning Bolt Solutions

CHAPTER 13

Salesforce CMS

Salesforce CMS is a curious player on the stage among the many other sizable announcements from Salesforce over the past few years. It operates under the radar, to a degree, but it fills a critical gap on the platform. It is very late to the party (in terms of content management in general not being new), yet Salesforce is doing its best to inject some degree of innovation into it. And, while it was originally released specifically for digital experiences (sites), it has shifted to technically become a platform-wide offering.

More important than piquing your interest with the idiosyncrasies, however, is making sure the value of CMS is clear. So, let's ask it: Why should anyone care about Salesforce CMS? There are a few reasons:

- *Centralization of content*: Content can easily be used and shared across various interfaces/destinations.

- *Granular administrative control*: Admins have the ability to control which interfaces have access to specific content.

- *Clicks, not code*: Admins can declaratively apply and configure content within Lightning components.

- *Extensibility*: Ability to structure custom content (content types).

- *Platform gap*: Existing platform alternatives do not suffice for the preceding items (Files, Libraries, Attachments, Documents, Static Resources, etc.).

Note   CMS Connect will be covered in this chapter (see end), but it should be noted that it's not really a part of the core CMS offering. It does have CMS in the name, but is essentially a separate feature.

© Philip Weinmeister 2022
P. Weinmeister, *Practical Guide to Salesforce Experience Cloud*, https://doi.org/10.1007/978-1-4842-8132-1_13

Overview

There are three key parts to understand to get a solid picture of Salesforce CMS overall: basic concept, structure, and components.

Basic Concept

At the most basic level, Salesforce CMS allows organizations to centrally manage content and surface that content via different areas of the Salesforce platform, with a particular emphasis on use within Experience Cloud. Figure 13-1 shows a basic diagram of how CMS works.

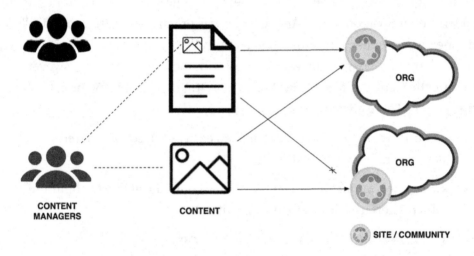

Figure 13-1. *Salesforce CMS allows content to be managed by various individuals and rendered within different interfaces*

Structure

Salesforce CMS is set up with a very clear structure that allows for simple management of the content in use. The primary container for content is called a "workspace." A workspace enables two key settings: (1) definition of content managers for the enclosed content and (2) definition of supported interfaces through what is referred to as "channels." Folders can be established within a workspace, but those are only used for organizational purposes. Figure 13-2 shows an overview of this structure.

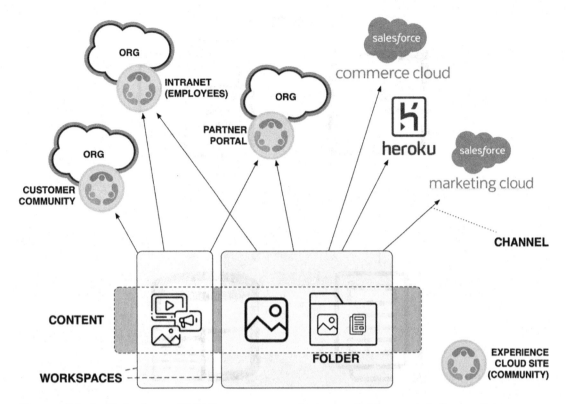

Figure 13-2. *Salesforce CMS leverages workspaces, folders, and channels to manage and distribute content*

Components

So far, we've focused on the storage and management of content within CMS. What about displaying the content? Well, of course, there's the high-code option; you can absolutely leverage content within custom solutions. On the declarative side, Salesforce provides a few components that allow one or more pieces of content to be displayed without requiring any code. Excluding CMS Connect components, Salesforce provides the following standard components to display content:

- CMS Single Item
- CMS Single Item (Detail)
- CMS Collection

Figure 13-3 shows a basic view of CMS Single Item and CMS Collection.

COMPONENTS

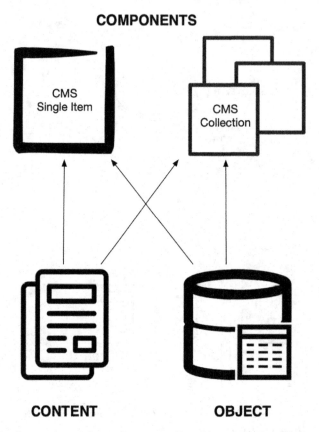

Figure 13-3. Salesforce provides a few standard/out-of-the-box components to display content

Did you notice anything interesting in Figure 13-3? In addition to seeing content as one of the sources for the components, I have an object as a second source. That's right—Salesforce showed excellent vision to make their CMS components multipurposed and support the display of CMS content *and* actual CRM records. Very powerful.

Setup and Configuration

Let's walk through the complete process of setting up Salesforce CMS and displaying related content via an Experience Cloud site.

Digital Experiences App

Ensure that you have access to the "Digital Experiences" app. Click App Launcher, search for "Digital," and select "Digital Experiences." Note that this app was previously labeled "Salesforce CMS." See Figure 13-4 for a look at each step.

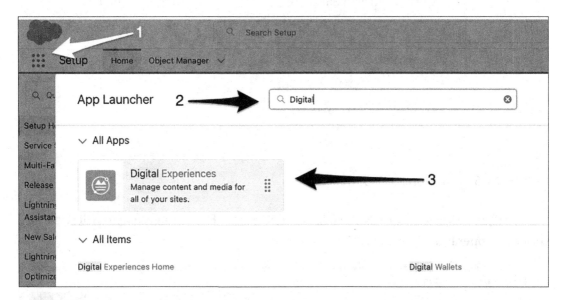

Figure 13-4. *Accessing the Salesforce CMS app*

Digital Experiences Tabs

Next, ensure you have access to the appropriate tabs, including "Digital Experiences Home," "CMS Channels," "CMS Workspace," and "All Sites." Make sure the tabs are in the app by navigating to App Manager. See Figure 13-5 to see the applicable tabs.

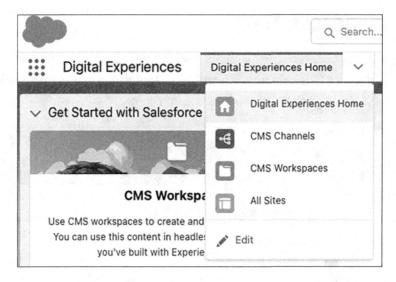

Figure 13-5. *Salesforce CMS tabs*

See Figure 13-6 for a look at the Digital Experiences Home page, which will serve as your main operational page for CMS.

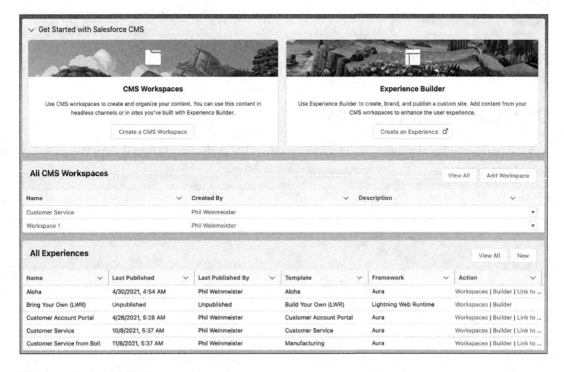

Figure 13-6. *CMS Home page*

Workspace Setup

In this section, I'll walk through all steps needed to create a functional workspace.

Get Started

To start, click "Add Workspace" in the "All CMS Workspaces" section, as shown in Figure 13-7.

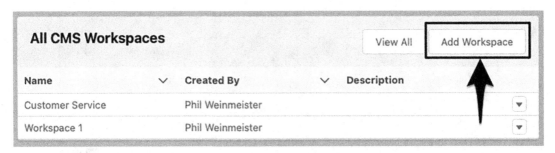

Figure 13-7. *Click "Add Workspace" to create a new workspace*

Step 1: Basic Info

In the first step, you'll need to provide a name and, optionally, a description for your workspace; see Figure 13-8.

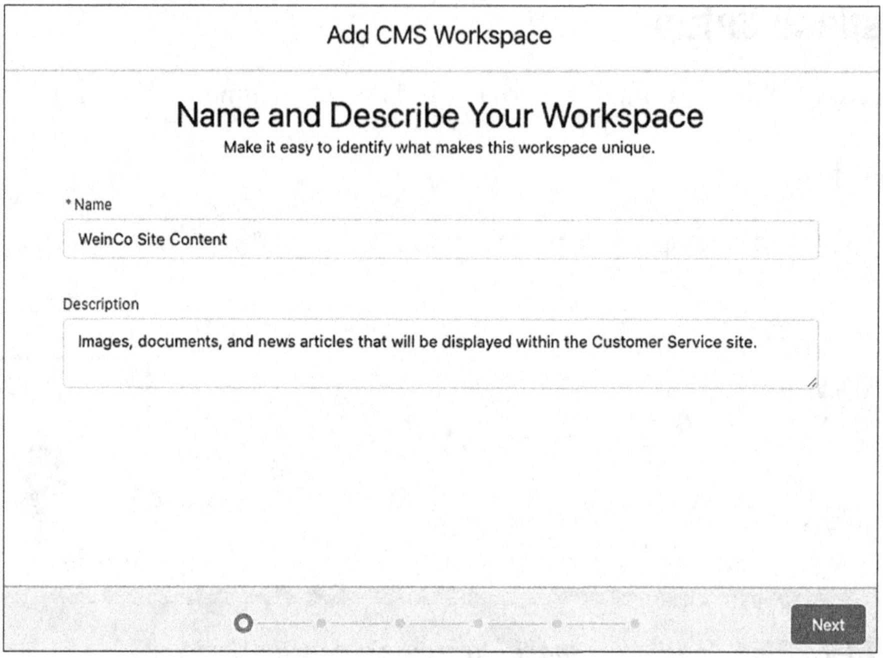

Figure 13-8. *Name and describe your workspace*

Step 2: Add Channels

In this step, you'll identify the channels in which this content may be used/leveraged/
displayed. In our case, we are only going to allow this content to be used in the Customer
Service Experience Cloud site. See Figure 13-9 for step 2.

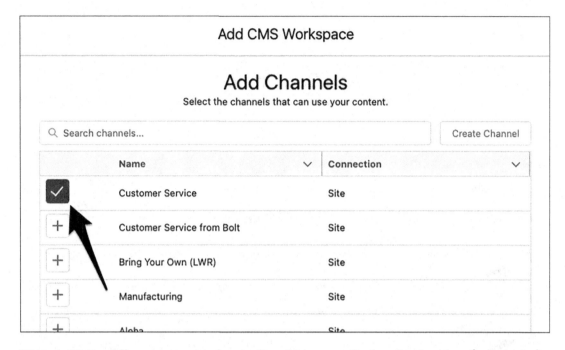

Figure 13-9. *Allow content to be surfaced in a particular destination (e.g., a site) by selecting it as a channel for a workspace*

Step 3: Add Contributors

Once you've established your channel(s), you'll need to determine who should have increased access to this workspace. Search for and click on those users to select them. See Figure 13-10; in this case, I've selected Cyndee and Nathaniel to be contributors.

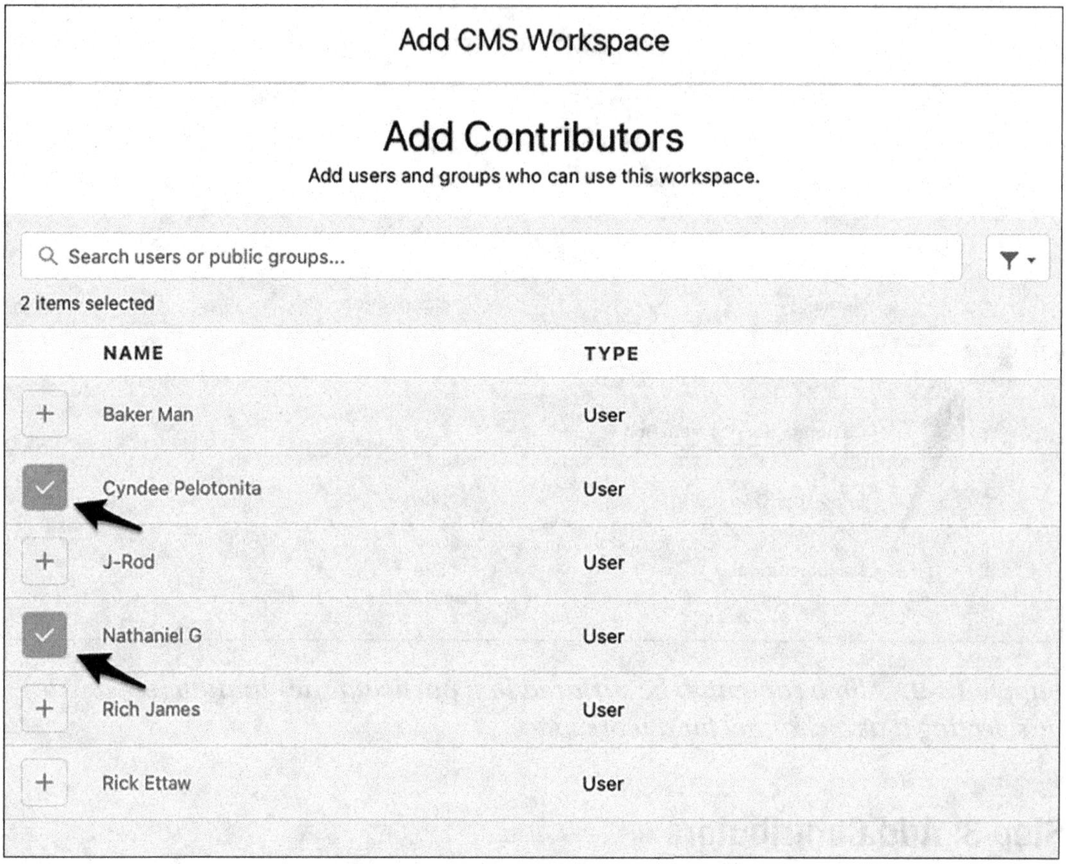

Figure 13-10. *Define your workspace contributors*

Step 4: Set Contributor Access

After identifying contributors, you'll now need to determine which level of access they have. See Figure 13-11; here, I've granted Cyndee admin access and Nathaniel manager access.

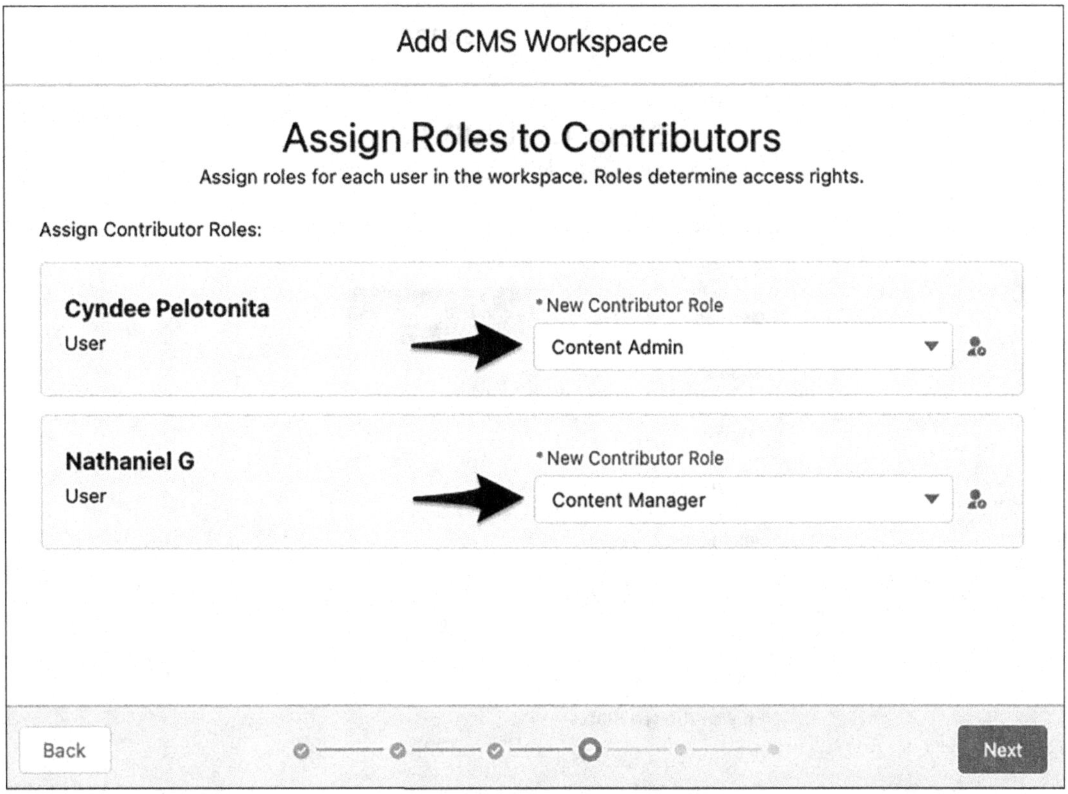

Figure 13-11. *Establish which roles the workspace contributors will have*

Step 5: Set Languages

To facilitate configurability later, Salesforce has you identify which languages will be used with your content in the next step. Select translation languages and also the default language. See Figure 13-12 for a look at the languages step.

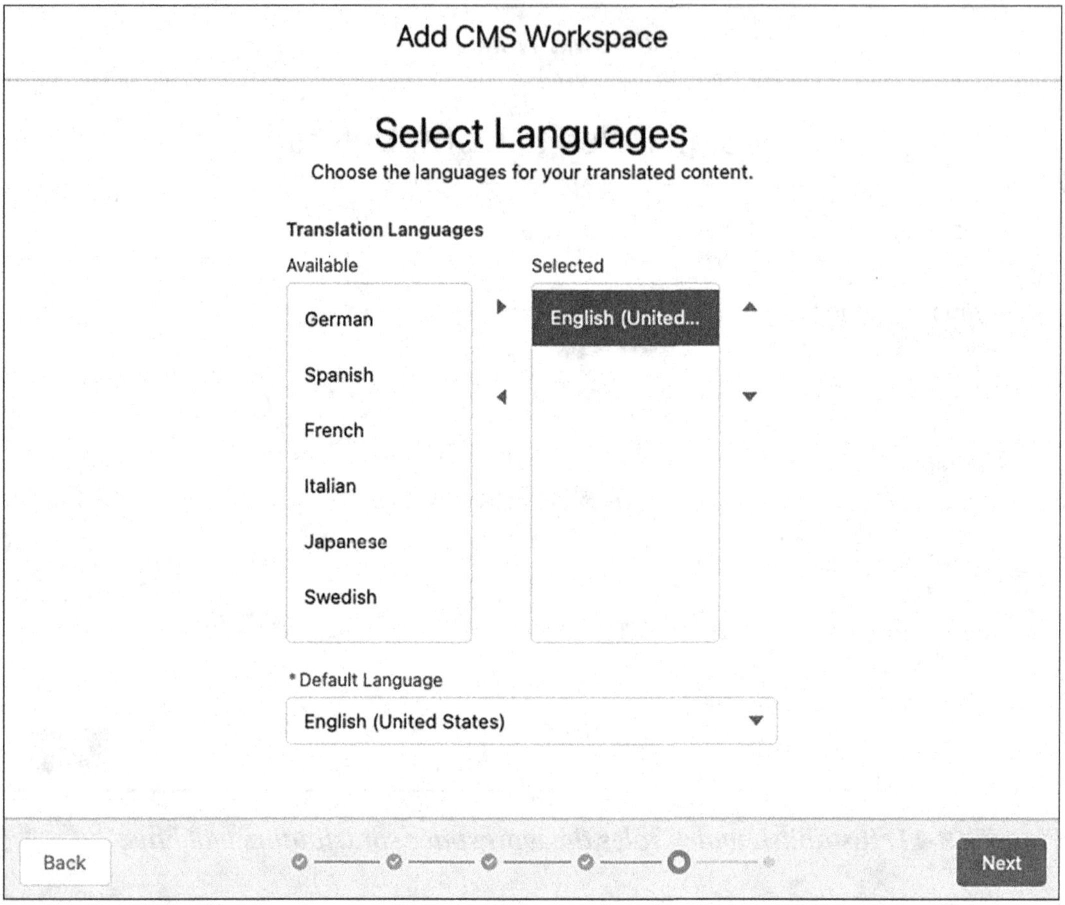

Figure 13-12. *Establish your translation languages and default language*

Step 6: Review and Save

In the last step, review your selections. When ready, save and create your workspace; see Figure 13-13.

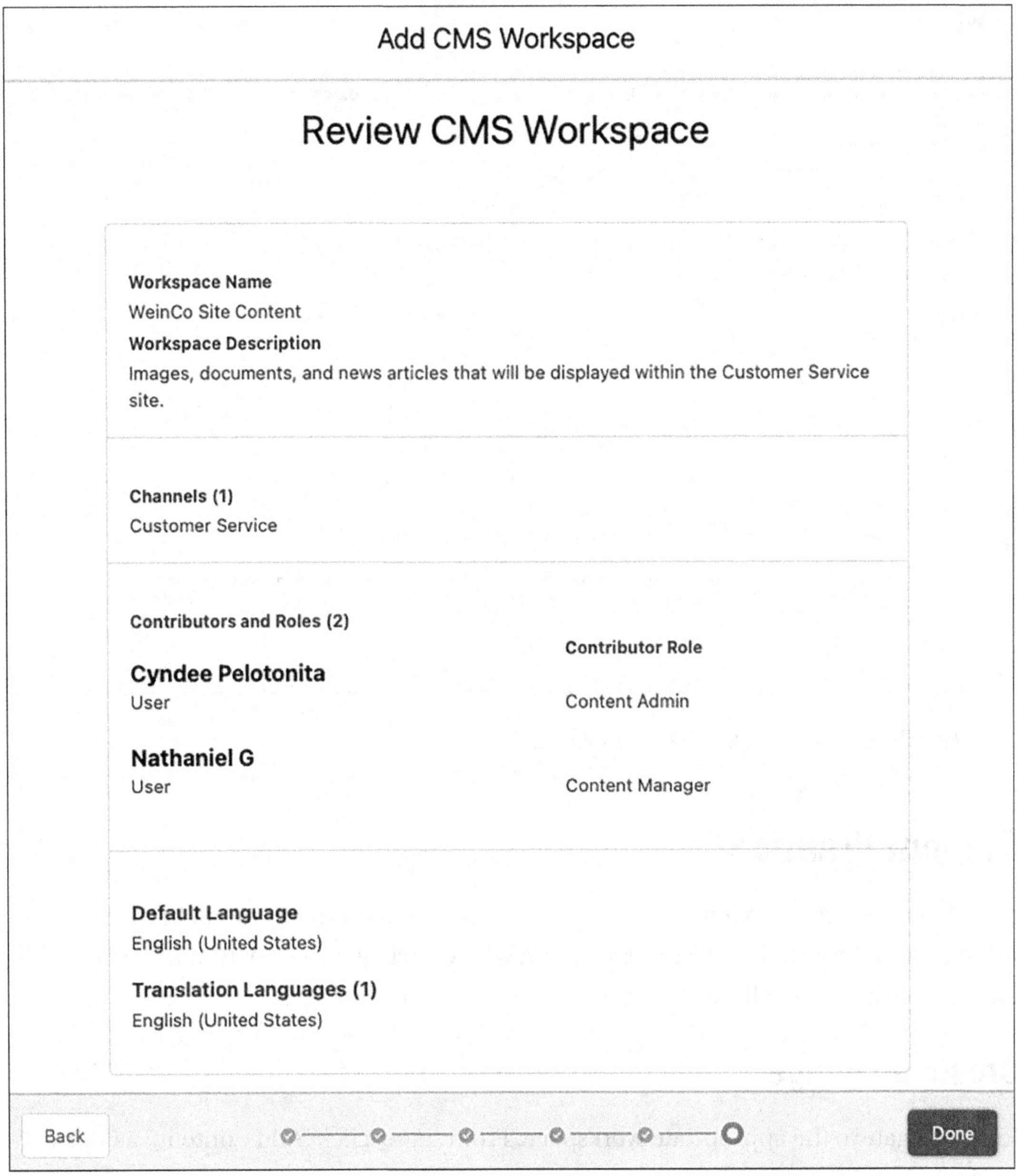

Add CMS Workspace

Review CMS Workspace

Workspace Name
WeinCo Site Content
Workspace Description
Images, documents, and news articles that will be displayed within the Customer Service site.

Channels (1)
Customer Service

Contributors and Roles (2)

	Contributor Role
Cyndee Pelotonita User	Content Admin
Nathaniel G User	Content Manager

Default Language
English (United States)

Translation Languages (1)
English (United States)

Back   Done

Figure 13-13. *Review your new workspace*

At this point, a workspace has been successfully created. See Figure 13-14 for the new workspace.

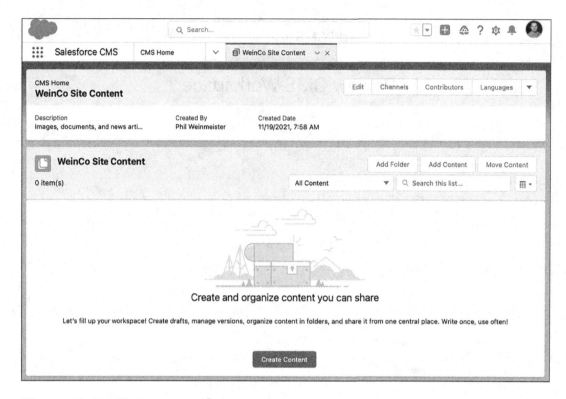

Figure 13-14. *Your new workspace page*

Content Creation

Now that we have set up our workspace, we need to create some content. In this workspace, we'll author content related to space. We will establish a number of images and one news article. I'll walk through the process for one of each.

Create an Image

First, navigate to the appropriate workspace. From there, click "Add Content," as shown in Figure 13-15.

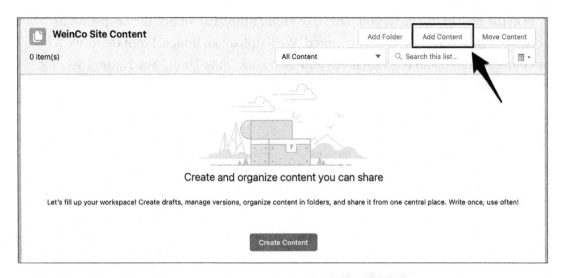

Figure 13-15. *Click "Add Content" to get started with content creation*

Select the type of content. In this case, "Image" will be selected. Once selected, click "Create." See Figure 13-16 for the Create content modal.

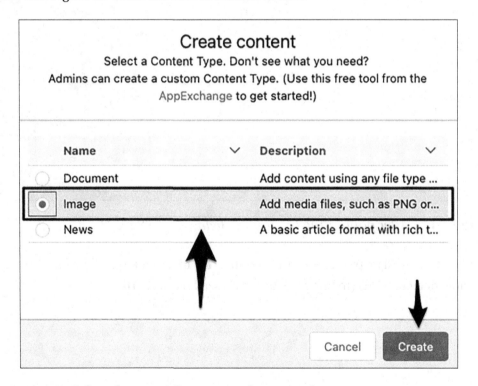

Figure 13-16. *Select the type of content to be created*

On the new image page, you'll need to either upload an image file or specify an accessible URL where the image is stored. We'll upload an image. From there, we'll fill out other required and relevant fields and then click "Save Draft." See Figure 13-17 for the new image page.

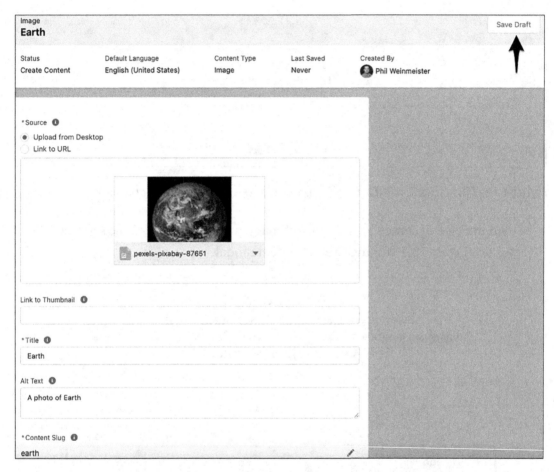

Figure 13-17. *After populating the content fields, click "Save Draft"*

Our last step will be publishing the content. This makes it accessible/usable within the established channels (in this case, our site); see Figure 13-18.

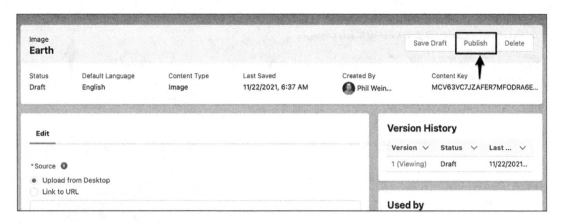

Figure 13-18. *Publish the new content*

Create News

We'll create a news article. The process is essentially the same, with two key differences:

1. The nodes (fields) are different. For example, news content contains a "Body" field, which images do not.

2. A banner image node allows for an existing piece of content (of type image) to be selected.

The second item is a big deal. It means that you can manage an image that is embedded in numerous other pieces of content without touching them; you can modify the image once, and your changes will be reflected in the content containing that image. See Figure 13-19 for a look at the News creation page. The bottom arrow in the screenshot shows where we've embedded an existing piece of content for the banner image.

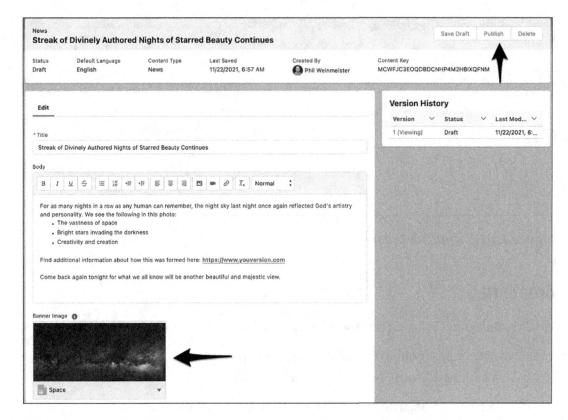

Figure 13-19. *For News content, image content can be embedded*

Content Display

We've established our workspaces and created our content, but we're still missing a big piece of the puzzle: the display of the aforementioned content. Let's look at a few standard (OOTB) components and leverage them to display our content.

CMS Single Item

Let's go ahead and display our news content with the CMS Single Item component. First, establish the page you'll be using. Then, find the list of CMS components in the component tab. Drag and drop the "CMS Single Item" component on a page region. See Figure 13-20.

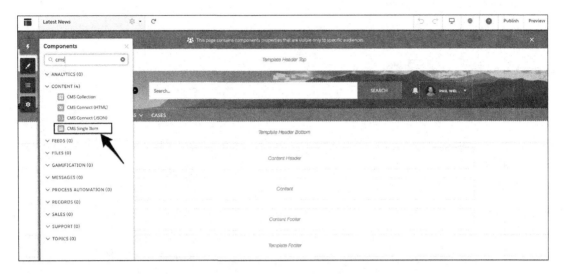

Figure 13-20. *Select and place the "CMS Single Item" component*

Once the component is on the page, content will need to be associated with it. Click "Add Content" within the property editor, as shown in Figure 13-21.

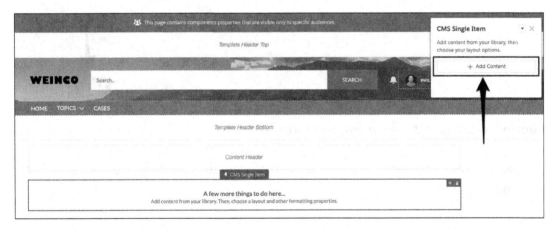

Figure 13-21. *Click "+ Add Content"*

Select the desired content and click "Save"; see Figure 13-22.

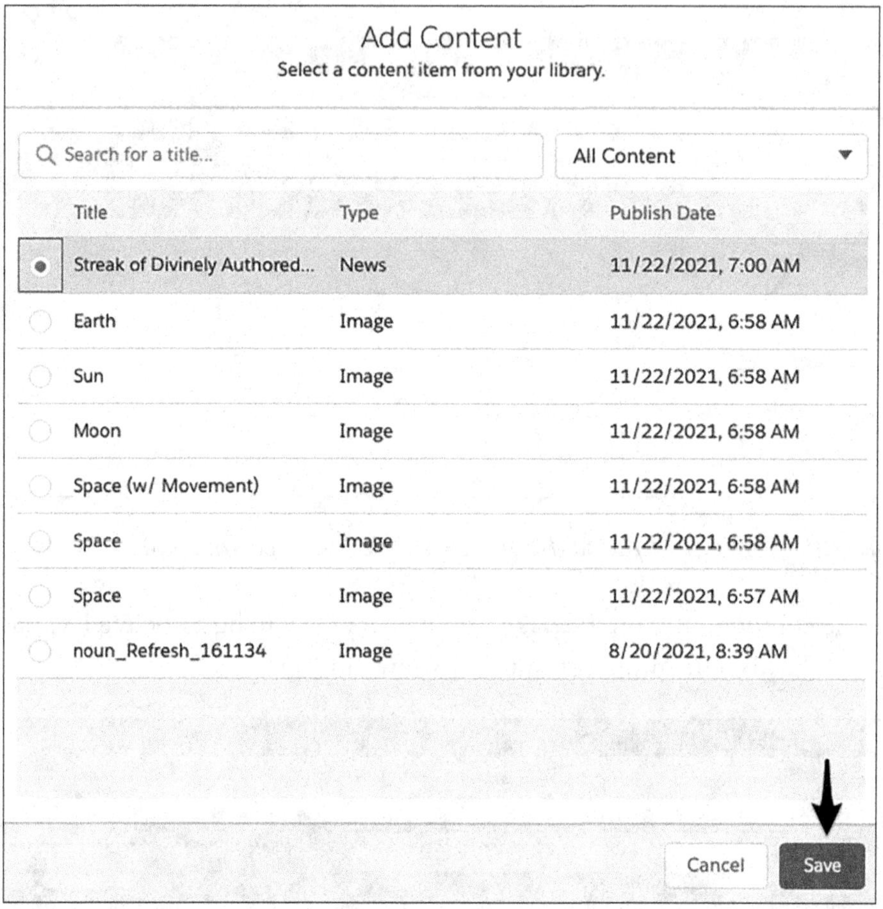

Figure 13-22. *Select the content to be displayed*

The experience we see in Figure 13-23 isn't too exciting, although we'll address that in a moment.

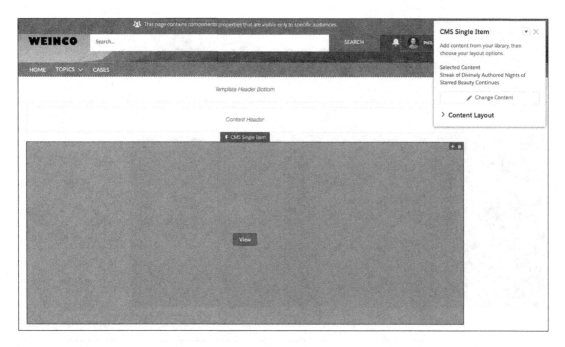

Figure 13-23. *A first look at the new content*

Now that the component is in place, we can map fields to the component to display the actual content. Click "Content Layout," click "Field Mappings," and then map fields to the different front-end elements of the component, as shown in Figure 13-24. In this case, map the following:

- Headline ➤ Title

- Subheading ➤ Excerpt

- Image ➤ Banner Image

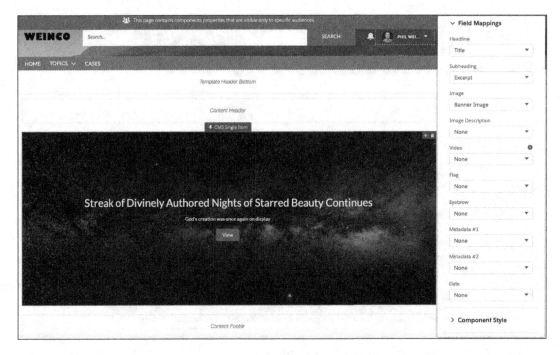

Figure 13-24. *Configure field mappings to bring the CMS component to life*

Success! Also, do note that there are tons more configurations that can be applied, and I highly encourage you to explore these to tweak how the component looks and behaves.

CMS Collection

The CMS Collection is a bit different, supporting both CMS Content and CRM data. Let's dive in.

CMS Content

For our content-driven collection, we're going to display a few space-related images that have already been uploaded. However, before we drag and drop the CMS Collection component onto a page, we need to define a collection. First, as shown in Figure 13-25, navigate to the Content Management workspace and then click the Collections tab.

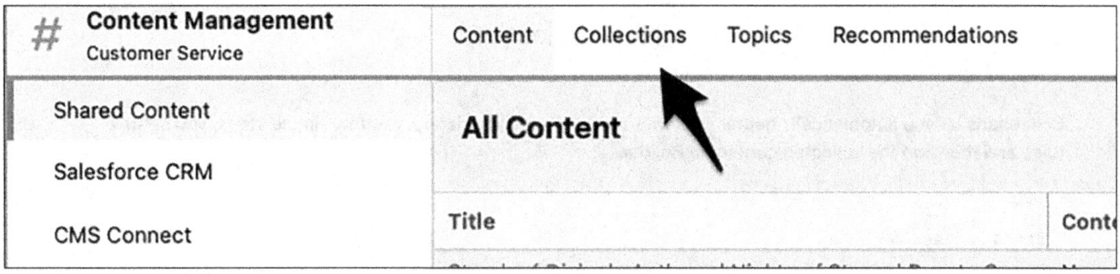

Figure 13-25. *Navigate to the Content Management workspace, then click the "Collections" tab*

Then, click "New" (see Figure 13-26).

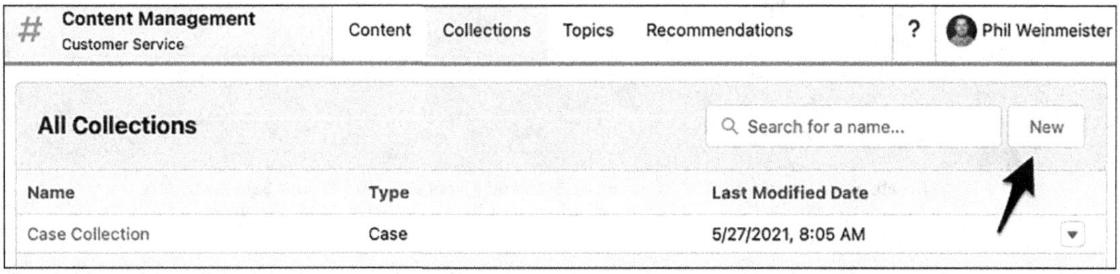

Figure 13-26. *Click "New" to create a new collection*

Next comes the content source (content vs. CRM data). In this case, we're using content, so select CMS Content (see Figure 13-27).

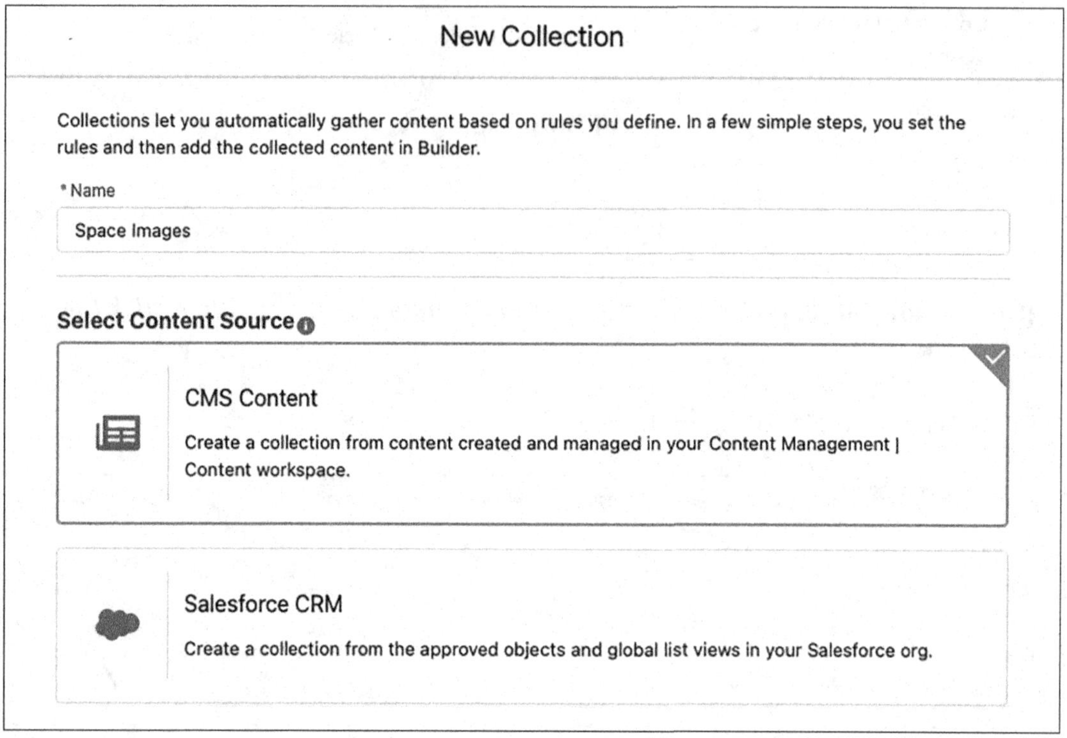

New Collection

Collections let you automatically gather content based on rules you define. In a few simple steps, you set the rules and then add the collected content in Builder.

* Name

Space Images

Select Content Source ⓘ

CMS Content

Create a collection from content created and managed in your Content Management | Content workspace.

Salesforce CRM

Create a collection from the approved objects and global list views in your Salesforce org.

Figure 13-27. *Select "CMS Content" as the content source (as opposed to selecting CRM records)*

Salesforce gives us the ability to select content manually or conditionally for our collection. Think of the manual option as fixed, or static; you select specific pieces of content, and that content never changes. On the other hand, conditional collections are like list views, which are dynamic; they will show whatever records (or, in this case, content) fit the criteria. That is an extremely powerful option, but we'll just go with a manually compiled collection here; see Figure 13-28.

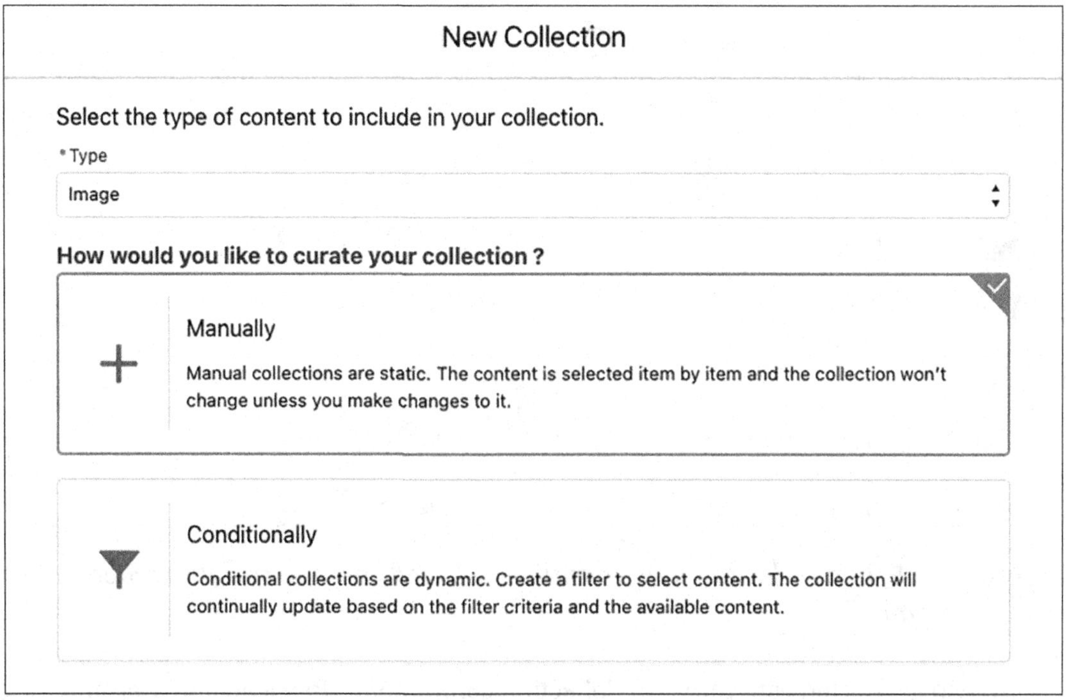

New Collection

Select the type of content to include in your collection.

* Type

| Image | ▲ ▼ |

How would you like to curate your collection ?

+   **Manually**

Manual collections are static. The content is selected item by item and the collection won't change unless you make changes to it.

▼   **Conditionally**

Conditional collections are dynamic. Create a filter to select content. The collection will continually update based on the filter criteria and the available content.

Figure 13-28. *Salesforce provides a choice of static or dynamic collections. In this example, select "Manually" (static)*

After identifying a content type (Images), we are presented with available image content. In this case, I'll select three images. See Figure 13-29.

	Title	⌄	Publish Date	⌄
✓	Earth		11/22/2021, 6:58 AM	
✓	Sun		11/22/2021, 6:58 AM	
✓	Moon		11/22/2021, 6:58 AM	
+	Space (w/ Movement)		11/22/2021, 6:58 AM	
+	Space		11/22/2021, 6:58 AM	

New Collection

🔍 Search for a title...

Figure 13-29. *In a collection with manually selected content, specific content will need to be added*

Time to get started with the CMS Collection component. Go ahead and drag and drop it onto a desired region; see Figure 13-30.

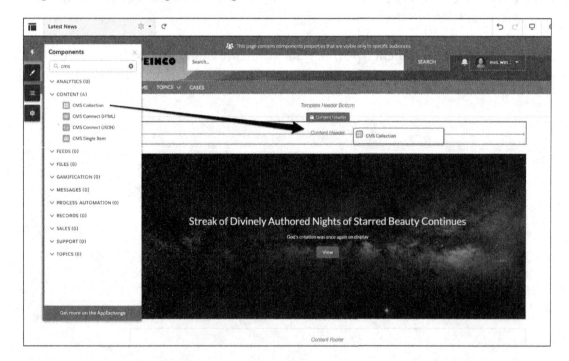

Figure 13-30. *Drag and drop the "CMS Collection" component onto the page*

Next, click "+ Add Collection." See Figure 13-31.

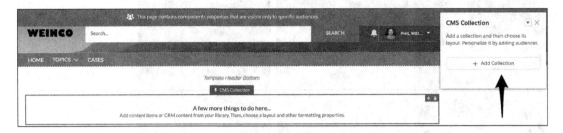

Figure 13-31. *Select a collection of content by clicking "+ Add Collection"*

Now, we'll select the collection we previously created. See Figure 13-32.

Add Collection
Select a collection from your library.

Q Search for a title...		All Collections ▼

Name	Type	Last Modified
● Space Images	Image	11/22/2021, 8:09 AM
○ Case Collection	Case	5/27/2021, 8:05 AM

Figure 13-32. *Select a specific collection of content*

After clicking the property editor and configuring the field mappings as shown in Figure 13-33, we see our content!

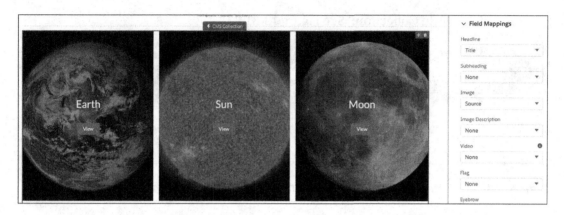

Figure 13-33. *Map fields to bring the component to life and see rich content*

However, the dimensions of the images are such that I can't see the full images within the available rectangle. To rectify that, I decrease banner height in the Component Style section, as shown in Figure 13-34, and my images display as desired.

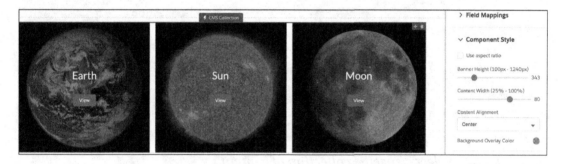

Figure 13-34. *Adjust banner height to change the content dimensions*

And we've finished our page. See Figure 13-35.

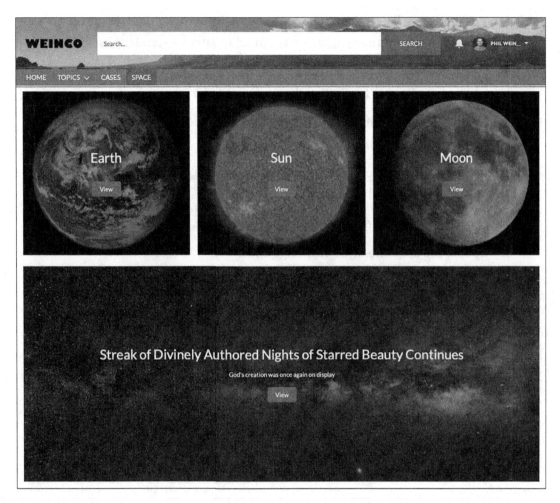

Figure 13-35. *A look at the completed page, showing both the CMS Collection component (top row) and the CMS Single Item component (bottom row)*

CRM Data

It's important to understand that the CMS Collection component can be used with CRM data as well. To make it work, we simply need to ensure that the appropriate data points are available for mapping.

For our example, we'll keep it simple. Let's say we want to highlight featured accounts in a way that is more engaging and compelling than a standard list view. To do this, I'll first complete the following steps:

1. Obtain logo images for each of the accounts to be featured.

2. Upload the images to any hosting platform (including Salesforce) that provides a publicly accessible URL.

3. Add the domain(s) of the uploaded images to the content security policy (CSP) trusted sites list.

4. Create a new custom field to hold the image URL.

5. Update the accounts with the image URL.

6. Create a list view to show the featured accounts.

Figure 13-36 shows the list view that I've created after doing all the necessary prework.

Figure 13-36. *A list view (with applicable fields shown) must first be created in order to utilize a collection based on Salesforce CRM data*

Now, let's create the appropriate CRM Connection before creating the collection itself. Navigate to the Content Management workspace and click "Salesforce CRM" on the left, then "Add CRM Connections." See Figure 13-37.

Figure 13-37. *To create a connection from the Content Management workspace, click "Salesforce CRM" on the left and then "Add CRM Connections" on the right*

In this case, select "Account" for the object, then click Save. See Figure 13-38.

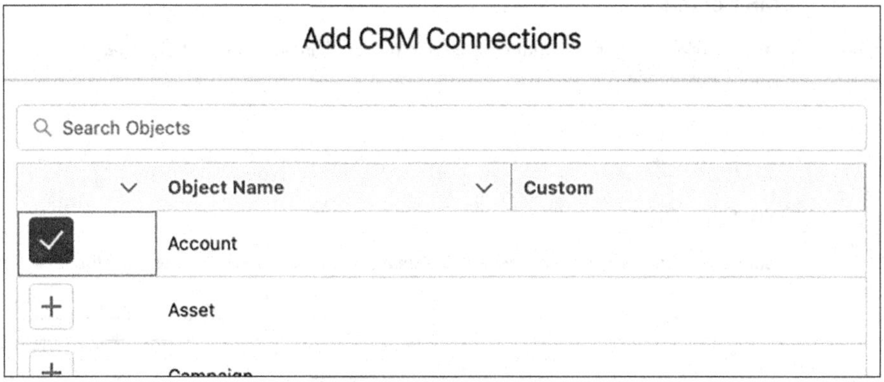

Figure 13-38. *Select the desired object to utilize in the connection*

Now, click the "Collections" tab at the top, followed by the "New" button on the right. See Figure 13-39.

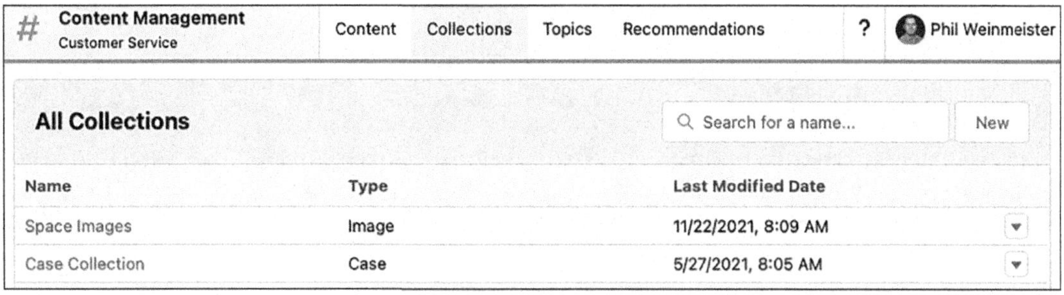

Figure 13-39. *Navigate to the Collections tab, then click "New"*

For content source, we'll select "Salesforce CRM" this time. See Figure 13-40.

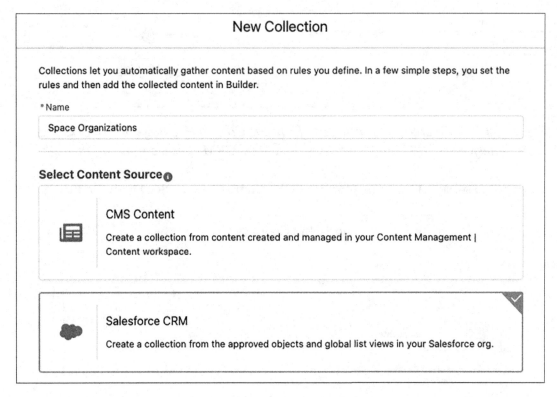

Figure 13-40. *Select "Salesforce CRM" to leverage Salesforce data in the collection*

Select "Account" and then click the desired list view (from our prework). See Figure 13-41.

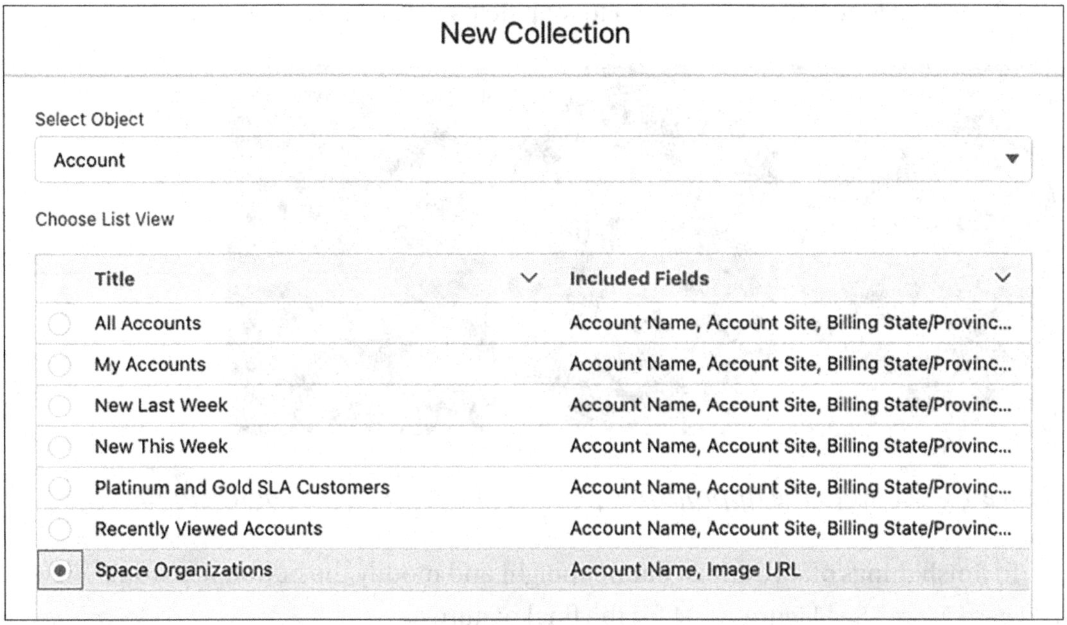

Figure 13-41. *Select the appropriate object and corresponding list view for the collection*

Let's drag and drop the CMS Collection component onto the page and then click "+ Add Collection," as we did in Figures 13-30 and 13-31. Select the appropriate collection; see Figure 13-42.

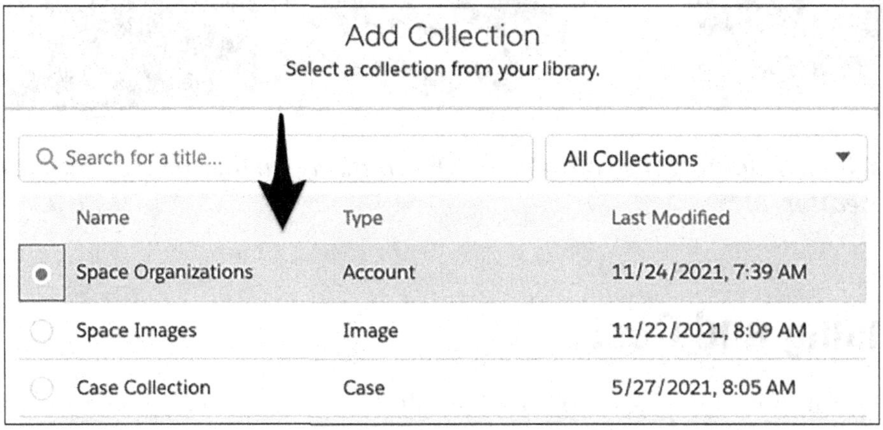

Figure 13-42. *Once the "CMS Collection" component has been dropped on the page, associate it with data by clicking "+ Add Collection" and selecting the appropriate collection*

Like we've done before, we'll need to map fields properly; see Figure 13-43.

Figure 13-43. *Map the appropriate fields to the property editor attributes*

To finish things off, we adjust banner height and modify the button text from "View" to "Learn More." See Figure 13-44 for the final picture.

Figure 13-44. *A look at the component after making further modifications via the property editor*

Licensing and Costs

As of 2022, Salesforce provides two "tiers" of Salesforce CMS licensing: free and paid. Since licensing changes so rapidly on the Salesforce platform, I won't include current costs here. However, I will make the following simple recommendations:

- Start with the free trial and explore Salesforce CMS.

- Once you have a clear picture of how you plan to use Salesforce CMS, take inventory of your expected usage (number of records and types, specifically).

- Reassess your trial in light of the new numbers.

- If necessary, upgrade to the paid version for unlimited usage.

- Go to `www.salesforce.com/editions-pricing/cms/` for more.

Recap

In this chapter, we took a detailed dive into the world of Salesforce CMS, looking at content from a conceptual perspective, the CMS app and tabs, creation of different types of content, and applying content to a digital experience via the standard "CMS Single Item" and "CMS Collection" components. By far, the best way to get experience with Salesforce CMS is just to dive in and create an experience with content yourself. Go ahead and get started today!

CHAPTER 14

Experience Cloud Certification

For anyone who has been a part of the Salesforce ecosystem for some time, it's clear that becoming Salesforce certified is highly valued by employees and employers alike. Experience Cloud is no exception to the slew of "clouds" featuring its own certification exam, and, if you're serious about developing your skills building digital experiences on the Salesforce platform, I'd highly recommend setting your sights on becoming a Salesforce Certified Experience Cloud Consultant.

In this chapter, I'll walk through the following aspects of this certification:

- An overview of the exam structure and contents (the "what")

- The case for obtaining this certification (the "why")

- My strategy and advice for study/preparation (the "how")

Exam Overview

Like with many areas of Salesforce, certification exams do change over time. While this particular exam hasn't seen drastic changes since its inception (the closest would be the rename from Community Cloud Consultant to Experience Cloud Consultant), it's very important to double-check the very latest regarding the exam at `https://trailhead.com`. Navigate to the exam info by clicking Credentials ➤ Certifications ➤ Salesforce Consultant ➤ Experience Cloud Consultant. And, if that path changes, you can always just Google "Salesforce Experience Cloud Consultant credential."

© Philip Weinmeister 2022
P. Weinmeister, *Practical Guide to Salesforce Experience Cloud*, https://doi.org/10.1007/978-1-4842-8132-1_14

Now that we've covered how to make sure you have the latest information, let's dive into the key details:

- 60 multiple-choice/multiple-select questions that determine the exam taker's official score (multiple-select indicates a selection of multiple choices from a larger set; e.g., select 3 of 5).

- Up to five additional questions that are unscored. These questions are included to gather feedback for potential future inclusion. Exam takers are not informed of whether a question is scored or not.

- A score of 65% is needed to pass the exam. This equates to correctly answering 39 of 60 questions correctly.

- 105 minutes, or 1 hour and 45 minutes, is provided to complete the exam.

- The exam costs $200, with retakes (any attempts following the initial one) costing $100.

- The Salesforce Administrator credential is required in order to take the Experience Cloud exam.

- Depending on physical testing center availability, the exam can be taken online or in person.

- All other standard exam stipulations and rules apply (e.g., no hard-copy or online materials may be used, the exam can be taken online or in person, etc.).

To take the exam, you'll need to use Webassessor. Take a look at Figure 14-1 for a view of the exam within the Webassessor interface.

— Salesforce Certified Experience Cloud Consultant (WI22)	The Salesforce Certified Experience Cloud Consultant exam is for individuals who want to demonstrate their skills and knowledge in designing, configuring, building, and implementing Salesforce Communities applications, using the declarative customization capabilities of the Communities platform. The credential is relevant to customers, partners, employees, and anyone interested in demonstrating competence with the Salesforce Experience Cloud. Learn more about the exam here: https://trailhead.salesforce.com/credentials/experiencecloudconsultant	*multiple*
Salesforce Certified Experience Cloud Consultant (WI22)	Retake Policy :	Onsite Proctored	USD 200.00
Salesforce Certified Experience Cloud Consultant (WI22)	Retake Policy :	Online Proctored	USD 200.00

Figure 14-1. *The Salesforce Certified Experience Cloud Consultant exam*

Exam Value

Many in the ecosystem may not realize how popular the Salesforce Certified Experience Cloud Consultant credential is, relatively to its peers. Based on data from Artisan Hub in late 2021, it was the tenth most common credential (out of 40+ exams) possessed by Salesforce experts. Within the subset of "Consultant" credentials, it was the third most common, following only Sales Cloud and Service Cloud.

Why does this data matter? It matters because the volume of each credential, to a degree, represents the demand. Let me explain. In the world of Salesforce certifications, the supply is, to a large degree, driven by demand. It's a common situation for a consultant (general term, lowercase "c") to be staffed or groomed for an upcoming project and have management express the need for a credential to legitimize a specific set of skills. Along the same lines, those who have already been doing a specific line of work for years will naturally want to show that they are capable in a specific area of the Salesforce platform. So, in other words, the volume of past and upcoming work directly impacts the number of certified consultants. One can make a decision on this exam knowing that plenty of Experience Cloud work is out there.

All of this points to the fact that the Experience Cloud credential, specifically, is a valuable one. Add that to the fact that Salesforce certifications in general have become a standard—even an expectation—in many cases, and I think the argument to push for this particular certification is an easy one for anyone who wants to build digital experiences on the Salesforce platform.

Anecdotally, I can also say that the consultant exams, Experience Cloud included, can have a direct impact on compensation. I have personally experienced this, and I've known others to experience the same; certifications can (potentially) lead to an increase in salary. And why shouldn't they? The best-paying individual contributor jobs—typically consulting roles—need good people. The Salesforce credential is the best possible way to establish an individual's skill level quickly. One additional reason why employers care about this so much is that the "Consultant" credentials hold a special value for partners, as they are considered "partner-level" certifications and contribute additional points to a Salesforce partner's partner program score. This score is absolutely critical to partners, since it determines their overall partner level.

Exam Approach

So, what's the best way to obtain the Salesforce Experience Cloud Consultant credential? I suggest three key pieces to successfully become certified:

- Hands-on experience

- Augmentation with learning materials

- A bold test-taking strategy

Hands-on Experience

I will admit that I have taken some certification exams before without studying or performing any relevant hands-on experience…and passed. I've also taken the same approach other times and fell far short of a passing score. Why share this with you? I'm sharing this to acknowledge that some exams, for long-time experts of the Salesforce platform, may not require the same amount of preparation as others. Let me be clear: the Experience Cloud exam absolutely warrants a level of hands-on experience. This is not an exam to be taken on a whim, even for a solid test-taker.

Hands-on experience can be split into two groups: actual project work (in the wild) and self-study (classroom work). Actual live work with Experience Cloud has no perfect substitution. If you have any opportunity to work with Experience Cloud at your organization or for a client, seize it. Get your hands dirty. You'll force yourself to solve problems that will probably be tougher than anything you'd come up with yourself. Now, with that said, that scenario is a luxury. If your organization isn't currently doing anything with Experience Cloud, you can't just hop in and start building a site in their Salesforce org. You can, however, do whatever you want in a dev org. If you are reading this book, you probably have a dev (developer) org already; if you don't, google "Salesforce developer org" and get started now. If you're taking the developer org approach, the next section will provide a guide for how to decide what to actually work on/build.

Learning Materials

I am going to keep this simple. I will recommend four *proven* resources that you can use to prepare for your Experience Cloud certification exam:

1. Trailhead

2. Focus on Force

3. *Practical Guide to Salesforce Experience Cloud* (this book)

4. Pluralsight

Trailhead does seem obvious, but it's probably my weakest recommendation of the four, based on real-world feedback. Don't misinterpret that; it's a key resource, but the other three will really set your studying apart. Trailhead is great because there is a direct link between the material in exams and what is shared on `https://trailhead.com`, especially with the content from each new release. There's not a plethora of information on Experience Cloud within Trailhead, though, and that's one of the reasons why I feel so strongly about the next three options.

Martin Gessner of Australia formed "Focus on Force" years back, and it has been instrumental in helping individuals to get certified on the Salesforce platform. He has had an Experience Cloud for some time, and it's quite popular. I have not viewed any of the material myself, but I can absolutely recommend this material. Why? I don't even know how many certified consultants have told me that they used Focus on Force to prepare for the Experience Cloud exam. I've only heard positive feedback, and people are passing after using the material. That's enough for me.

While it's a bit funny to include my own book (the one you're reading) here, I'd be remiss to exclude it. It has been a true honor and privilege to have had many individuals use this book to study for the exam, pass the exam, and then tell me how critical the content was in obtaining the certification. So, great decision, and soak this content up.

Pluralsight is a growing video-based learning platform that has seen a significant expansion of Salesforce-related material in the past few years. It has some great Experience Cloud–related courses that cover some of the material on the exam.

Test-Taking Strategy

I have a few pieces of advice on how to approach the exam itself. First, if your organization doesn't already do it, convince them to pay for the exam registration fees. This is now extremely common and such an easy, obvious win for the organization. A few hundred dollars to have a credentialized consultant? That's a no-brainer.

Having your organization pay for the registration fees helps with the next piece: be okay with/prepared to fail. Really, failing a Salesforce certification exam is not a big deal. No one will even know that you failed except Salesforce, the person approving your exam fee reimbursement, and you. Of course, study and prepare to the best of your ability; your goal should always be to pass on your first try. My point is to avoid mental paralysis by studying for months and months with the hopes of achieving a perfect score. There's actually one more, extremely valuable, way to prepare for the exam in addition to content like Trailhead, Focus on Force, and this book: it's taking the exam itself. There's nothing better for getting a feel for the exam material.

I'll wrap this up by sharing a practical activity that can be done after failing an exam that is extremely helpful. I know, because this is something I've done that has yielded great results (psst...this is the first time I've publicly shared this advice). Before submitting your exam (assuming you have a few minutes), quickly go through all the questions. Try your very best to remember any questions that gave you pause or concern. Then, if you see "FAIL" after submission, close out the exam, open your favorite notes application, and start unloading. Type out everything you can remember: words, phrases, questions, choices, etc. Don't stop until you have typed out everything that comes to mind. Next, organize the information into cohesive bullet points. Then, a few days later, come back and turn those bullet points into a mini-study guide. Find out everything you can about each bullet point and be ready with potential corresponding answers. While it's obviously a major issue to record or capture any information during an exam, Salesforce completely supports learning through the test-taking process itself (i.e., using one's memory). It is tempting to just step away and clear your mind after a failed test, but I'd highly recommend you stick around for five to ten minutes and write down your thoughts.

Recap

In this chapter, I provided a take on the what, why, and how related to the Salesforce Experience Cloud Consultant certification exam. It's a valuable credential for anyone serious about building digital experiences on the Salesforce platform. If you don't yet have it, there's no better time to start planning than today.

CHAPTER 15

The Best of the Rest: Additional Experience Cloud Topics

The breadth of Experience Cloud is a microcosm of the Salesforce platform. As new features and capabilities are introduced with each release, it has become increasingly difficult to maintain comprehensive expertise on Salesforce overall, let alone this single "cloud." As such, there is a significant amount of information that can be covered within the realm of Salesforce sites, and individual chapters could be written about a number of additional topics. To balance the need for breadth across Experience Cloud areas of focus and the unwieldy and awkward nature of a 600-page book, I've identified a number of specific topics that I'll be covering in brief throughout this chapter. My goal is to provide a practical starting point or common reference from which readers can explore additional detail via Salesforce Help and Training and other resources. Specifically, I'll cover the following in this chapter:

- Analytics

- Moderation

- Deployment

- Salesforce mobile app

- Search

- Messages

- Notifications

- Chatter streams

© Philip Weinmeister 2022
P. Weinmeister, *Practical Guide to Salesforce Experience Cloud*, https://doi.org/10.1007/978-1-4842-8132-1_15

- Lightning Web Runtime

- Microsites

- Mobile Publisher

- Additional items (Guided Setup, Marketing Cloud, Quip, Einstein, CMS Connect)

Analytics

The appropriate starting point for any discussion regarding analytics in a Salesforce site is the Community Management Package for Sites app from Salesforce. The full name includes the release name, and two versions exist (depending on whether Chatter is enabled):

- Salesforce Community Management Package for Sites with Chatter (e.g., Spring '21 Salesforce Community Management Package for Sites with Chatter)

- Salesforce Community Management Package for Sites without Chatter (e.g., Winter '19 Salesforce Community Management for Sites without Chatter)

Figure 15-1 shows the Spring '21 version of the app with Chatter.

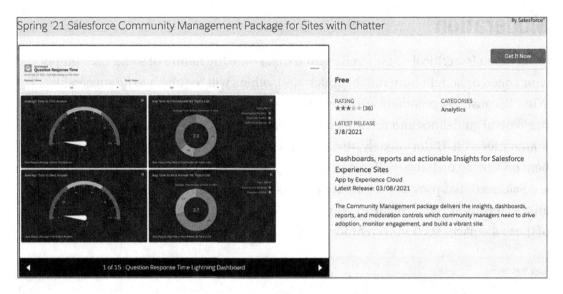

Figure 15-1. Community Management Package on AppExchange

This app has some serious meat to it, including many custom report types, dashboards, and reports. Once installed, an administrator of the site can navigate to Workspaces ➤ Dashboards and view a suite of valuable dashboards that bring the site to life. See Figure 15-2.

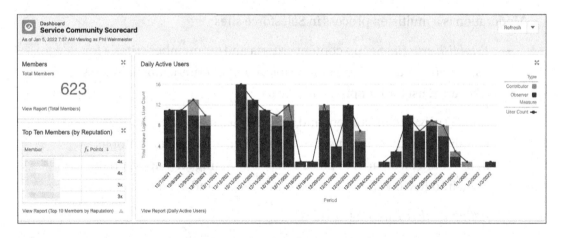

Figure 15-2. Service Community Scoreboard

Moderation

Moderation is a critical consideration for a site. While the nature of some sites simply won't need or benefit from much moderation, others will require it to be successful. Why? Because site members are people! While members of most sites will honor the general guidelines and rules of engagement, there are those who may push the boundaries a bit. Unfortunately, there are also those who are simply destructive and are bent on stirring up havoc within a site.

Salesforce has provided a number of tools to help with moderation. To access these, an administrator can navigate to Workspaces ➤ Moderation. See Figure 15-3 for a view of the workspaces section with Moderation.

Figure 15-3. *Moderation in My Workspaces*

Moderation is a multistep process in Salesforce sites:

- *Establish criteria*: Set up content criteria and/or member criteria for use in moderation rules. For example, content criteria might involve a keyword list for inappropriate words.

- *Create rules*: Create content and/or rate rules to enable automated handling of activities that satisfy the defined criteria. For example, a rule could be created to place a post containing an inappropriate word into Review status for moderator review and action.

- *Activate rules*: Turn on the rules.

- *Review/manage*: Stay on top of flagged discussions, files, messages, and members by using the provided analytics and dashboards.

- *Take action*: Unless an action is fully automated, a decision will need to be made on flagged items, and that decision may require some action.

Figure 15-4 shows an example of a rule that uses content criteria and automatically blocks profane words within a site.

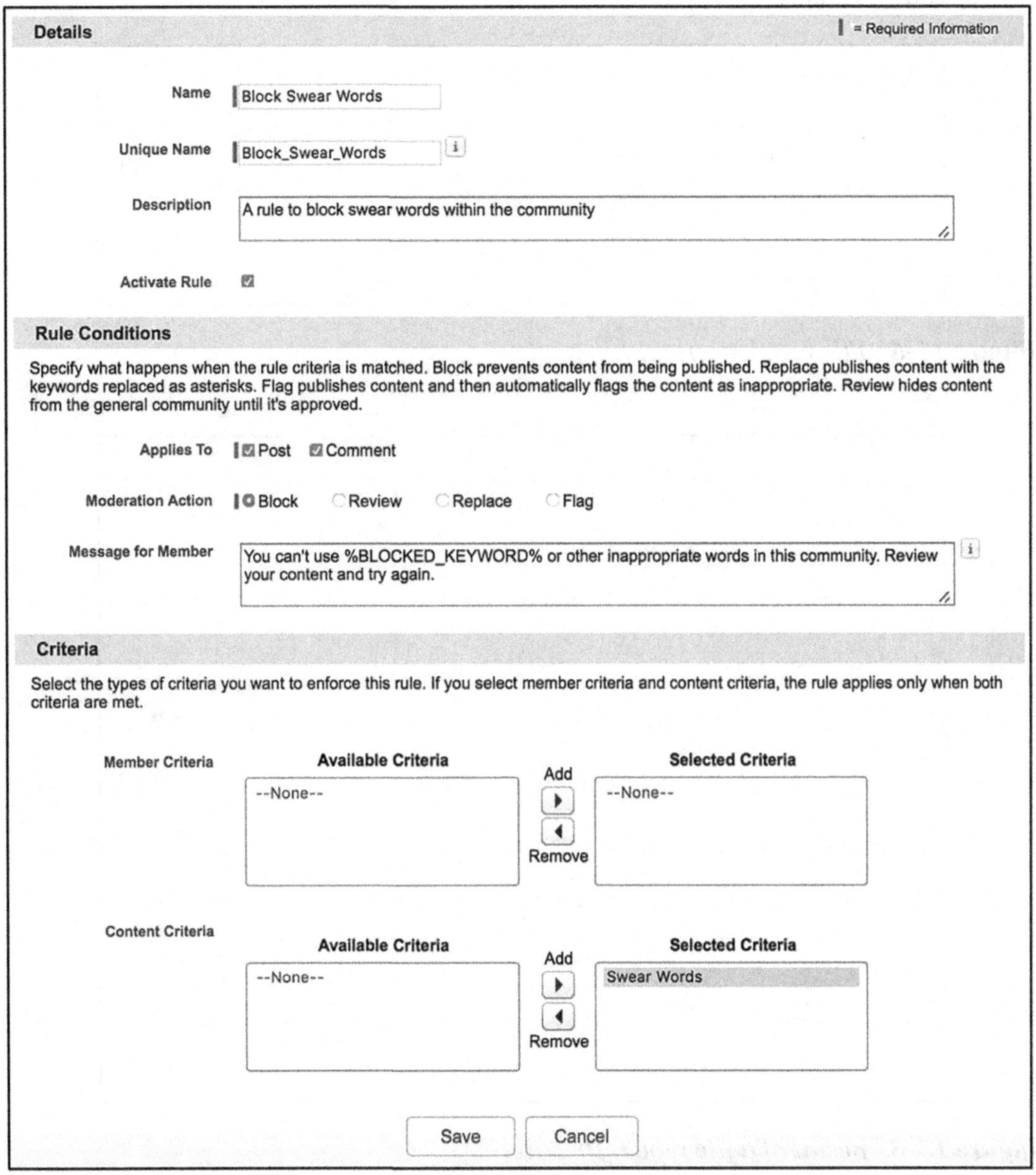

Figure 15-4. *A site moderation rule that blocks any text strings found in the defined content criteria ("swear words")*

Note that, in the preferences section within the Administration workspace, file types and sizes can be moderated as well. See Figures 15-5 and 15-6 for the settings and the corresponding result.

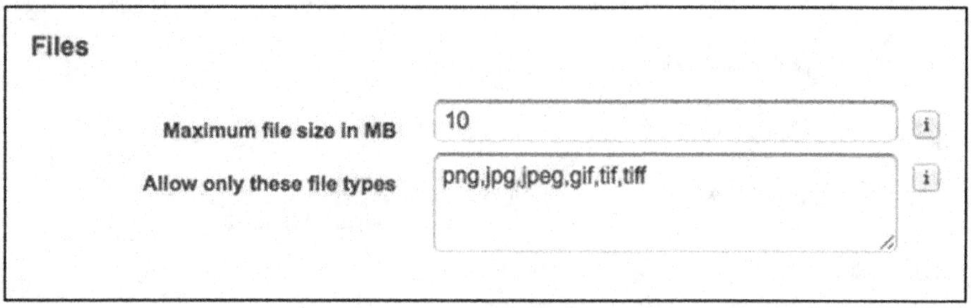

Files

Maximum file size in MB	10
Allow only these file types	png,jpg,jpeg,gif,tif,tiff

Figure 15-5. *File restrictions within a site*

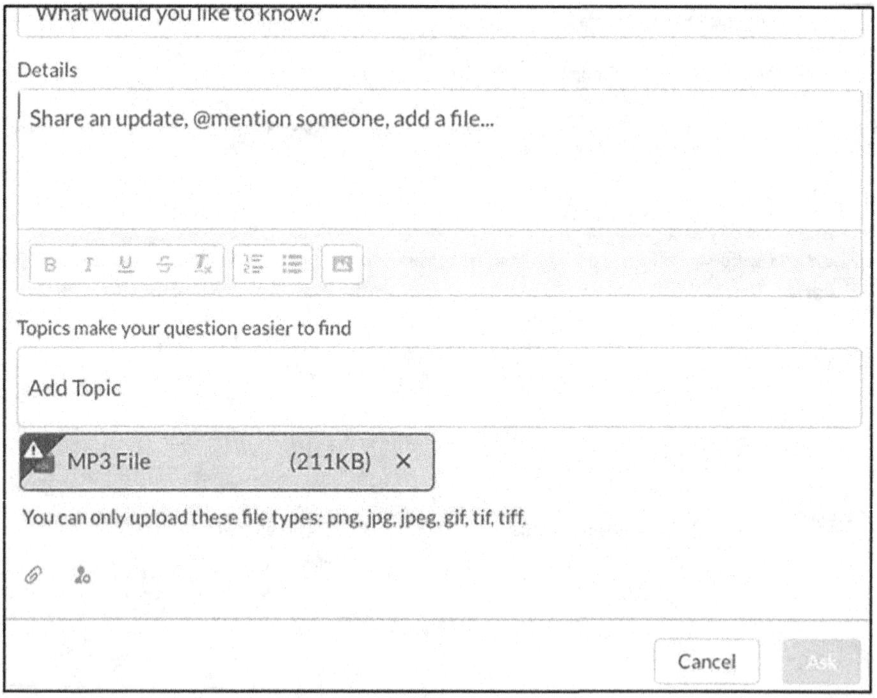

What would you like to know?

Details

Share an update, @mention someone, add a file...

B   I   U   S   Tₓ

Topics make your question easier to find

Add Topic

⚠ MP3 File   (211KB)   ×

You can only upload these file types: png, jpg, jpeg, gif, tif, tiff.

Cancel   Ask

Figure 15-6. *Result of a file type restriction*

Deployment

Deployment is a critical topic when it comes to Salesforce sites. While deployment of "standard" platform elements and entities, such as objects, fields, workflow rules, Apex classes, and so on, has become a fairly well-known and mature process, sites have required different processes and have not always fit into standard deployments. In this section, I won't be giving a simple formula for all deployment scenarios; instead, I'll cover the available options and call out some key considerations.

Change Sets

Change Sets are an established platform element in the Salesforce ecosystem and allow the inclusion of sites for the purpose of deployment. The following are a couple key items to know about Change Sets, as they relate to sites:

- Change Sets require that a site with the same name as the source site exist in the target org.

- Change Sets work for both Lightning and Tabs + Visualforce sites.

As Change Sets are well known on the platform, I won't go into extreme detail on the process. However, I will call out the main "gotcha," which is that sites are represented as "networks" within Change Sets. See Figure 15-7.

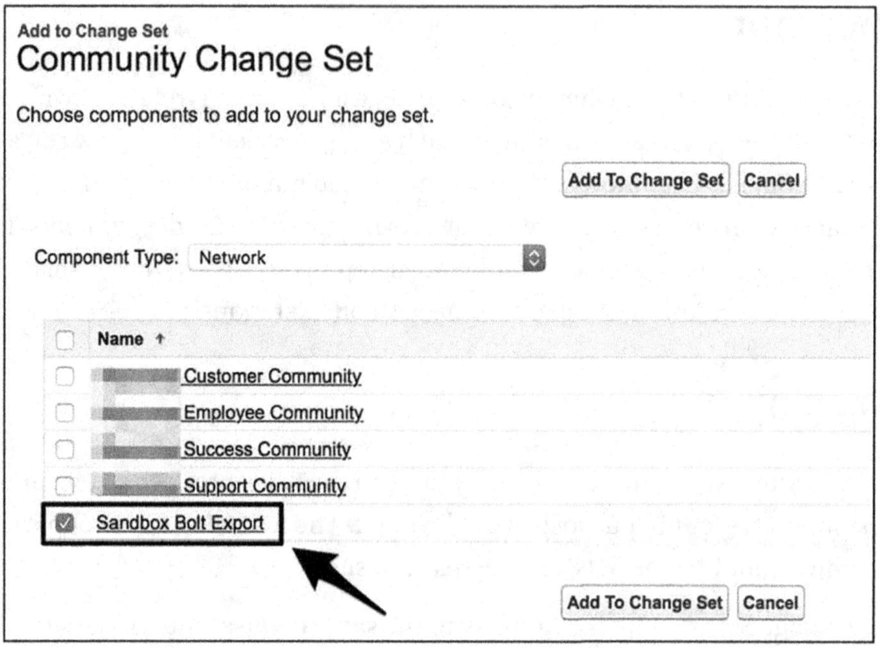

Figure 15-7. *Select a network (site) within a Change Set*

Overall, the Change Set process looks like the diagram shown in Figure 15-8.

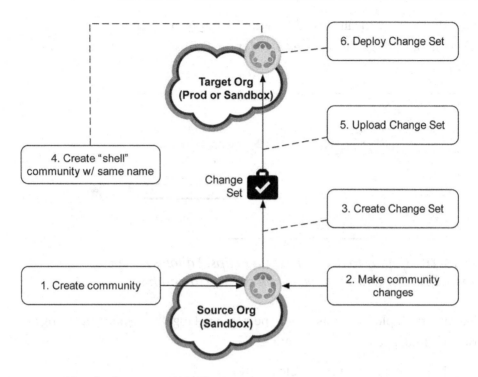

Figure 15-8. *Site deployment via Change Set*

IDEs and the Metadata API

Integrated development environments (IDEs) provide a means to save org contents to the cloud or a local server. An IDE (such as the Force.com IDE, used with Eclipse) uses the Salesforce Metadata API to extract and save a network (i.e., site) and all related content and then deploy it to a different org (see Figure 15-9).

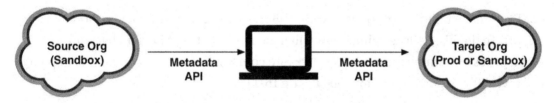

Figure 15-9. *Overview of leveraging an IDE to deploy a site from a source org to a target org*

Once contents are locally saved, an administrator can deploy the selected contents to a particular target org. See Figure 15-10 for the Eclipse menu option that allows this action.

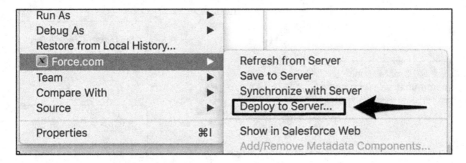

Figure 15-10. *Deploy to Server (within Eclipse) allows for specific contents, including a network, to be moved from one org to another*

Note that multiple elements should be deployed together when deploying an Experience Cloud site via the Metadata API:

- Network (an Experience Cloud site)

- CustomSite (domain and page setting information)

- ExperienceBundle *or* SiteDotCom (Experience Builder settings and site components. Highly recommended to enable ExperienceBundle and use that instead of SiteDotCom, as ExperienceBundle is human-readable and SiteDotCom is not)

Site.com Export

For Experience Builder sites only, Site.com allows a method for full site export and import. To do this, a site administrator will need to navigate to Site.com by going to Workspaces ➤ Administration ➤ Pages ➤ Site.com Studio. From there, the Settings cog will reveal the Export Site option. See Figure 15-11.

Figure 15-11. *Exporting an Experience Builder site via Site.com*

In the target org, a target site must exist. Following the same path to the Site.com Settings cog, an administrator will select Overwrite Site and select the exported file to import the file and update the site. See Figure 15-12.

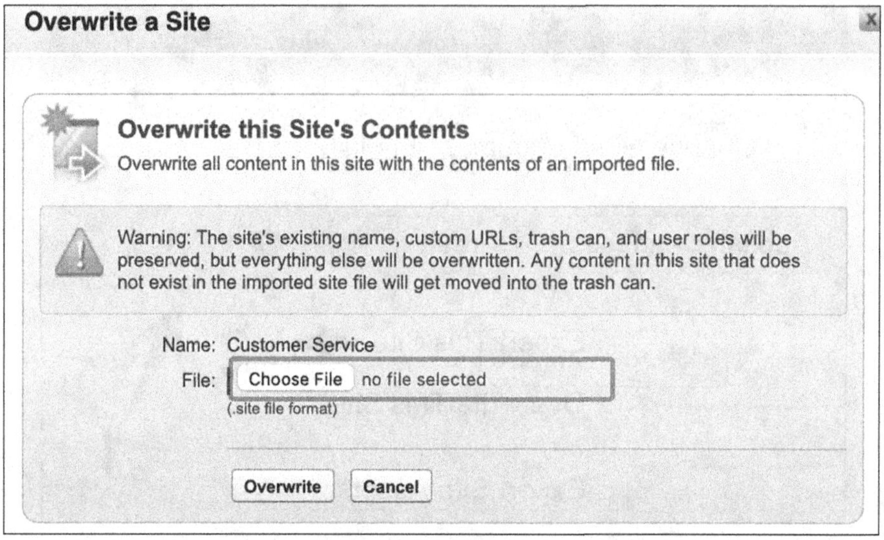

Overwrite a Site
Overwrite this Site's Contents
Overwrite all content in this site with the contents of an imported file.
Warning: The site's existing name, custom URLs, trash can, and user roles will be preserved, but everything else will be overwritten. Any content in this site that does not exist in the imported site file will get moved into the trash can.
Name: Customer Service
File:
Choose File
no file selected
(.site file format)
Overwrite
Cancel

Figure 15-12. *Overwriting a site requires the import of the site file that was previously exported from the source site*

Figure 15-13 provides an overview of the entire process.

Target Org
(Prod or Sandbox)
5. Site.com Import
4. Create "shell" community
3. Site.com Export
1. Create community
2. Make community changes
Source Org
(Sandbox)

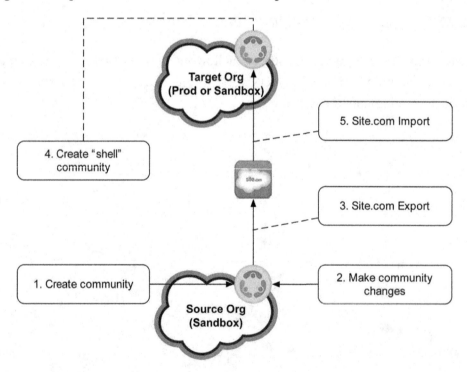

Figure 15-13. *Overview of the Site.com export/overwrite process*

While Site.com export is an option, I wouldn't recommend it above the previously mentioned options (Change Sets/Metadata API). It is not an area seeing any investment and shouldn't be seen as reliable going forward.

Packaged Lightning Bolt

Custom Lightning Bolts, covered in Chapter 12, are fairly new and continue to evolve at the time of this book's publication. While you won't find any documentation listing the use of Lightning Bolts as an established site deployment method, they do provide a means to export a site in its current state. The export can then be either packaged (and then installed) or migrated via the Metadata API. The concept of the Lightning Bolt framework is that it allows the output of a site starting point (i.e., a template). Ultimately, though, a bolt captures everything about a site at the point an export is created, and it could absolutely be used to "move" a site from one org to another.

Again, I don't recommend this as a standard deployment approach, but there is value in understanding how Lightning Bolt technology can potentially facilitate site deployment.

Manual Replication

With all of the other deployment tools available, manual replication is not generally recommended as an approach; however, it is an option. The only advantage to this approach is that it does put all the control in the hands of the individual or individuals doing the deployment, down to each aspect of the site. In other words, if an individual wants to make sure that everything is moved properly and set up in the same way as it was in the source org, this might provide a level of comfort. It does not increase the likelihood of success, though. Rather, it introduces many potential opportunities for manual mistakes.

Salesforce Mobile App for Sites

Since Lightning sites provide an out-of-the-box responsive, mobile-friendly UX, the Salesforce app doesn't play a prominent role in the mobile experience for sites. However, there are some use cases I've run into where the app has come into play. I'd like to share a few tips that could be relevant:

- *Usage in a LEX-based employee site*: There are times when it makes sense to build a LEX-based employee site/portal vs. one leveraging Lightning sites (e.g., an HR help desk because of the nature of case visibility). In these situations, the app will potentially apply. See Figure 15-14.

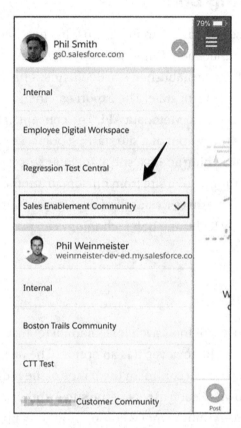

Figure 15-14. *Selection of a site from within the Salesforce app*

- *Security/network limitations*: I have encountered a situation where employees are not able to access the site on a mobile browser on their phone, for security-related reasons. In that situation, the Salesforce app provides a means to access some elements of the site that are not prohibited by security configurations.

- *Flexible Lightning approach*: The Salesforce app provides a great use case for building Lightning components in a flexible way to be used via different mediums. Any component that includes implements="force:appHostable" in the aura:component tag can be surfaced as a Lightning component tab in the app.

- *Modifying the tab menu*: In setting up the Salesforce app to work for a user of a Lightning site, I found myself struggling to figure out how to actually manage the app tab menu. The answer was not obvious; you have to make the Tabs menu within Administration visible and then set up the tabs there. See Figures 15-15 and 15-16 for the result of a custom tab set for a site within the app.

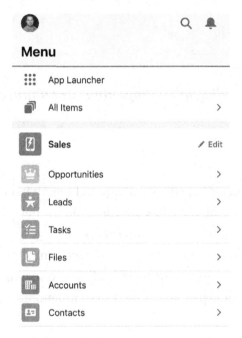

Figure 15-15. *Tabs, as shown in the Salesforce app*

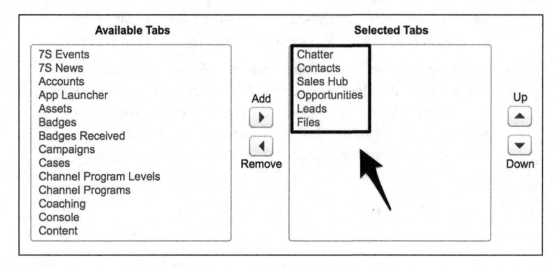

Figure 15-16. *Corresponding tab settings from site administration*

Search

I covered some of the component-specific aspects of search in earlier chapters but thought it was important to call out a few additional items here. Figure 15-17 shows an example of some search results on the standard results page available within sites. The fact that a site admin can prevent an accessible object from showing up in the search results is a welcome feature, but no one would call native search capabilities "advanced." I point this out to set proper expectations for a site implementation and to show that the options are limited.

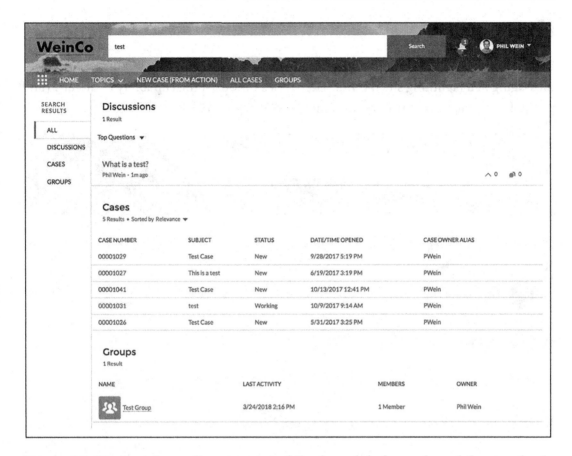

Figure 15-17. *Search results using out-of-the-box global search and the standard search results component*

One nice enhancement added a few years back was the ability to filter search results. Now, as an admin, you can configure specific fields that can be used by a user to restrict the set of records displayed.

If the native search features don't satisfy the needs of a particular organization, a couple options are available. First, there's the custom development approach. Custom search functionality can absolutely be provided, either through Visualforce or through Lightning. Additionally, admins may want to consider third-party options. AppExchange has a few site-enabled search apps that can be installed and configured to override the standard search experience.

Messages

Direct messages through Chatter have been available for some time, but direct messaging in a Lightning site has not. There does now exist the capability to directly (and privately) message other users within the site. See Figure 15-18.

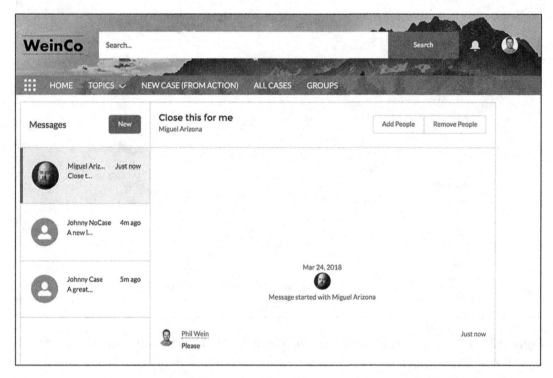

Figure 15-18. *Direct message home page within a Lightning site*

Although the messages page can't be directly added to the navigation menu without specifying a message ID, there is a messages page that can be referenced. The relative URL is /s/messages/Home and will default to the first message when the page is loaded.

Notifications

The need to surface notifications and allow site users to easily manage them was a feature gap for a while, but that gap was filled a few years back. Now, a setting exists that can show or hide notifications within the standard header. See Figure 15-19.

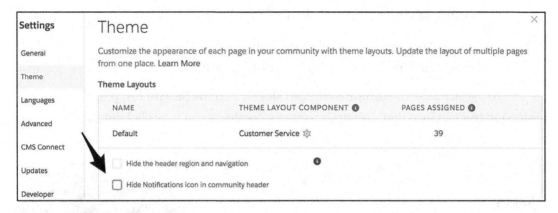

Figure 15-19. *A setting on the Theme page allows the notification icon to be shown or hidden*

If the notification icon is enabled, users will be able to review any event that triggers a notification. See Figure 15-20 for a view of the Notifications menu with content.

Figure 15-20. *Notifications menu with an example notification displayed*

Chatter Streams

Chatter streams are a feature that might be useful for more collaborative organizations. Chatter streams basically allow a user to create a custom feed that provides these two functions:

- Cuts through the noise that is found in the main site feed

- Allows for an aggregation of individual feeds to allow a user to hand-select feeds from multiple entities/records

To enable streams, an administrator can simply add the Stream List page to the navigation menu. Once that's set up, a user can create a stream by clicking the New button. See Figure 15-21.

Figure 15-21. *Clicking New on the Streams home page allows a site member to create a new stream*

To assemble the stream, identify the objects and the corresponding records whose feeds will make up the fully aggregated feed. See Figure 15-22.

Figure 15-22. Different records can be selected when creating a stream

Once the brief setup is done, the feed will start to show the tailored content selected by the end user. See Figure 15-23 for an example of a live Chatter stream.

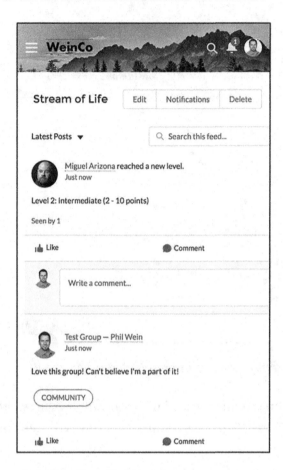

Figure 15-23. *A completed, active Chatter stream*

Lightning Web Runtime

A few years ago, Salesforce realized that their current version of Lightning components (Aura) was not going to be as performant as desired and, as a result, started developing a new runtime platform. That has provided us with what is referred to as the Lightning Web Runtime platform, or LWR. LWR has a very specific application in the context of Experience Cloud. It can be used under two conditions:

- Zero Aura (Lightning) components are needed in the applicable site.

- An LWR template (e.g., Build Your Own (LWR)) is used (see Figure 15-24).

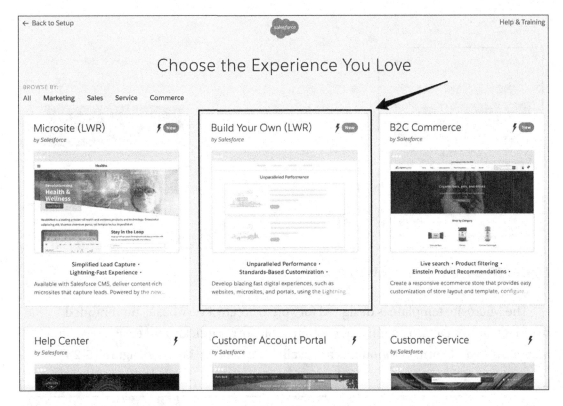

Figure 15-24. Build Your Own (LWR) template

If you are able to satisfy these requirements, then you can take advantage of the speed that LWR offers. However, be aware that a large number of standard Experience Builder components are still not available for LWR as of early 2022. If you make the leap to use Build Your Own (LWR), you'd better make sure that your use case fits. A highly customized, highly performant site is an ideal candidate for using an LWR template.

Microsites

Multiple times over my career, I've had a need for a very basic, one-page "site" for a form of some sort on Experience Cloud. It's overkill to create a full Customer Service site, and Build Your Own isn't even always the right fit. Fortunately, Salesforce finally came out with a template that addresses this need: Microsite. See Figure 15-25 for a look at the selection page.

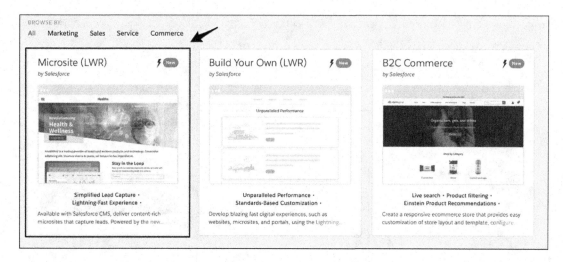

Figure 15-25. *Microsite (LWR) template*

The Microsite template is designed for you to create a very basic, but branded, site that features calls to action and customizable forms quickly and easily. Lead and Marketing Cloud Form components are available out of the box (see Figure 15-26).

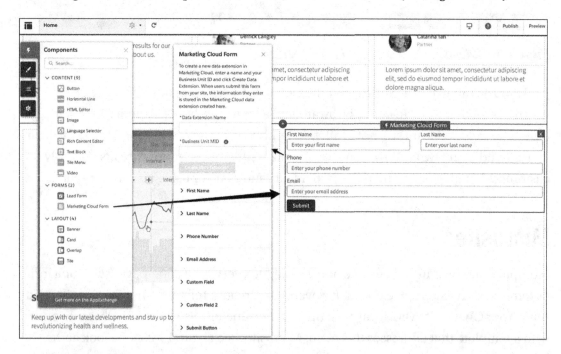

Figure 15-26. *Marketing Cloud Form standard component in a Microsite*

However, there is a bit of a catch here. You will need to subscribe to a paid Salesforce CMS license to access Microsites. My suggestion? If you need it, a business case shouldn't be too hard to put together. Come up with the benefits and cost savings and encourage your organization to leverage CMS and Microsites, if there's value there for you.

Mobile Publisher

Mobile Publisher was released in 2019. This offering enables organizations to release a branded app on the Apple App Store or Google Play Store that showcases a Salesforce digital experience. See Figure 15-27 for an example site that leveraged Mobile Publisher.

Figure 15-27. *A site viewed via a Mobile Publisher app*

Mobile Publisher is essentially a managed process that produces an app version of a Salesforce site to be listed in one of two places: the Apple App Store and Google Play Store. It's important to understand that this is not a Salesforce product in the typical sense, in which everything is contained within Salesforce itself. See Figure 15-28 for a look at the process.

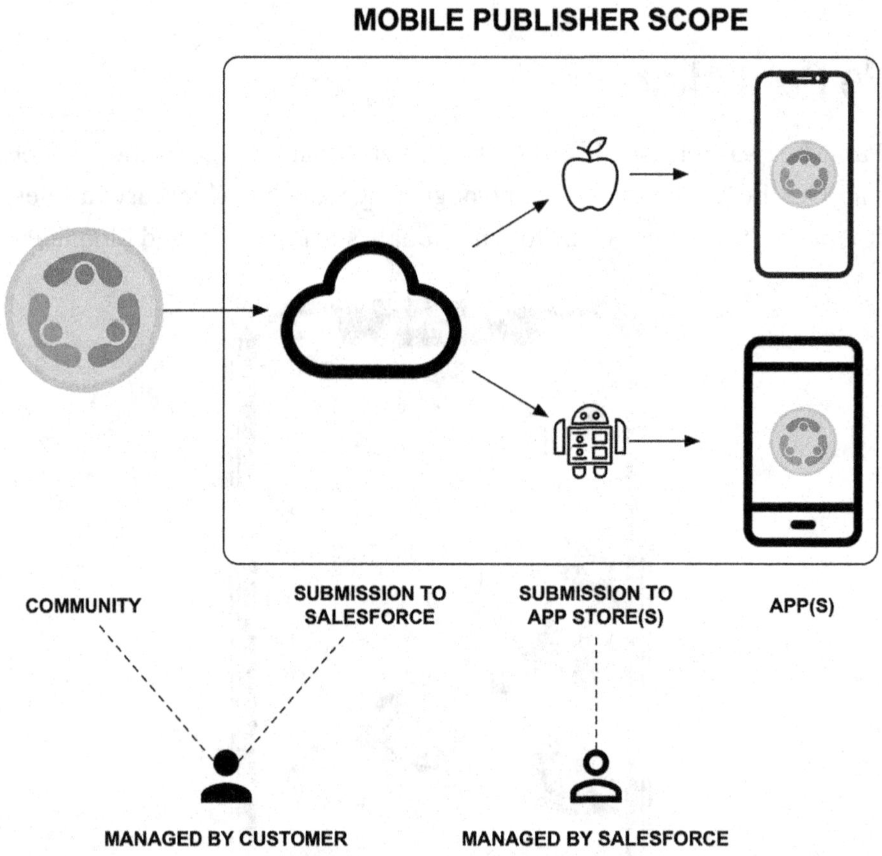

Figure 15-28. *The Mobile Publisher submission process*

Mobile Publisher is a paid product, calculated at the aggregate level via a summary of per-user charges. Note that there is a minimum annual charge per Mobile Publisher instance, so organizations with potentially small projected app user audiences might need to think through the long-term value before diving in.

One of the great things about Mobile Publisher is that changes made through Experience Builder do not require a resubmission to App Store or Play Store. Changes to the "container" (e.g., icon, splash screen) would require a new app version.

In terms of whether Mobile Publisher requires a special "mobile-ready" site to qualify, that's a bit nuanced. Technically, there is not a distinct, unique path that must be followed during site development in order to take advantage of Mobile Publisher. For example, a "normal" custom component built for a site would not necessarily require additional work to successfully pass through the entire Mobile Publisher process. This contrasts with the requirement to modify a custom component built for communities to work in Lightning Experience, Flow, etc. (via the interfaces specified in the component's "implements" attribute).

However, there is another take to this. All elements (components) of a site that will be submitted through Mobile Publisher *must* be developed to be appropriately responsive for a mobile device (or, really, for any device). If not, you will have a problematic app—or one that does not make it through the process due to a poor user experience.

However, building digital experiences with responsive design in mind should be happening already. So, while responsiveness *is* critical for a digital experience that will leverage Mobile Publisher, it should also be critical in your site independent of Mobile Publisher.

The takeaway here: When approaching the development and design of your community—whether for Mobile Publisher or not—consider responsiveness and ideal user experience as a top priority.

One of the critical pieces to understand with Mobile Publisher is that an approval from Apple or Google is not guaranteed whatsoever. Salesforce is owning the submission, not the content submitted. While they can provide guidance, they will not guarantee review approval.

Since it's possible that a submission can get rejected, it's important to maximize your chances of approval from the onset. To do this, you'll need to get to know the guidelines for both Google and Apple. Make sure you find the appropriate documents that outline the process and guidelines for the corresponding platform.

While there isn't a one-size-fits-all approach that secures approval, there are some particular areas to consider that you can address with wisdom. Let's take the Apple App Store. One particular section that can be problematic for Mobile Publisher reviews is **4.2 Minimum Functionality** ("Your app should include features, content, and UI that elevate it beyond a repackaged website").

While Apple's guidelines aren't terribly specific, the applicable section appears to suggest that the app's experience is not sufficiently differentiated from a Safari mobile web experience.

Apple may say that certain iOS features "are not enough," including push notifications, "core location," and sharing. However, there are other approaches. One strategy would be to enable biometric ID (fingerprint/Face ID).

It is possible to test an app before submission. Salesforce has released a "playground" that allows users to test out their Mobile Publisher app before the app is ready from the App/Play Stores. As a part of the Mobile Publisher submission process, organizations will have access to the Beta build (with branding and configuration) via Apple's TestFlight and Google's Alpha track. Additionally, an admin may invite others to view and test this build.

Note that a Mobile Publisher app does *not* have to be distributed as a public app in the Apple App Store or Google Play Store. It is possible to privately distribute the app. Take a look at Salesforce Help articles for more info.

Ultimately, the value of Mobile Publisher will be determined by how it is used. There are obviously costs involved, both the time required to work through the process and maintain the app (which could be minimal) and the required recurring fee. However, based on my personal experience, it is safe to say that this meets a critical gap for customers and, in summary, Mobile Publisher's closure of that gap makes this a worthwhile investment.

Other Capabilities

Site builders will continue to find powerful new site capabilities with each Salesforce release. In this section, I will call out additional capabilities that will warrant more research and consideration for many organizations.

Guided Setup

Guided Setup is an additional workspace that corresponds to partner sites, walking administrators through a series of steps to help set up the site quickly and thoroughly. Figure 15-29 shows a view of the Guided Setup landing page.

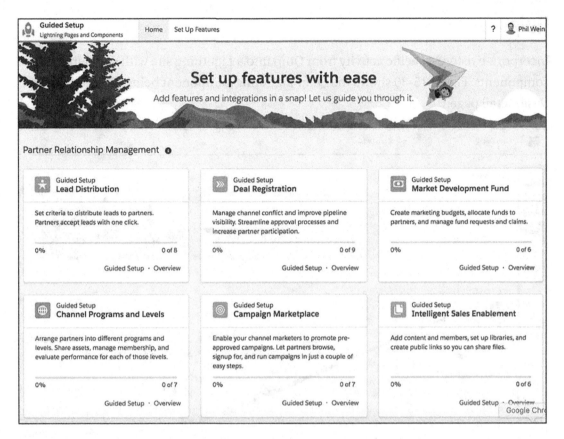

Figure 15-29. *Guided Setup landing page*

Marketing Cloud

For organizations leveraging Marketing Cloud, Experience Cloud now offers built-in tools for direct integration with a site:

- Distributed marketing allows for the creation of personalized partner campaigns.

- Journey Builder for sites enables the configuration of marketing journeys for site members.

Quip

Incorporate record-specific activity from Quip into a Lightning site with standard Quip components. Figure 15-30 shows the Quip Lightning component being dropped onto a Case Detail page.

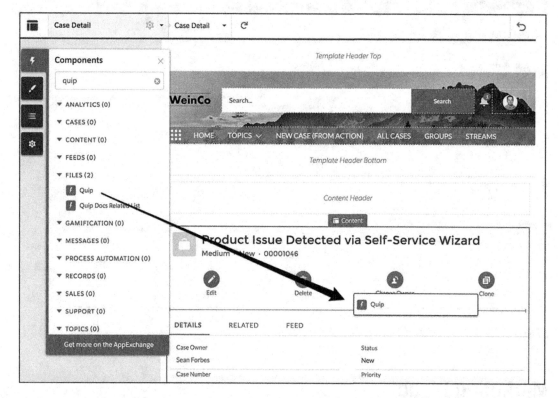

Figure 15-30. *Dragging the standard Quip component onto a Case Detail page*

Einstein for Sites

Einstein functionality, once fully released, will provide an enhanced engine for recommending responses to questions submitted within a Salesforce site. This will have significant value for self-service scenarios by increasing the probability that those following the question will truly find the information that they are looking for. Stay tuned to this space.

CMS Connect

CMS Connect is a major addition to Experience Cloud. It has evolved rapidly and will likely continue to see significant investment for some time. CMS Connect allows organizations to connect to HTML, JSON, CSS, and JavaScript from third-party content management systems to provide consistent branding and UX across multiple sites. The following providers are explicitly supported: Adobe Experience Manager, Drupal, Sitecore, WordPress, and SDL. Any other CMS server that supports HTML/CSS/HTTP standards should work, too.

Figure 15-31 shows the New CMS Connection page, while Figure 15-32 shows the standard CMS Connect (HTML) component available within Experience Builder.

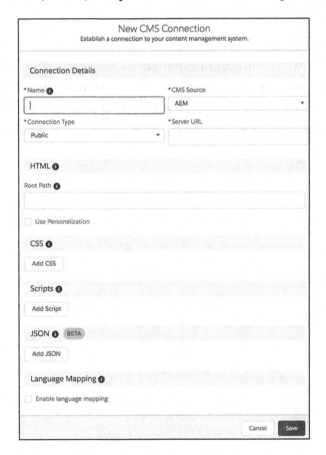

Figure 15-31. *New CMS Connection page*

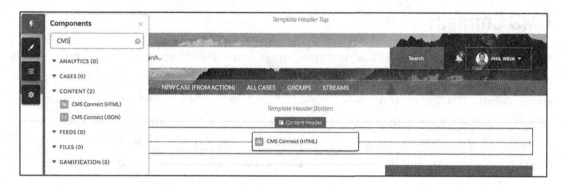

Figure 15-32. *The standard CMS Connect (HTML) component*

Recap

In this chapter, I reviewed a number of Experience Cloud capabilities that round out the majority of the full site feature set available on the Salesforce platform. Topics covered included analytics, moderation, deployment, search, and more. The information in this chapter was intended to provide a starting point for understanding these areas.

Index

© Philip Weinmeister 2022
P. Weinmeister, *Practical Guide to Salesforce Experience Cloud*, https://doi.org/10.1007/978-1-4842-8132-1

Printed in the United States
by Baker & Taylor Publisher Services